MW00777923

Terrorism and Counterterrorism Studies

Comparing Theory and Practice

EDWIN BAKKER AND
JEANINE DE ROY VAN ZUIJDEWIJN

Terrorism and Counterterrorism Studies

Comparing Theory and Practice

Second, revised edition

LEIDEN UNIVERSITY PRESS

First edition, 2015
Second, revised edition, 2022

Cover design: Sander Pinkse
Lay-out: Coco Bookmedia BV

ISBN   978 90 8728 389 6
e-ISBN   978 94 0060 435 3
DOI   10.24415/9789087283896

NUR   686

Contents

List of boxes & figures

11

Preface

The field of terrorism and counterterrorism studies has grown exponentially since the attacks on the United States on September 11, 2001. The terrorist attacks on that day are among the defining features of the 21st century and terrorists are still making headlines worldwide, threatening or attacking governments and ordinary citizens. In some parts of the world, terrorism has been one of the most important threats to peace, security and stability. Yet in most parts it received a lot of attention without constituting a primary threat, let alone a strategic threat. But what does this mean? What is the nature of this threat and how does it 'work'? Who or what is threatened, how, by whom and why? And what can be done about it, or how can we at least limit the impact of terrorism and make sure that terrorists do not manage to spread fear, dread or anxiety?

These are just a handful of questions that we address in this revised textbook that accompanies the Massive Open Online Course on Coursera and FutureLearn: 'Terrorism and Counterterrorism: Comparing Theory & Practice'. This undergraduate level course was first launched in September 2013 and has attracted over 180,000 participants from more than 80 countries. The course and this handbook have been completely revised in 2022. The revised edition discusses recent trends and developments and uses many new studies that shine a different light on certain topics. Additionally, it pays more attention to the important question what we can do to deal with the impact of terrorism on politics and society. The input from the course participants from all across the world and students at Leiden University helped us to develop our thoughts for this revised edition.

The aims of both the online course and this textbook are to learn more about:
- The notion of terrorism as an instrument to achieve certain goals.
- The difficulties and importance of definitions of terrorism.
- The state of the art of terrorism studies.
- Theoretical notions and practical examples to better understand the phenomenon of terrorism.
- Theoretical notions and practical examples to better understand and critique approaches to counterterrorism.
- How to deal with the impact of terrorism.
- Possible futures of terrorism and terrorism studies.

The textbook consists of seven chapters. The first one focuses on the definition of terrorism and explores some of its main features and the difficulties of defining the phenomenon – think about the phrase: 'one man's terrorist is another man's freedom fighter'. This is followed by a chapter on the history of terrorism and one on the state of the art in terrorism and counterterrorism studies. Since '9/11' the number of such studies has grown exponentially, reflecting the rise in perceived threats and the needs of the authorities to deal with terrorism. But what have academia and think tanks come up with? What theories, assumptions and conventional wisdom have they produced that could be of help in understanding this phenomenon and dealing with it? In chapter four (on terrorism) and chapter five (on counterterrorism), we examine the most interesting results and compare these with empirical evidence with the aim to either stress their importance or to debunk them as myths. The sixth chapter of this book builds on what was explored and discussed in the previous chapters. It zooms in on the question how we can best deal with terrorism, investigating concepts such as resilience, fear and impact management. The final chapter looks at trends and developments in (counter)terrorism. First, we explain why it is important to monitor trends and look ahead. We will then discuss un- and under-researched topics and identify persisting challenges. We end with some thoughts on a possible future research agenda.

The target audience of this book is the same as that of the Massive Open Online Course: 'Terrorism and Counterterrorism: Comparing Theory & Practice', including practitioners working in the field of terrorism and security, as well as students, journalists and a wide range of other people with a strong interest in terrorism and counterterrorism.

This textbook offers essential reading for the above mentioned target audience. Next to the online course material, this textbook provides additional readings, concrete examples of cases of terrorism and counterterrorism and other insights that help the reader to discuss, analyse and understand the complex phenomena of terrorism and counterterrorism.

About the authors

Prof. dr. Edwin Bakker is professor in terrorism studies at Leiden University and works for the Netherlands Police Academy. He is an advisor and editor to several journals in the field of security studies and provides courses for university students as well as security professionals. His research interests include jihadist terrorism and (the impact of) counterterrorism policies. Many students worldwide have participated in his massive open online course on terrorism and counterterrorism on Coursera and FutureLearn.

Dr. Jeanine de Roy van Zuijdewijn is assistant professor in terrorism studies at Leiden University. She is a member of several international networks in the field of counterterrorism and serves as an associate editor of one of the main terrorism journals. Her research interests include dealing with the impact of terrorism, threat perceptions, foreign fighters and lone-actor terrorism. She aims to make academic knowledge relevant for wider audiences, ranging from the general public to policymakers and politicians.

Acknowledgements

The authors of this textbook gratefully acknowledge the support of a number of people in writing this book and organising the MOOC on terrorism and counterterrorism. Without their help, neither the book nor the MOOC would have materialised. First there is the team that helped starting this project by introducing MOOCs to Leiden University and those who continued this important work with a high level of professionalism and enthusiasm: we would like to mention the Tanja de Bie in particular. We would also like to thank the panel of students from the track terrorism studies in the Master Crisis and Security Management of Leiden University. For the research of the first edition of this book, Reinier Bergema and Furlan Funke-Kaiser played a crucial role, as did the staff of the Institute of Security and Global Affairs (formerly known as the Centre for Terrorism and Counterterrorism, CTC) and the International Centre for Counter-Terrorism (ICCT), who proofread the text. The same holds for the team of Leiden University Press, three anonymous reviewers and prof. dr. Alex P. Schmid who provided valuable feedback on the first edition of this book.

1

Definition and nature of terrorism

1.1   Introduction

Terrorism is a highly complex, highly subjective and politically sensitive topic. In this chapter we will address some of this complexity, subjectivity and sensitivity. We will show why and how terrorism is receiving much attention from both the media and governments and how it has affected societies. After discussing the geographical distribution of attacks and casualties, we will arrive at the problem of defining terrorism. We will explore the questions of what can be labelled terrorism and what not, and why it is actually important (and difficult) to define the term. Finally, we will discuss the nature of terrorism: what it is about, what it does to society, and how it works.

That terrorism indeed has an impact on society we can read in the papers and see on television and the internet. In fact, terrorism makes headlines almost every day and almost everywhere around the globe. In recent years, major attacks have taken place in many parts of the world, leaving hardly any region untouched. The most lethal and most 'spectacular' attacks have not only received national attention, but in many cases have made headlines across the world. For instance, the Paris attacks on 13 November 2015 not only were breaking news in France and the rest of Europe, but also resulted in headlines in newspapers as far away as Indonesia. Readers of *Media Indonesia* were confronted with a picture of the attack and its victims with a headline saying, 'Europe on alert after the Paris tragedy'. Other examples are international responses to the many attacks by the terrorist organisation Boko Haram in

Nigeria. Their kidnapping of young girls in April 2014 made it to the front pages of newspapers around the world. The US-based *CBS News* reported, '100 schoolgirls kidnapped in Nigeria by suspected extremists', and the newspaper *China Daily* reported, 'China condemns Nigeria kidnappings'. US First Lady Michelle Obama and Pope Francis were among the various international figures who joined the #BringBackOurGirls social media campaign. Also in 2014, the rise of Islamic State (formerly known as Islamic State of Iraq and the Levant - ISIL) and the atrocities committed by that organisation led to worldwide condemnation. That resulted in a United Nations Security Council Resolution 2170 (15 August 2014) in which the Council deplored and condemned 'the terrorist acts of ISIL' in the strongest terms.

But what makes the acts by Islamic State or Boko Haram, and, for instance, the Paris attacks 'terrorist acts'? When and why do we use that label to describe certain acts of violence? We will discuss this very important question after further exploring the deadliness and geographical scope of attacks that have been labelled terrorist attacks.

1.2 A worldwide phenomenon

Whatever definition one uses, unfortunately, there has not been a single day in recent history in which 'extremists' or 'terrorists' have not killed or wounded civilians, military personnel, police or others. In the past decade, terrorism has left almost a quarter of a million dead in many parts of the world. The Global Terrorism Database (GTD) (see box 1.01) of the University of Maryland is one of the very few databases that have collected data on terrorism for a long time. According to that database, there were 106,301 acts of terrorism between 2010 and 2019 – defined as intentional acts of violence or threats of violence by a non-state actor meeting two of the following three criteria:

1. The violent act was aimed at attaining a political, economic, religious or social goal;
2. The violent act included evidence of an intention to coerce, intimidate or convey some other message to a larger audience (or audiences) other than the immediate victims; and
3. The violent act was outside the precepts of International Humanitarian Law.

Using these criteria, these acts have led to more than 243,000 fatalities and 284,000 injuries in a ten-year timespan between 2010 and 2019. It should be noted that other sources provide different figures, partly depending on the definitions and methodologies they use, which we will discuss later in this book.

The Global Terrorism Database (GTD)

The University of Maryland does extensive research on both trans- and international terrorist events and presents its data annually in its Global Terrorism Database (GTD), starting in 1970. The GTD is currently maintained by the National Consortium for the Study of Terrorism and Responses to Terrorism (START) and consists of over 200,000 terrorist attacks, with information on dozens of variables, such as the nature of the attack and the number of casualties, but also the motive of the perpetrators and the amount of ransom paid in regard to kidnappings. For 2019 it lists 8,495 terrorist attacks, resulting in 20,329 fatalities (and 18,714 injuries) across 61 countries. However, around 40 per cent of the total casualties occurred in just one country: Afghanistan (8,249). Nigeria followed with 1,718 and Yemen suffered 1,223 deaths because of terrorism. Together, more than half of the total casualties were found in these three countries. The actual datasets, along with additional information on research and the methodology of the GTD, can be accessed via their website at http://www.start.umd.edu/gtd/.

BOX 1.01 THE GLOBAL TERRORISM DATABASE

Yet not all parts of the world are as much troubled by acts of terrorism as others. In fact, terrorism is a strategic threat – seriously challenging the existing political and social order – in only a limited number of countries. Among the countries that in the last few years have been confronted by extremely high numbers of terrorist attacks are Iraq, Afghanistan, Nigeria, Pakistan, Syria, Somalia, Yemen and the Philippines.

If we take the incidents reported by the GTD for the period between 2000 and 2019, we see several countries that suffered many more fatalities than others. Iraq heads the list with about 80,000 fatalities in those two decades, followed by Afghanistan with about 57,000, while Nigeria has counted around 27,000 deaths. The fourth on the list is Pakistan with about 22,000 people killed, followed by Syria (17,000), Somalia (12,000), Yemen (12,000) and India (11,000).

Parts of the world with much lower numbers of fatalities and injured people include most western countries. For instance, Europol, the EU's law enforcement agency, reported 21 fatalities across the 27 member states in the year 2020. The US and Canada also suffered very few deaths because of terrorism in the same period. The same holds for other states in the western hemisphere, such as Brazil and Mexico, which are relatively safe from the terrorist threat (not counting criminal kidnappings or other forms of violence that might 'terrorise' the population). The same holds for the largest state in the world in terms of population, the People's Republic of China. The Chinese are occasionally confronted by fatal terrorist attacks. Nonetheless, the number of reported incidents and casualties has, until recently, been relatively low.

The GTD's data provide a good overview of the physical threat of terrorism. But there are other ways to measure its seriousness. By combining the data of the GTD, in particular the number of fatalities and injuries, with the amount of property damage the Global Terrorism Index provides a broader picture of the consequences of terrorism. It shows a number of hotspots of terrorism: most parts of Southeast Asia and the Middle East, the Russian Federation and most regions within Africa. These parts of the world are more often confronted by terrorist attacks and their consequences than a number of other regions where terrorism is less of a security issue. Moreover, they are confronted by counterterrorism measures – including the use of violence by states – which add to terrorism-related insecurity. The relatively more fortunate parts of the world in this respect include the remaining parts of Asia, Southern Africa, the Americas, Australia and Europe. In these regions and countries terrorism is a low physical and strategic threat. It does not cause a lot of victims nor does it pose a serious threat to the existing political order. Nonetheless, rightly or wrongly, it is often perceived as a serious threat to societies. Moreover, terrorist attacks, especially major ones such as those on 9/11, have provoked strong counterterrorism measures worldwide.

Key points
- Terrorism has a worldwide impact.
- Although terrorism is a worldwide phenomenon, there are important regional differences.
- Most terrorist attacks take place in Southeast Asia, the Middle East, Russia and various parts of Africa.
- Many parts of Asia, the southern part of Africa, the Americas, Australia and Europe are less frequently troubled by terrorism.
- Nonetheless, even in countries with relatively few terrorist attacks, it is often perceived as a serious threat to security.

1.3 Terrorism leading to strong responses around the globe

As mentioned above, not only in the countries where terrorists strike most often, but also in parts of the world where they pose a low physical and strategic threat, terrorism ranks high on the political agenda. It is considered one of the most important and pressing security issues that requires the full attention of politicians and policymakers. Major attacks often result in strong counterterrorism measures, including quite a few that have received criticism linked to fundamental questions about their legitimacy and proportionality.

Human rights organisations in particular believe that much of the post-9/11 counterterrorism legislation is dangerously over-broad and has undermined civil liberties and fundamental human rights. Others have pointed to issues related to efficiency and effectiveness or unwanted negative side effects of counterterrorism. A number of the most controversial measures need mentioning. One of them is the 2001 'Uniting and Strengthening America by Providing Appropriate Tools Required to Intercept and Obstruct Terrorism Act', better known by its acronym, the 'PATRIOT Act', which expanded the investigatory instruments of American law enforcement agencies in their combat against terrorism. In the UK, after the 2005 London bombings, Parliament passed several Acts including the 'Terrorism Act 2006', which extended police powers to deal with the encouragement of terrorism both on- and offline, the preparation of terrorist acts and terrorist training, amongst others. Additionally, the Act extended police powers to hold terrorist suspects without charge, doubling the time allowed from 14 to 28 days. Similarly, the rise of western foreign fighters joining the ranks of IS and other jihadist groups in Syria and Iraq from 2013 onwards was followed by extraordinary measures in several countries. This included laws aimed at revoking the passports or even the citizenship of these fighters.

As these examples indicate, major terrorist attacks or developments can lead to more and more far-reaching counterterrorism legislation. This not only holds for western countries, but strong reactions have also happened in many other parts of the world. The case of India is a clear example. Since its independence in 1947, this country has had a turbulent history of terrorism, having been confronted with, among other things, separatist and Islamist groups in Kashmir, separatist movements in the Punjab and the north-eastern regions, and communist groups in the central part of the country. In response to an attack on India's parliament building in December 2001 by members of Lashkar-e-Taiba and Jaish-e-Mohammed, both separatist and Islamist groups, the Parliament of India passed the 'Prevention of Terrorism Act' (POTA). Like the US 'PATRIOT Act', POTA faced substantial criticism because of its broad definition of terrorism, rigorous detention procedures and vast investigatory powers. It should be noted that in 2004, after multiple reports of abuse (including cases of detention without charge, police misconduct, lack of judicial and administrative oversight), POTA was repealed by a newly elected government. This was possible in part because the Act had a built-in sunset clause – an expiry date three years after its commencement (see box 1.02).

Sunset clause

Sunset clauses are provisions of law which provide for the expiry of a law at some point in the future. They are employed especially for controversial legislation, passed quickly in response to a crisis such as after a major terrorist attack. They are used to prevent the normalisation of exceptional measures and to allow for democratic accountability through review mechanisms when the law expires. Sunset clauses can take different forms. They can simply state a date on which the legislation will cease to exist. They can automatically trigger a review of legislation, such as an evaluation of its effectiveness and (negative) side effects. Or they can provide for legislation to lapse on a certain date unless there are good reasons to believe that the law should be extended. Sunset clauses and review mechanisms have been recommended by human rights organisations and several international organisations, including the United Nations Counterterrorism Implementation Task Force (CTITF). See for instance the CTITF's 'Basic Human Rights Reference Guide: Conformity of National Counterterrorism Legislation with International Human Rights Law', published in 2014.

BOX 1.02   SUNSET CLAUSE

When looking at these cases, we see a trade-off between security and human rights. Especially after major attacks, in order to gain more security state actors are more willing to compromise on fundamental rights, such as the freedom of expression, the right to privacy and the principle that a prisoner is released from detention when there is a lack of sufficient cause or evidence. Non-governmental organisations (NGOs) such as Amnesty International and Human Rights Watch (HRW) have repeatedly expressed their concern about draconic and disproportional counterterrorism measures by states, especially after large or shocking terrorist attacks.

As terrorism is not only a worldwide, but also a trans-border phenomenon, not only individual countries but also international organisations have come up with strong measures in reaction to terrorist attacks. The question of how terrorism can best be prevented has been on the agenda of important international organisations, ranging from the United Nations (UN) to the North Atlantic Treaty Organization (NATO), and other regional (security) organisations, such as the Association of Southeast Asian Nations (ASEAN). In the wake of 9/11, the UN Security Council adopted Resolution 1373 (see box 1.03), which obliges all UN member states to criminalise a number of terrorism-related activities, such as providing financial support for or facilitating terrorist actors. Further measures of the UN to prevent and combat terrorist attacks were defined in its 2006 'Global Counterterrorism Strategy' and include the intensification of cooperation in regard to information exchange and strengthening coordination and collaboration among UN member states in regard to crimes connected to terrorism (such as drug trafficking, money laundering, the illicit arms trade, etc.).

Resolution 1373

Security Council Resolution 1373 (2001), which was adopted unanimously on 28 September 2001 in the wake of the 11 September terrorist attacks in the US, requested countries to implement a number of measures intended to enhance their legal and institutional ability to counter terrorist activities at home, in their regions and around the world, including taking steps to:

- Criminalise the financing of terrorism; freeze without delay any funds related to persons involved in acts of terrorism; deny all forms of financial support for terrorist groups.
- Suppress the provision of safe havens, sustenance or support for terrorists.
- Share information with other governments on any groups practising or planning terrorist acts.
- Cooperate with other governments in the investigation, detection, arrest, extradition and prosecution of those involved in such acts; and criminalise active and passive assistance for terrorism in domestic law and bring violators to justice.
- The Resolution also calls on States to become parties, as soon as possible, to the relevant international counterterrorism legal instruments.

BOX 1.03   RESOLUTION 1373

In the EU, the 2004 Madrid train bombings in which almost 200 people died provoked strong measures to improve ways to prevent such attacks from happening again. In the wake of the bombings, the Council of the EU felt the need for a body that could foster closer cooperation and coordination in the field of counterterrorism. Among others, it appointed an EU Counterterrorism Coordinator who, as the name suggests, would coordinate the work of the EU bodies in the field of counterterrorism and improve cooperation between member states. The Madrid bombings also speeded up the process of developing a European-wide strategy. This strategy, the 'European Union Strategy Counterterrorism Strategy. Prevent, Protect, Pursue, Respond', was adopted by the Council a year later. Among other things, it set out to disrupt the activities of networks and individuals who draw people into terrorism and it contained an action plan with new measures. The Madrid bombings and the subsequent London bombings (2005) also sparked a debate on the need to criminalise various terrorism-related offences in all EU member states, such as recruitment and training for terrorism.

Terrorist attacks can also provoke one of the most extraordinary measures: foreign military interventions. Think of the US-led intervention in Afghanistan (2001-2021) and more recent military interventions by (coalitions of) foreign powers to counter terrorism in Somalia (2011), Mali (2013), Libya (2014), Syria and Iraq (2014), to mention just a few. Some of these operations have received not only a lot of attention, but also a lot of criticism from those who regard these measures as disproportional and counterproductive, leading not to less, but to more terrorism, or because they lack a legal mandate. Also making headlines are the many military operations by armed forces in Colombia, Iraq, Israel, Nigeria, Pakistan, the Philippines, Russia, Turkey and many other countries. These operations cause casualties not only among terrorists – or rebels, insurgents or 'opposing forces' – but also among innocent civilians.

Key points

- Terrorist attacks can provoke strong counterterrorism measures.
- Many countries have come up with new and sometimes extraordinary measures after terrorist attacks.
- As terrorism is a global phenomenon, international organisations have also developed new measures, policies and strategies in response to terrorist attacks.
- Military interventions are among the most far-reaching of measures taken after terrorist attacks.
- Some of the strong measures taken after terrorist attacks have been criticised as they have an impact on fundamental rights or cause casualties among innocent civilians.

1.4 The use of the term 'terrorism'

As mentioned earlier, terrorism makes headlines almost every day in many parts of the world. The words we use to describe attacks and define this phenomenon differ around the world depending on political views, languages, cultures and other factors. Moreover, the way we use the term terrorism today differs from the way we talked about political violence and related groups in previous eras.

In the past certain violent acts, which we might nowadays call acts of terrorism, were not labelled as such. The assassination of William McKinley, the 25th president of the United States, in 1901 is such an example. In the name of anarchism, Leon Czolgosz shot the US president twice at a public appearance in Buffalo. Although McKinley initially seemed to recover, he died as a result of gangrene. In its aftermath, newspapers used different terms to describe the attack. The *Philadelphia Record*, a local paper, simply stated that McKinley was shot twice by an anarchist. It reported that 'Washington was stunned by the blow' and it featured a drawing showing where the President was hit. However, the term 'terrorism' or 'terrorist' was never mentioned.

This is just one example showing how different terms have been used at different times to describe violent political acts by non-state actors. Think of the term 'freedom fighters', which is associated with anti-colonialism and the struggle against oppressive regimes. While these fighters were labelled 'terrorist' by the authorities, the local population would often see them as honourable defenders who rebelled against an oppressor. Obviously, it depends from what side you look at it or, as the historian Walter Laqueur (1987, p. 7) put it, '[o]ne man's terrorist is another man's freedom fighter'. This often-mentioned phrase can, of course, also be read the other way around. For a critique of the idea that the use of the label 'terrorist' or 'freedom fighter' is simply a matter of personal opinion, it is worth reading Boaz Ganor's article (2002) 'Defining Terrorism: Is One Man's Terrorist another Man's Freedom Fighter?'.

The notion of 'terrorist versus freedom fighter' is also visible in the report of a British newspaper, *The Dundee Courier*, on Mohandas Gandhi and the state of India in the early 1920s (see box 1.04). The newspaper used terms such as 'serious anxiety', 'open violence', 'bloodshed' and 'the murder of Britishers', and referred to Gandhi and his following as a 'gang of terrorists'. Gandhi's notion of civil disobedience was equated with 'open violence' and he was considered a threat to the stability of the UK and its colonial territory. Roughly a week after the publication of this report, the authorities convicted Gandhi of sedition and sentenced him to six years in prison. Nowadays, Gandhi is considered one of the world's greatest non-violent leaders and his name is mentioned in the same breath as those of other pioneers of civil rights campaigns, like Dr. Martin Luther King.

'The Peril in India – Fruit of Doctrinaire Policies'
'The international state of India gives cause for serious anxiety, and any reduction of the army is impossible. ... The infamous Gandhi ... is still at liberty. The distinction between his "civil disobedience" campaign and open violence is purely academic. It has led to much bloodshed, and although its author has once more "repented" no reliance can be placed on his promises. ... Now its spread has been so insidious that all our military forces in India might at any time be required to cope with an outbreak of violence. Seditious propaganda has been at work among our native troops, and among the civil population public lectures are openly given advocating the murder of Britishers. ... The loyal population, native as well as European, is at the mercy of gangs of terrorists and assassins.'
Quotation from *the Dundee Courier*, Fruit of Doctrinaire Policies, 9 March 1922.
BOX 1.04 'THE PERIL IN INDIA – FRUIT OF DOCTRINAIRE POLICIES'

As in the 1920s in Gandhi's case, contemporary media play an important role in attributing the labels 'terrorism' and 'terrorist' to certain acts of violence and militant armed groups. By using emotional and denigrating labels, media are able to influence the perception of their audiences and contribute to shaping public opinion. Often, the media are criticised for this. Reporters and editors have been blamed for being irresponsible, making the threat of terrorism or specific incidents larger or more dramatic than they are, thereby contributing to increased levels of fear among the public. The media have also been blamed for contributing to polarisation or, worse, heightened tensions between various ethnic, religious or political groups.

It should, however, be noted that there are also numerous examples in which media have shown restraint. Perhaps in a reaction to the negative image of the media in relation to terrorism, some (but certainly not all) media outlets are becoming more aware of the sensitivity of using the terms 'terrorist' and 'terrorism', and some try to avoid using it altogether. *Reuters*, one of the leading news agencies in the world, is fully aware of the importance of impartiality and objectivity in the news business and claims to allow its readership to make its own assessments. In the section on terrorism in the

Reuters 'Handbook on Terrorism Journalism' (2014), the agency advises its reporters and editors to avoid the terms 'terrorism' and 'terrorist' whenever possible (see box 1.05). Although seemingly solid advice, it should also be stressed that it is both difficult and problematic to demand restraint from journalists and editors. Of course, the media are attracted by terrorist acts and can and should not ignore them or play down these incidents as it is their duty to report on any major event. They are also attracted by terrorism because the dramatic and spectacular aspects of this phenomenon fascinate their audience, the general public. However, terrorists aim to influence that same audience and themselves try to make use of the media. The staging of extreme and spectacular attacks is partly done to attract the maximum attention and to make headlines around the globe.

In recent years, there seems to be more awareness of the importance of limiting the platform that terrorists might seek and often get. In the aftermath of the Christchurch mosque shootings in 2019, where an extreme right-wing terrorist killed about 50 people in two mosques, New Zealand's Prime Minister, Jacinda Ardern, phrased it as follows: the attacker 'sought many things from his act of terror, but one was notoriety – that is why you will never hear me mention his name'. Similarly, after a jihadist killed French school teacher Samuel Paty, who had discussed cartoons of the prophet Mohammad in class, French President Emmanuel Macron said that he would not talk about such 'cowards' who committed such attacks: 'they no longer even have names'. Limiting the platform of terrorists was restricted not only to their names. After the attack in Nice in 2016, the French newspaper *Le Monde* announced that it would no longer publish pictures of the perpetrators to avoid possible glorification.

The *Reuters* 'Handbook on Journalism'

'We may refer without attribution to terrorism and counterterrorism in general but do not refer to specific events as terrorism. Nor do we use the word terrorist without attribution to qualify specific individuals, groups or events. Terrorism and terrorist must be retained when quoting someone in direct speech. ... Terror as in terror attack or terror cell should be avoided, except in direct quotes. Report the subjects of news stories objectively, their actions, identity and background. Aim for a dispassionate use of language so that individuals, organizations and governments can make their own judgment on the basis of facts. Seek to use more specific terms like "bomber" or "bombing", "hijacker" or "hijacking", "attacker" or "attacks", "gunman" or "gunmen" etc.'

BOX 1.05   THE *REUTERS* 'HANDBOOK ON JOURNALISM'

The use of the term 'terrorism' and its definitions and connotations have changed over the years. Some anarchists were proud to use the term to describe themselves, whereas the militants of the anti-colonial wave regarded themselves as freedom fighters and strongly rejected the label 'terrorist'. The use of the term is very subjective. While the victims of an attack or hostage taking are likely to perceive this event as an act of terrorism, for which there is no justification, the perpetrators often consider their actions to be justifiable within their own system of beliefs and values, or as part of a (defensive) struggle against aggression or oppression. Finally, there is disagreement over the question whether or not states can or should be labelled terrorists or whether we should use a different word for states or regimes using the instrument of terror. Think of the many demonstrations after the invasion of Ukraine by Russia with people holding signs saying 'Putin is a terrorist'. Can a head of state be labelled a terrorist or are there other labels more apt to describe political leaders who use violence against civilians? In the next section we will concentrate on this and other difficult questions regarding the definition of terrorism.

Key points

·   The use of the word 'terrorism' has changed over the years.
·   In history we have seen events that we did not at the time label terrorism, but we would now.
·   Yet the opposite has also happened: events and individuals we used to refer to as terrorism and terrorists are now perceived differently.
·   Media are important actors as regards the framing of specific events and actors.
·   Some, but definitely not all, contemporary media outlets have become more aware of the subjectivity and impact of the use of the term 'terrorism'.

1.5   Why is there no generally accepted definition?

Changes in the use of the term of terrorism across time and languages have created confusion and disagreement among both scholars and politicians about how to define the term. But why is it so difficult to agree on a functional, let alone a legal, definition? This is perhaps best explained by Alex Schmid, one of the most renowned scholars in the field of terrorism and counterterrorism studies. In his article, 'Terrorism – The Definitional Problem' (2004), he gives four reasons for the fact that there is no generally accepted definition: (1) 'Terrorism is a "contested concept" and political, legal, social science and popular notions of it are often diverging'; (2) 'the definition question is linked to (de-)legitimization and criminalization'; (3) 'there are many types of "terrorism", with different forms and manifestations'; (4) 'the term has undergone changes of meaning in the more than 200 years of its existence'.

Let us have a closer look at each of these four reasons, starting with the notion that terrorism is a rather contested concept. According to Schmid, it has a strong emotional and moral undertone which makes it difficult to apply to specific events or groups. An individual who is considered to be a terrorist by one conflict party is often considered to be a freedom fighter by the others. It is to some extent a matter of perspective whether a certain act can be regarded as an act of terrorism or as a part of a legitimate struggle for freedom. The late Yasser Arafat, former President of the Palestinian National Authority, received the Nobel Peace Prize in 1994 for his role in the Oslo Peace Accords, along with the Israeli politicians Yitzhak Rabin and Shimon Peres (see box 1.06). However, the Palestine Liberation Organisation (PLO), of which he was the chairman from 1969, was considered a terrorist organisation by both Israel and the US at least until 1991.

Yasser Arafat

Yasser Arafat was a chairman of the PLO, an organisation founded in 1964 with the purpose of creating an independent Palestine. It tried to achieve this goal by using violence against a wide variety of targets, both inside and outside Israel. This made the PLO one of the most renowned or infamous armed non-state organisations in the world. Its leader was, for some, the archetypical terrorist or freedom fighter, depending on one's position as regards the PLO. Arafat operated from several Arab countries such as Jordan, Lebanon and Tunisia. His organisation gradually transformed into a quasi-state actor that started to accept Israel's right to exist in peace and to reject the use of violence and terrorism. In response, Israel officially recognised the PLO as the representative of the Palestinian people and the Palestinian National Authority of which Arafat became the first President. Later in his career, Arafat engaged in a series of negotiations with the government of Israel. For his constructive role in these he received the Nobel Peace Prize in 1994. Arafat's award was the subject of controversy. In the eyes of most Palestinians, Arafat was a heroic freedom fighter for their cause, while many Israelis continued to regard him as an unabashed terrorist.

BOX 1.06   YASSER ARAFAT

Another example of the ambiguity surrounding a rebel, insurgent or 'terrorist' leader when it comes to terminology is Abdullah Öcalan, the imprisoned leader of the Kurdistan Workers' Party (PKK). Despite the fact that the PKK is listed as a terrorist organisation in Turkey, the EU and the US, he is considered a hero and a freedom fighter by many people with a Kurdish background. Even with regard to Osama bin Laden, the late leader of al-Qaeda who was held responsible for the attacks on 9/11 and other terrorist attacks, there is no unanimity over the use of the label 'terrorist'. He had many followers: among them people who admire him for his stand against western foreign policy and 'infidel' and corrupt regimes in the Islamic world. In many countries in that part or the world one could buy t-shirts or posters of the leader of al-Qaeda that would glorify him.

Turning to the western hemisphere, a similar ambiguity existed with regard to Che Guevara. He was an Argentinian Marxist revolutionary and a major figure of the Cuban Revolution of 1959 which overthrew the regime of the corrupt Cuban President, Fulgencio Batista. 'Che' became a symbol of rebellion in the 1960s and today his picture is still a frequently seen icon in popular culture. It is entirely plausible that if he were to conduct his paramilitary activities today, many governments would be quick to label him a terrorist.

An example of a self-proclaimed fighter for independence is Anders Breivik. In 2011, he bombed a government building in Oslo, Norway, and subsequently opened fire on members of the youth organisation of the Norwegian Labour Party on the island of Utøya, killing 77 people in cold blood. Breivik claimed to be acting in self-defence, calling himself a resistance fighter. He justified his crime by claiming that his victims were part of a 'conspiracy' that was trying to 'deconstruct' the cultural identity of Norway by embracing immigration and multiculturalism. In 2012, Breivik wrote a letter to the far-right extremist, Beate Zschäpe of the National Socialist Underground (NSU), who had been involved in murdering nine people with an immigrant background and a police officer in Germany. Breivik called her a 'courageous heroine of national resistance' and said that they both were 'martyrs for the conservative revolution'.

A second reason why it is so difficult to agree on a universally accepted (legal) definition is its link to the (de)legitimisation and criminalisation of the individual or group that receives the label of terrorist. Organisations that are registered on national or international lists of designated terrorist organisations are considered to be criminal. This gives governments a number of instruments to combat them, such as freezing their assets or arresting their members. The US, as well as supra- and international organisations such as the UN and the EU, maintains such lists. Governments and international organisations are put under pressure by other governments, lobby groups or activists to list or delist certain groups. It should be noted that groups are more frequently listed than delisted.

One organisation that has been confronted with repeated calls to be put on the EU list of terrorist organisations is the Lebanese organisation Hezbollah, a Shi'a Islamist militant group and political party. Advocates of listing Hezbollah as a terrorist organisation refer to its alleged involvement in violent activities both inside and outside Lebanon, such as the terrorist attack on Israeli tourists in Bulgaria in 2012, or its involvement in conflicts in different parts of the Islamic world, such as the civil war in Syria. As a consequence of its alleged involvement, the EU blacklisted the military wing of Hezbollah in 2013, 16 years after it was designated a terrorist organisation by the US State Department. Other states, such as Iran, do not regard Hezbollah as a terrorist organisation, expressed their concerns about adding it to the list and continue to back the group. A second example is the Gülen movement, led by Muslim preacher Fethullah Güllen, who has been living in the United States for more than 20 years. The government of Turkey refers to the group as the Fethullah Terrorist Organisation and proscribed it as a terrorist organisation, a move that was followed by Pakistan and the Gulf Cooperation Council (GCC). Yet, many other countries disagree and the group does not feature on the EU or UN list of terrorist organisations.

The third reason Schmid has identified as complicating the process of finding a common legal definition is the fact that there are many types of 'terrorism', with different forms and manifestations. For example, Europol, the EU's law enforcement agency, identifies five different ideological strands of terrorism: (1) religiously-inspired terrorism; (2) ethno-nationalist and separatist terrorism; (3) left-wing and anarchist terrorism; (4) right-wing terrorism; and (5) single-issue terrorism.

To make things more complicated one could add a sixth category, that of attacks by small groups or individuals with a very vague political idea or ideology, who are mainly inspired by personal issues and (foiled) ambitions that one could label 'personal terrorism' or 'ego terrorism' (see box 1.07).

'Ego terrorism'

Terrorist acts committed by actors who operate more or less on their own initiative with little or no support from others are not new. In the past decade their numbers have grown. Many of them are often indirectly linked to groups and ideologies. However, there are quite a large number who do not fit into one of the categories of terrorism. Their ideological background is not clear and they seem to be primarily driven by personal grievances and motivations. One could label this group of perpetrators examples of 'personal terrorism' or 'ego terrorism'. This development seems to be in line with trends in society: individualisation and 'de-ideologisation'. It is also in line with the basic need and societal pressure to be successful, to be seen in a society that puts pressure especially on young people. The main motivation of ego terrorists is to deal with personal issues and to be seen by conducting attacks on targets that can be linked to a political issue. Think of the case of the attack on the queen of the Netherlands (see box 1.12). The phenomenon can be compared to school shootings except that the target is of a political nature.

BOX 1.07 'EGO TERRORISM'

Think, for instance, of 'incels', an abbreviation of 'involuntary celibates'. This term refers to a (mostly online) movement of predominantly men who are frustrated at being unable to get a romantic partner. 'Incels' have been involved in various acts of violence. In the Canadian city of Toronto in 2018, Alek Minassian drove over various people with his van, killing 11. Some scholars say that such attacks should be labelled as terrorism because they are motivated by an ideology of male supremacy and misogyny, while others say that the centrality of personal grievances and lack of a clear political ideology mean that they should not be considered as such. Perhaps a seventh category, and a politically sensitive one, is that of state terrorism, also referred to as regime terrorism. Some protesters against the invasion of Ukraine see Vladimir Putin as an example of a leader who not only suppresses his own people, think of opposition leaders, war protesters and – in the past – the Chechen minority, but also those of neighbouring countries. For more on terror by states see box 1.08.

Bruce Hoffman on terror by states

In this textbook we understand terrorism to mean certain violent acts by non-state entities. Many might disagree with this limitation, claiming that a number of states also use the instrument of terror. Interestingly, the term 'terrorism' was initially used to refer to the 'regime de la terreur' after the French Revolution. The new regime under Maximilien de Robespierre aimed to consolidate its rule by terrorising counter-revolutionaries and other dissidents. According to Bruce Hoffman in *Inside Terrorism* (2006, pp. 15-16), '[c]ertainly, similar forms of state-imposed or state-directed violence and terror against a government's own citizens continue today. The use of so-called "death squads" ... in conjunction with blatant intimidation of political opponents, human rights and aid workers, student groups, labour organizers, journalists and others has been a prominent feature of the right-wing military dictatorships .... But these state-sanctioned or explicitly ordered acts of internal political violence directed mostly against domestic populations – that is, rule by violence and intimidation by those already in power against their own citizenry – are generally termed "terror" in order to distinguish that phenomenon from "terrorism", which is understood to be violence committed by non-state entities'.

BOX 1.08   BRUCE HOFFMAN ON TERROR BY STATES

The fourth and final reason given by Schmid to explain the difficulties in defining terrorism is the fact that the term 'terrorism' has several times changed its semantic focus. Originally, 'terrorism' referred to the phenomenon of state terror during the 1793-1794 'Reign of Terror', initiated by the authorities when they feared that the French Revolution might be crushed by foreign interventions. According to Schmid (2004) terrorism was initially not used to describe the use of political violence against the state. This changed in the second half of the nineteenth century. In other words, what is meant by the term partly changed, together with the methods and targets of terrorism. The nature of the phenomenon today is in many respects different from the terrorism during the Reign of Terror at the height of the French Revolution. Then the iconic weapon of regime terrorism was the guillotine. Today, it is the suicide bomber with sticks of explosives around his or her body.

Key points

- Scholars and politicians do not agree on how to define terrorism.
- Terrorism is a contested concept: 'one man's terrorist is another man's freedom fighter'.
- It is difficult to come to a generally accepted definition because of the (de)-legitimisation and criminalisation of the phenomenon.
- Another complicating factor is that there are many types of terrorism with different forms and manifestations.
- Finally, the nature of terrorism has changed through the course of history.
- Some terrorists today might be primarily motivated by personal issues and ambitions; we might label this 'ego terrorism'.
- Violence by states against their own citizens is usually not labelled as terrorism.

1.6 The need for a definition

In the previous sections we discussed some difficulties with regard to arriving at a universally accepted or legal definition of terrorism. This lack of consensus is problematic, as such a definition would be extremely valuable from both an academic and a societal perspective. The need to reach a common definition is manifest in three different domains: (1) that of international cooperation; (2) the legal domain; and (3) the academic domain.

First, in order to achieve success within the international domain, states need to agree on what terrorism consists of. As we have witnessed, terrorism is a transnational issue which requires international cooperation, since most individual states do not have the instruments to track and deal with terrorism outside their domestic territory. However, international cooperation, for example the sharing of terrorism-related data, requires a certain level of consensus on what terrorism is. Cooperating states need to find agreement on questions such as: who are we fighting, and what is a terrorist organisation or network? We already highlighted some difficulties with regard to the listing of certain groups as designated terrorist organisations. A lack of cooperation due to the absence of a general definition can also result in the refusal of certain states to share information on terrorists and extradite terrorist suspects. A universal legal definition of terrorism and consensus as to which groups to label terrorist and which not would be highly beneficial to international cooperation.

Second, within the legal domain there is the need to develop a common legal definition of terrorism. According to human rights organisations, the lack of a precise definition of terrorism is an invitation to abuse. When terrorism is not strictly defined it can open the political space for government agencies to use the term in a way that suits their special interests. It is very tempting, especially for more authoritarian regimes, to stretch the definition of terrorism in order to achieve certain goals that have nothing to do with countering terrorism. For instance, by labelling demonstrations or other types of political action as terrorism, authoritarian regimes are able to silence all kinds of opposition groups. These governments can charge those groups with terrorism-related activities and arrest and convict their leaders and supporters. Non-governmental organisations such as Human Rights Watch (HRW) have expressed concern about human rights violations committed as a result of vaguely worded definitions of terrorism. The overly broad nature of these definitions allows the authorities to enforce them rather arbitrarily.

An example is provided by HRW in its report, '"In a Legal Black Hole" Sri Lanka's Failure to Reform the Prevention of Terrorism Act' (2022). For 40 years the country used the Prevention of Terrorism Act (PTA) mostly to fight the Liberation Tigers of Tamil Eelam (LTTE, also known as 'Tamil Tigers') which was active between 1976 and 2009 and aimed to get an independent Tamil state in Sri Lanka. In 2022, the Sri Lankan government finally changed its counterterrorism policies in response to strong criticism. While HRW applauded some developments, it noted that the amended PTA still does not provide a clear definition of the term 'terrorism'. This means that it can be used to target ethnic and religious minorities and curtail political dissent. Human rights organisations have noted such patterns with regard to counterterrorism legislation in many countries. A wide range of activities are often considered as terrorist activities or terrorism-related activities, with the consequence that ordinary crimes such as murder, assault and kidnapping are now treated under terrorism laws. Given these broad definitions, it is easier for regimes with malicious intent to label common protestors terrorists. A generally accepted and clear-cut definition could limit certain abuses by governments.

A commonly accepted legal definition is also important for private companies. Increasingly, they can be held accountable if they provide services to terrorists. Think of the role of social media companies that need to remove content linked to terrorism (see box 1.09) or banks that have to combat the financing of terrorism and can do so only when they can properly check what organisation or individual should be regarded as a terrorist. A generally accepted legal definition and commonly accepted lists of terrorist organisations are essential to being able to do this in an effective way and without unintended side effects. Think of innocent customers who might be excluded from certain financial services because they belong to groups in society that are associated with terrorism, or aid organisations or other NGOs that work in areas where there is a lot of terrorism.

Taking down online extremist content

The Christchurch mosque shootings revived debates on the policies of hosting service providers in relation to taking down extremist content. The attacker had livestreamed his violence and the footage had been widely shared across various platforms on the internet. Representatives of states and hosting service providers met in Paris in May 2019 for the Christchurch Call to Action Summit, where they expressed their commitment to 'eliminat[ing] terrorist and violent extremist countries online'. While progress has been made, companies still struggle with detecting such videos in time. A few months after the summit, a right-wing extremist in the German city of Halle livestreamed his attack on a synagogue and kebab shop for 35 minutes before it was taken down. In 2021, after years of debate, the European Parliament adopted a law that forces hosting services to remove terrorist content within one hour after receiving a notification. While there is widespread support for the principle of removing terrorist content, critics argue that this might lead to the over-removal of content as companies do not want to run the risk of getting fined, and so limiting freedom of expression. Others raised worries that more authoritarian regimes could flag content by the political opposition as terrorism propaganda, forcing online platforms to remove it quickly.

BOX 1.09   TAKING DOWN ONLINE EXTREMIST CONTENT

The third domain, academia, would also benefit from a generally accepted definition of terrorism. Researchers in the field of terrorism studies are often confronted with different definitions that hamper, for instance, comparative studies. An example that clearly illustrates this problem is the discrepancy in the number of casualties of terrorism counted by different sources, such as the US State Department, Europol and the GTD. This discrepancy is the consequence of the different definitions adopted by those institutions. In practice, this entails that some cases are included in one dataset and excluded in another, which results in different representations of terrorism. Because these institutions adopt different definitions as the basis of their research, it is difficult to compare their findings and make statements on contemporary terrorism (see box 1.10).

Definitions and methodologies and comparative research

Various organisations try to monitor the number of people killed because of terrorism worldwide. Three of the most well-known ones are the GTD, the US Department of State (DOS) and the Global Terrorism Index (GTI) published by the Institute for Economic & Peace. Using different definitions and methodologies leads to different figures. For the year 2019 the number of fatalities was 25,000 (DOS), 21,000 (GTD) and 14,000 (GTI). In other words, the highest estimate reports 80 per cent more fatalities than the lowest one. Also important to note is that some databases sometimes change the definition that they use. For instance, the country reports on terrorism by the DOS employed three different ways to calculate terrorism deaths between 2010 and 2019. This makes it very complicated for researchers to compare data and to carry out a proper analysis of these figures. That is why it is important always to look at the methodology sections of databases and statistical reports.

BOX 1.10   DEFINITIONS AND METHODOLOGIES AND COMPARATIVE RESEARCH

It should be noted that definition problems are not unique to the study of terrorism and counterterrorism. In social sciences, defining any social phenomenon is a challenge, let alone agreeing on a single functional definition. Take, for instance, 'poverty', 'happiness' or 'discrimination'. There are many ways to define these phenomena, resulting in different approaches or policies to deal with them.

Key points

- Although it has proven to be difficult to reach consensus on a definition of terrorism, one would be very valuable.
- A definition would improve international cooperation, as it would help states and international organisations to agree on whom and what to fight.
- A clear-cut definition would also limit the abuse of legal instruments by states under the pretence of counterterrorism measures and would help private actors to avoid delivering services to terrorists without negative side effects to other customers.
- An academic consensus definition of terrorism could improve the quality of research, especially comparative research.

1.7   Definition attempts

Although it has been impossible to reach consensus on a definition of terrorism, the previous section has highlighted why such a consensus would be extremely valuable. The importance of a single legal definition of terrorism has not gone unnoticed, as leading public figures have made an attempt at crafting one (see box 1.11). Former Secretary General of the UN Kofi Annan tried to grasp what he considered to be the nature of terrorism and translate it into a viable working definition. In late 2006 UN member states agreed on a common strategy for combating terrorism titled 'Uniting Against Terrorism – Recommendations for a Global Counterterrorism Strategy'. Despite this UN strategy, an attempt to reach consensus on a definition of terrorism failed miserably. Such a definition has hitherto not been formulated due to some of the difficulties outlined above. The definition of the Secretary-General's 'High-level Panel on Threats, Challenges and Change' (2004) read as follows, '[a]ny action, in addition to actions already specified by the existing conventions on aspects of terrorism, the Geneva Conventions and Security Council Resolution 1566 (2004), that is intended to cause death or serious bodily harm to civilians or non-combatants, when the purpose of such an act, by its nature or context, is to intimidate a population, or to compel a Government or an international organization to do or to abstain from doing any act'. However, in light of the conflicts between Israel and its Arab neighbours, and that between India and Pakistan over Kashmir, some Muslim states hold that under certain circumstances, in particular foreign occupation, violence is not necessarily unjustified, and therefore should not be labelled as terrorism. According to these member states, a legal definition of terrorism should include state terrorism and make allowances for the struggle for self-determination. However, accepting such conditions would affect not only the Israeli-Palestinian conflict but also disputes over other contested territories.

This brings up the question of the context in which certain 'terrorist' or 'terror' acts take place. Can we speak of terrorism in an ongoing war or war-like situation? Is terrorism only a peace-time phenomenon, and should we speak of insurgencies or guerrilla warfare within the context of war? The Supreme Court of India once adopted Schmid's suggestion to choose a restricted legal definition of terrorist acts being the peacetime equivalents of war crimes. According to Schmid (1993, p. 12), 'such a definition might exclude some forms of violence and coercion (such as attacks on the military, hijackings for escape and destruction of property) currently labelled "terrorism" by some governments'. It should be stressed that any attempt to take this approach will run into another problem; that of defining war and answering the related crucial question of what forms of organised, politically focused violence constitute war.

Examples of definitions of terrorism

- Political scientist Martha Crenshaw: '[t]errorism is a conspiratorial style of violence calculated to alter the attitudes and behaviour of multitude audiences. It targets the few in a way that claims the attention of the many. Terrorism is not mass or collective violence but rather the direct activity of small groups'. Crenshaw, M. (1995), *Terrorism in Context*, University Park: Penn State University Press, 4.
- Israeli Prime Minister Benjamin Netanyahu: '[t]errorism is the deliberate and systematic assault on civilians to inspire fear for political ends'. Netanyahu, B. (1995), *Terrorism: How the West Can Win*, London: Weidenfeld and Nicholson.
- UN Secretary General Kofi Annan: '[a]ny action constitutes terrorism if it is intended to cause death or serious bodily harm to civilians and non-combatants, with the purpose of intimidating a population or compelling a Government or international organization to do or abstain from doing an act'. United Nations News Centre. (2005).

BOX 1.11   EXAMPLES OF DEFINITIONS OF TERRORISM

While the international community is still unable to agree on a universal *legal* definition of terrorism, a somewhat higher degree of agreement has begun emerging in the academic community since Schmid made several efforts to bring academics to the same page. In the 1980s Schmid identified 22 components that could be found regularly in various academic, administrative and legal definitions of terrorism. Based on these frequently used elements, he composed the following definition in 1988 with Albert Jongman (p. 28): '[t]errorism is an anxiety-inspiring method of repeated violent action, employed by (semi-)clandestine individual group or state actors, for idiosyncratic, criminal or political reasons, whereby, in contrast to assassination, the direct targets of violence are not the main targets. The immediate human victims of violence are generally chosen randomly (targets of opportunity) or selectively (representative or symbolic targets) from a target population, and serve as message generators. Threat- and violence based communication processes between terrorist (organization), (imperiled) victims, and main targets are used to manipulate the main targets (audience(s)), turning it into a target of terror, a target of demands, or a target of attention, depending on whether intimidation, coercion, or propaganda is primarily sought'.

In 2011 Schmid revised his academic consensus definition again, based on a new round of consultations with members of academia and others. He included the most prominent elements, such as the political nature of the threat, and the use or threat of use of force, but also elements such as arbitrariness of target selection (e.g. targets of opportunity, representative or symbolic nature) and mechanisms (e.g. intimidation, coercion, propaganda). What is remarkable, and of course up for debate, is the inclusion of states as potential terrorist actors. So far, this particular issue has divided academia, the UN, experts in international law and many others.

Nonetheless, the search for a definition continues … and continues to get lost. Or, as Brian Jenkins in an interview with Lisa Stampnitzky (2013, p. 5) put it: '[d]efinitional debates are the great Bermuda Triangle of terrorism research. I've seen entire conferences go off into definitional debates, never to be heard from again'. And even with a proper definition, defining certain groups and events remains difficult. For instance, as the academic consensus definition of Schmid shows, many regard terrorism not to be primarily or ultimately aimed at the direct victims. Instead, it is widely considered a practice or doctrine of using physical violence to instill fear in order to get a political message across. Yet what message is not always very clear (see box 1.12).

How would you label this?

In 2009, The Netherlands was shaken by the live images of a car sweeping through a crowd during the festivities on 'queen's day' in the city of Apeldoorn. The footage of bodies flying through the air reached millions right in their living rooms. The perpetrator drove his car into the crowd in the direction of a bus with most members of the royal family in it. He missed the open-topped bus by only a couple of metres and crashed into a monument. He accused the crown prince of being a fascist and a racist, just before he died in his crashed car. The question is how to label such an incident: as an act of terrorism or something else? The Dutch authorities were quick to say that it was not a terrorist attack. At the press conference some four hours after the attack, the public prosecutor stated that while they had reason to assume that the attack was premeditated, there was no reason to assume any link to terrorism. Investigations into the perpetrator did not provide many clues about why he had wanted to attack the royal family. He left no note or anything else that could link him to a certain group or movement or political ideology. Was this a terrorist incident or not? He did target one of the ultimate symbols of politics in The Netherlands, the queen and the soon to-be king, in other words, the head of state. The GTD included the attack in its database as a terrorist incident. How would you have labelled the attack?

BOX 1.12   HOW WOULD YOU LABEL THIS?

Fortunately, there are a number of governmental and academic definitions that are used quite often. Think of Schmid's definition, the definition used by the GTD and the EU's. Nonetheless, these and others remain contested. Yet the search for a generally accepted definition will undoubtedly continue in the years to come.

Key points

- There have been various attempts to arrive at a generally accepted definition of terrorism over the past decades by academics and by the UN.
- Although there is no consensus on a universal legal definition, there appears to be some agreement on a number of key elements of terrorism.
- These elements are the idea that terrorism is a tool, a mechanism or an instrument to spread fear by the use of violence in order to affect politics and society as a whole.

Key elements of terrorism

In the previous section we discussed attempts to arrive at a generally accepted definition. We observed that although there is no consensus on a universal legal definition, there appears to be some level of agreement on the idea that terrorism is a tool, a mechanism or an instrument to spread fear by the use of violence to affect politics and society as a whole. So there is more or less agreement on the idea that terrorism is an instrument or a tactic of certain actors to achieve certain political goals. The use of force or violence is an important part of this instrument or tactic.

Terrorists use force or the threat of force to intimidate their opponents. The most common weapons and methods of attack that terrorists use as part of their 'modus operandi' – method of operating – change over time. Terrorists perpetrate attacks by shooting, stabbing or using various explosives. In recent decades, as we will discuss in the next chapter, terrorists have increasingly engaged in suicide bombings. They have also used items that are not traditionally seen as weapons; think of the use of aeroplanes (the attacks on 9/11) and trucks and other vehicles. In some cases terrorists have also used biological and chemical substances, and the sum of all fears is that terrorists might get their hands on nuclear weapons. Some terrorist groups have shown an interest in using these substances or have tried to acquire weapons of mass destruction, and trends in technology have increased worries over what is called CBRN terrorism (see box 1.13).

Worries over CBRN terrorism

CBRN terrorism is the name for terrorism in which the perpetrators make use of chemical, biological, radiological or nuclear weapons or materials. The UN Counterterrorism Centre (UNCCT) regards the prospect of terrorists gaining access to and using chemical, biological, radiological and nuclear materials and weapons of mass destruction as a serious threat to international peace and security. The UNCCT observes that, over the years, terrorist groups have tested new ways and means to acquire and use more dangerous weapons to maximise damage and incite terror, including weapons incorporating CBRN materials. It also sees that, with advancements being made in technology and the expansion of legal and illegal commercial channels, including on the dark web, some of these weapons have become increasingly accessible.

BOX 1.13   WORRIES OVER CBRN TERRORISM

Not all forms of terrorist violence are lethal or aimed at causing serious bodily harm. Examples of these kinds of attack are kidnappings and hostage takings. Terrorists have often used such forms of violence to receive ransom or to pressure governments to meet their political demands. There are also various examples of terrorists using hostage takings to press for the release of their imprisoned companions. Some definitions of terrorism also include the credible threat of force as an act of terrorism. A topic of contention is the question whether something like 'cyberterrorism' exists. While cyberattacks might not necessarily lead to physical harm, they could disrupt the fundamental structures of societies and could influence political decision-making and influence political opinion in a non-democratic and illegal way. Think of the use of ransomware and spreading fake news that forces governments to do something or to refrain from doing something or which influences public opinion.

A well-known scholar who was one of the first to emphasise that terrorism is not primarily about killing people is Jenkins. In 1975, he wrote that terrorists want a lot of people watching, not a lot of people dead. His statement is still true for most cases of terrorism. Although it looks as if at least some of today's terrorists 'also want a lot of people dead' – as Jenkins himself noted after the attacks on 9/11 – the essence of terrorism is sending a message to people other than the direct victims.

Connected to this is the fact that the use of violence is not a goal in itself. In other words: terrorists do not kill just to kill, but to have an impact on those who continue to live: society, you and me, and politics. In some cases, however, the goal is to kill certain individuals, political leaders, journalists or religious leaders. But even in these cases these individual targets represent something bigger – a political party or a state, the elite or specific groups in society, or a particular religion.

This means that the direct targets of terrorists are often not the main targets. The almost 3,000 victims of the 9/11 attacks were not the prime targets of the al-Qaeda terrorist cells. The main targets were those watching the footage and pictures of the people killed in New York, Washington D.C. and Pennsylvania. In the eyes of al-Qaeda their chosen locations – the 'capitalist' World Trade Center and the 'imperialist' Pentagon – had high symbolic value and served as a means, rather than an end, as hard as that may sound to the families and friends of those who died. To terrorists, the direct targets are hardly ever the main targets and the violence is aimed at the audience, rather than at the casualties directly affected. In a way, the main target is us, and the terrorists' strategy is to kill a few in order to frighten many others.

Terrorists want to hurt not only those they attack, but also many others. They want people to be afraid, to be angry, to overreact. Unfortunately, they often manage to frighten many people, not only in major attacks, but also with smaller ones. The impact of terrorism on society can sometimes be very high. Media are very important in spreading fear. UK Prime Minister Margaret Thatcher once called media attention the 'oxygen' for the terrorists. But the same holds for politicians and public figures, who often tend to overreact. Terrorists want to spread a political message and aim to provoke certain strong reactions. As a result, terrorism poses a significant threat to many countries, but not in physical terms – although too many people die because of terrorism – but in socio-political terms. The impact of terrorism on politics and society – on our daily lives, how we live together, on relationships between communities and between countries – can be enormous. The impact of terrorism can also be very high in economic terms; think of the disruption to, for instance, tourism in countries where this is a major source of income. The impact of terrorism is thus mostly determined by what happens after an attack and how various actors respond to it. The attack itself is a means to set this process in motion.

Knowing this essential part of the workings of terrorism, maybe we should try harder not to be afraid, not to overreact. An example of such an attempt is the social movement and slogan 'we are not afraid'. In many different countries, citizens have expressed their resilience to terrorism after attacks by using this particular slogan or shown the terrorists in other ways that they will not give them what they want. In chapter 6 we will further elaborate on the need to deal with fear and to limit the impact of terrorism.

Key points
- Terrorism is a tool or tactic, not a goal in itself.
- Terrorists use different types of force or violence.
- The aim is to kill a few in order to frighten many others.
- Terrorists aim to have an impact on politics and society.

1.9 Conclusion

In this chapter we looked into the impact of terrorism and the definition of the term. First we showed how terrorism makes headlines around the world almost every day. We have also given an overview of the geographical distribution of terrorist attacks and the number of casualties. Discussing these data we learned that Iraq, Syria, Afghanistan, Yemen, Pakistan and Nigeria are among the countries that have been hardest hit by terrorism in recent years. Despite the fact that terrorism as a phenomenon is less common in the West, we saw that it is considered one of the most important security issues in the US and Europe, especially after 9/11. In these parts of the world and elsewhere, governments have invested in more and tougher counterterrorism measures. As a consequence, laws have been designed that have largely criminalised terrorism-related activities and expanded the investigatory instruments of national law enforcement agencies. While governments have generally tended to justify these changes by pointing to the success stories of disasters prevented, we also noted that others have expressed their concerns with regard to violations of human rights that have further added to the negative impact of terrorism on societies.

Discussing the number of attacks and victims we touched upon the issue of the definition of terrorism. What makes an incident a terrorist attack, and what makes a group a terrorist one? These are difficult questions as there is no generally accepted definition of the term. Many terms are used to describe comparable phenomena that some may label terrorism and others would give another name to. There are many reasons why defining terrorism is difficult. We described the dynamic nature of terrorism and explained how it has changed significantly throughout time and that it comes in many different shapes and sizes. Its subjective and politically sensitive nature further complicates reaching consensus on a definition. Ideally, we would arrive at a common legal definition, as it would improve, for instance, international cooperation in counterterrorism. We showed that within the academic world Schmid has accumulated many of the elements of definitions by scholars and crafted a definition that is generally considered to be the closest to consensus. According to Schmid, fear is a major component of terrorism. Moreover, rather than 'simply' killing a lot of people, terrorists are seeking some type of (political) change. In order to achieve this, terrorists try to instigate fear in society and to affect politics and societies. Following this argument, we should do more to limit this impact, the possibilities of which we will explore in chapter 6.

Bibliography

Bakker, E. (2006). Differences in Terrorist Threat Perceptions in Europe. In Manchke, D. & Monar, J. (eds.), *International Terrorism. A European Response to a Global Threat?* (47-62). Brussels: Pieter Lang.

Bruce, G. (2013). Definition of Terrorism – Social and Political Effects. *Journal of Military and Veterans Health, 21*(2), 26-30.

Council of the European Union. (2005). *The European Union Counterterrorism Strategy. Prevent, protect, Pursue, Respond.* Brussels: Council of the European Union.

Crenshaw, M. (1995). *Terrorism in Context.* University Park: Penn State University Press.

Europol. (2021). *European Union Terrorism Situation and Trend Report.* Luxembourg: Publications Office of the European Union.

Ganor, B. (2002). Defining Terrorism: Is One Man's Terrorist another Man's Freedom Fighter? *Police Practice and Research, 3*(4), 287-304.

Herschinger, E. (2013). A Battlefield of Meanings: The Struggle for Identity in the UN Debates on a Definition of International Terrorism. *Terrorism and Political Violence, 25*(2), 183-201.

Hoffman, B. (2006). *Inside Terrorism* (revised and expanded ed.). New York: Columbia Press University.

Human Rights Watch. (2012). *In the Name of Security Counterterrorism Laws Worldwide since September 11.* New York: Human Rights Watch.

Human Rights Watch. (2022). *"In a Legal Black Hole". Sri Lanka's Failure to Reform the Prevention of Terrorism Act.* New York: Human Rights Watch.

Jenkins, B. M. (1975). *Will Terrorists Go Nuclear?* Santa Monica: RAND Corporation.

Journal of International Criminal Justice. (2006). *Special Issue Criminal Law Responses to Terrorism After September, 4*(5).

Laqueur, W. (1987). *The Age of Terrorism.* Toronto: Brown and Company.

Merari, A. (1997). Terrorism as a Strategy of Insurgency. *Terrorism and Political Violence, 5*(4), 213-257.

National Consortium for the Study of Terrorism and Responses to terrorism (START). (2022). *Global Terrorism Database,* https://www.start.umd.edu/gtd/.

Netanyahu, B. (1995). *Terrorism: How the West Can Win.* London: Weidenfeld and Nicholson.

Reuters Press Agency. (2014). *Handbook of Journalism.*

Schmid, A. P., & Jongman, A. J. (1988). *Political Terrorism: A New Guide to Actors, Concepts, Data Bases, Theories & Literature.* New Brunswick: Transaction Publishers Inc.

Schmid, A. P. (1993). The Response Problem as Definition Problem. In Schmid, A., and Crelinsten, R., *Western Responses to Terrorism,* (7-13). New York: Frank Cass.

Schmid, A. P. (2004). Terrorism - The Definitional Problem. *Case Western Reserve Journal of International Law, 36*(2-3), 375-419.

Schmid, A. P. (2011). *The Routledge Handbook of Terrorism Research.* London: Routledge.

Stampnitzky, L. (2013). *Disciplining Terror.* Cambridge: Cambridge University Press.

United Nations Counterterrorism Centre. (2022). Chemical, biological, radiological and nuclear terrorism, https://www.un.org/counterterrorism/cct/chemical-biological-radiological-and-nuclear-terrorism.

United Nations General Assembly. (2004). High-level Panel on Threats, *A/59/565 Follow-up to the outcome of the Millenium Summit*. New York: United Nations.

United Nations General Assembly. (2006). *GA resolution A/RES/60/288 on the United Nations Global Counterterrorism Strategy*. New York: United Nations.

United Nations General Assembly. (2010). *GA resolution A/RES/64/297 on the Global Counterterrorism Strategy*. New York: United Nations.

United Nations News Centre. (2005, March 10). *Annan lays out detailed five-point UN strategy to combat terrorism*, https://news.un.org/en/story/2005/03/131322-annan-lays-out-detailed-five-point-un-strategy-combat-terrorism.

United Nations Security Council. (2001). *Resolution 1373*. New York: United Nations.

United Nations Security Council. (2005). *Resolution 1624*. New York: United Nations.

United Nations Security Council. (2014). *Resolution 2170*. New York: United Nations.

United States Department of State. (2022). *Country reports on terrorism*, https://www.state.gov/country-reports-on-terrorism-2/.

2

History of terrorism

2.1   Introduction

Although terrorism has received more attention than ever since the attacks on the US on 11 September 2001, the phenomenon is much older. In fact, there have been several periods in which (what we now call) terrorism ranked high on political and security agendas. In other words, the phenomenon is certainly not a new one. According to Walter Laqueur (2007), '[t]errorism appears in the Bible's Old Testament, and there were frequent incidents of political murder, even systematic assassination in Greek and Roman history'. What is often new is the size, shape, nature and impact of these acts, as well as how we label them. This has changed in the course of the long history of this phenomenon. The French Revolution and the 'Reign of Terror' in 1793-1794 are considered by many to be the starting point of modern terrorism. The Revolutionary regime used 'terror' to deal with its opponents. Terrorism in those days clearly referred to the actions of the state, something which would change in the centuries that followed.

Historians such as Laqueur have looked into the long development of terrorism, aiming to see patterns and trends (see box 2.01). In his book, *A History of Terrorism*, first published in 1977, Laqueur wanted to 'shed some light on certain problems such as the conditions under which terrorism tended to occur and the circumstances in which it prospered or failed' (2001, p. vii). At the same time, he warned that an analysis of the history of terrorism does not offer clear-cut lessons for today, as terrorism varies in time and no country or era could be directly equated with any other.

Walter Laqueur's *A History of Terrorism*

One of the first attempts to present the historical development of terrorism is Laqueur's book, *A History of Terrorism*. The work first appeared in 1977 and was translated into several languages. Today it is considered to be a classic on the history of terrorism, and is probably one of the most often reprinted books on the subject. In this pioneering and authoritative study of terrorism, Laqueur outlines the history of political terror from nineteenth-century Europe, through the anarchists of the 1880s and 1890s, the left- and right-wing clashes during the twentieth century, and the multinational operations of Arab and other groups of the 1970s. With the historical overview and analysis he aimed to shed some light on the conditions under which terrorism tended to occur and the circumstances in which it prospered or failed. Laqueur looked for common patterns, motives and aims, and, in a way, his book is as much a sociological study as a historical one. An expanded edition was published in 2016.

BOX 2.01   WALTER LAQUEUR'S *A HISTORY OF TERRORISM*

An influential attempt to categorise key developments in global terrorism in modern history is the work of David Rapoport (2004), a leading American political scientist. He organised global developments in relation to terrorism into various 'waves' of terrorism. Somewhat like Laqueur, he emphasises continuities and change. In particular with respect to international elements and factors, Rapoport shows that the different waves each have their own characteristics, such as ideological backgrounds, modus operandi, target selection and international audiences and supporters. Each of these four waves lasts a few decades before it peters out. These four waves are (1) the anarchist wave, starting in the 1880s; (2) the anticolonial wave that commenced in the 1920s; (3) the so-called new left wave with its beginnings in the 1960s; and finally (4) the religious wave that started in 1979. The name of each wave represents its dominant feature, but it should be noted that this single feature is not the only characteristic. These waves were connected by their international dimension and ideological character, as they occurred on a global scale.

Key points

- Terrorism is not a new phenomenon and many manifestations of today's terrorism are not new either.
- The history of terrorism shows continuities and change.

- What is often new is the size, shape, nature and impact of terrorist acts.
- Rapoport distinguishes four waves of terrorism, each with its own characteristics, such as ideological background, modus operandi, target selection, international audience and supporters.

2.2 The first wave of terrorism: the 'anarchist wave' (1880s - 1919)

The first wave distinguished by Rapoport is the anarchist wave, which started in tsarist Russia in the 1880s before it spread to other parts of Europe, the Americas and Asia. Initially, anarchism started as a doctrine and social movement inspired by revolutionary Russian writers such as Mikhail Bakunin and Pyotr Kropotkin. As Kropotkin, a former prince, wrote upon invitation in the *Encyclopaedia Britannica* in 1910, anarchism is essentially referred to as 'a principle or theory of life and conduct under which society is conceived without government' and whereby harmony came not from submission or obedience, but by voluntary agreements between (groups of) people (Kropotkin, cited in Jensen, p.8). While these writers played an important role in laying the ideological foundations of future terrorist organisations, many, such as Bakunin, did not support the use of violence. The failure of these non-violent anarchists to accomplish their goals, coupled with increasing police repression, eventually led to the rise of groups who wanted to use violent means. The invention of new technologies and communication tools, such as the telegraph, mass newspapers and railways, allowed these revolutionaries to promote their ideas among Russia's people.

Perhaps the most well-known example of an anarchist terrorist organisation was Narodnaya Volya, best translated as the People's Will. This group aimed to end the reign of Tsar Alexander II and implement political reforms that would bring power to the people. After some failed attempts, the group would eventually succeed in killing the Tsar (see box 2.02). These revolutionaries were often proud to use the term 'terrorist' to describe themselves. An example of this was found in the aftermath of an attack that received widespread attention, perpetrated by Vera Zasulich. Zasulich was a well-known revolutionary and had been in contact with Sergey Nechaev, the author of the infamous *the Catechism of a Revolutionary*, leading to her imprisonment in 1869. Eight years later, after her release, she shot a police commissioner, Fyodor Trepov, who was known for abusing political prisoners. Zasulich proclaimed that she was a terrorist, not a murderer. In a widely publicised trial, she claimed to have acted out of a sense of avenging an act of injustice. Public sympathy was clearly on her side and the trial soon focused more on the brutal behaviour of Trepov than on her attempt to kill him. The jury declared her not guilty and she was released, to the joy of an enthusiastic crowd that welcomed her outside the court in St. Petersburg.

Narodnaya Volya and the 1881 assassination of Tsar Alexander II

The assassination of Tsar Alexander II by Narodnaya Volya followed after a number of failed attempts, such as the use of new types of explosives to blow up the Tsar's train or destroying a bridge in St. Petersburg while Alexander II passed over it. Partly in reaction to these attacks, Alexander II promised the Russian people a constitution, while a special police unit would deal with the terrorist threat. Despite this promise and improved security measures, members of Narodnaya Volya threw two bombs at the Tsar's carriage during his weekly Sunday drive. Although Alexander initially escaped unscathed, the Tsar insisted on going back to check on the injured men, who had been hit by the bomb. While he was standing next to the victims, another bomb was thrown which killed him. After the assassination, Narodnaya Volya sent a letter to the authorities stating that they were willing to enter negotiations. The organisation would lay down its weapons in return for amnesty for political prisoners and an end to Russia's autocratic government.

For more on anarchism see Jensen, R.B. (2004). Daggers, Rifles, and Dynamite: Anarchism Terrorism in 19th Century Europe. *Terrorism and Political Violence, 16*(1), 116-153.

BOX 2.02   NARODNAYA VOLYA AND THE 1881 ASSASSINATION OF TSAR ALEXANDER II

The cases of Narodnaya Volya and Zasulich show the belief of these anarchists in the idea of 'propaganda by the deed'. Anarchists firmly believed that action speaks louder than words. Terrorism was a means, rather than an end, used in order to counter the repressive nature of the state. By eliminating political targets, the self-proclaimed terrorists tried to affect the public attitude to the state. They considered terrorism to be something noble: they saw themselves as heroes or martyrs who were sacrificing themselves for a greater purpose. As also seen in Zasulich's case, they did not consider themselves to be criminals. In addition to their attempts to overthrow the system, the Russian anarchists also assisted or trained foreign groups. Many Russian anarchists also fled the country and launched radical cells of exiles in other countries. Rapoport explains that partly as a result it eventually hit other parts of Europe, the Ottoman Empire and the Americas.

During the 1890s, in the period known as the 'golden age of assassination', the anarchist wave reached its peak. Monarchs, presidents and prime ministers were regular targets of anarchists. As mentioned earlier, US President McKinley was shot in 1901 by Leon Czolgosz, an American anarchist, who regarded him as a symbol of oppression. Other targets who were killed by anarchists were French President Carnot (1894), Empress Elisabeth of Austria (1898) and King Umberto of Italy (1900). Arguably the terrorist attack in modern history with the greatest consequences was the assassination of the Austro-Hungarian archduke Franz Ferdinand by Gavrilo Princip, a member of the Serbian Black Hand, in June 1914, which eventually ignited the First World War (1914-1918). Although this war resulted in overthrowing the systems in four of the warring empires (Germany, Austro-Hungarian Empire, the Ottoman Empire and Russia), the anarchists' political success remained rather limited.

Key points

· In Russia in the 1880s, an initial 'anarchist wave' appeared which continued for some 40 years.
· The Russian experience in the 1880s spread rapidly to other parts of Europe, the Americas and Asia before reaching its peak and receding.
· Rapoport argues that doctrine and technology explain the start of this wave, as well as transformation in communication and transport patterns.
· Monarchs, presidents and prime ministers were victims of the 'propaganda by the deed'.

2.3 The second wave of terrorism: the 'anti-colonial wave' (1920s - 1960s)

The second wave distinguished by Rapoport is the anti-colonial wave. Somewhat ironically, this wave was a response to the Versailles Peace Treaty of 1919, the (formal) outcome of World War I which, in its turn, was sparked off by the assassination of the Austro-Hungarian Archduke. Former European empires were broken up and borders were redefined, partly according to the principle of self-determination. US President Woodrow Wilson was one of the key proponents of this idea of self-determination, which quickly spread around the world. However, as Rapoport explains, this principle was initially not applied to the non-European territories which became mandates of the victors of World War I, until they were considered 'ready' for independence. Colonial rule triggered terrorist activity by organisations such as the Irish Republican Army (IRA), the Jewish Irgun and the Algerian Front de Libération Nationale (FLN). Their terrorist campaigns eventually contributed to the establishment of the Irish Republic and the states of Israel and Algeria.

In terms of their characteristics, there are a number of differences between the first and second waves of terrorism. First of all, Rapoport explains that due to the negative connotation of the term 'terrorist' as a result of first-wave terrorism, the rebels would refer to themselves as 'freedom fighters'. This new terminology adopted by these self-proclaimed freedom fighters was not merely a superficial decision, as their goal, independence, was considered much more legitimate than the goals of first-wave terrorist organisations. They considered themselves to be fighting 'government terror'. Imperialist governments, however, were also aware of the power of semantics, as they labelled these anti-colonial rebels 'terrorists' or, at best, 'guerrillas' in an attempt to win over public opinion. Second, rather than funds being collected via criminal acts, such as bank robberies, material resources were collected by the new 'freedom fighters' in diaspora groups. Irish rebels received funds, weapons and manpower from the Irish-American community. According to Rapoport, Irgun received similar support from the Jewish diaspora. In addition to these material resources, there was often foreign government support. The US government, for instance, exerted its political influence to bring about the establishment of an Irish and a Jewish state. The third element that differentiates second-wave terrorists from their colleagues from the first wave is the changing nature of their tactics. Assassination of public figures, so popular among anarchists in the previous wave, turned out to be rather counter-productive and did not help them in achieving their goals. Rapoport shows how the second-wave terrorist organisations adopted guerrilla-like tactics as government forces were attacked in hit-and-run attacks. In particular, they hoped that police and military forces could be lured into overreacting to their actions. The 'freedom fighters' could then claim that they were the victims of government terror who needed public support to fight a stronger enemy.

After the Second World War, growing attention within the United Nations (UN) for de-colonisation also helped the anti-colonial movements that had emerged from the 1920s onwards. Former colonial territories joined international organisations such as the UN. These newly independent countries gave the anti-colonial sentiment in that body more focus and opportunities. According to Rapoport, this second wave, in contrast to the first, can be considered to be relatively successful if we look at the goals that terrorist organisations were fighting for: Algeria and Israel were examples of countries that liberated themselves from foreign rule and became independent states. Yet, it is difficult to establish the exact contribution of terrorist organisations to the achievement of these outcomes. As is clear from the discussion above, norms and ideas about the independence of states were changing worldwide, and these organisations might actually have been riding that global wave of changing ideas about statehood.

Key points

- The 'anti-colonial wave' began in the 1920s, and by the 1960s had largely disappeared.
- Individuals and organisations would refer to themselves as 'freedom fighters'.
- They tried to gain public support by provoking overreactions and atrocities by law enforcement agencies.
- Guerrilla-like tactics were adopted, as government forces were attacked in hit-and-run attacks.
- Rapoport considers this wave to be the most successful wave.

2.4 The third wave of terrorism: the 'new left wave' (1960s - early 1990s)

The third wave distinguished by Rapoport is the so-called 'new left wave' that emerged in the 1960s. The international event that inspired many would-be terrorist organisations was the Vietnam War. The difficulties the American military encountered in its fight against the Vietnamese insurgents showed that regular military capabilities, which seemed superior from a technological perspective, were ill-suited to this type of asymmetrical warfare. The success of the Viet Cong (VC)'s guerrilla tactics and the American atrocities did not go unnoticed in the western world. Particularly among the youth, there was widespread criticism of the behaviour of western powers abroad, as well as the capitalist and consumerist culture at home. Western-based groups, such as the West-German Rote Armee Fraktion (Red Army Faction; RAF), the Italian Brigate Rosse (Red Brigades; RB) and the Nihon Sekigun (Japanese Red Army, JRA), considered themselves to be vanguards for people in developing countries – what we now call the Global South and what used to be called the 'Third World'.

That same Third World was also confronted with terrorism at home. Latin America in particular suffered from widespread violence. Colombia saw the rise of the Revolutionary Armed Forces of Colombia (FARC) in the late 1960s. The FARC found its origins in Communist resistance and militia movements that fought against the Colombian government. According to the GTD database, FARC actions caused about 2,500 casualties in the period between 1970 and 1990. In Peru another movement with communist roots started to draw attention to itself in the 1980s. The Sendero Luminoso (Shining Path; SP) movement, Maoist in terms of ideological orientation, was led by a former university professor and sought to establish a rural communist state through a combination of terrorist attacks and guerrilla warfare. While founded as early as in 1969, the group launched its 'people's war' years later, in 1980. In the years that followed, the group would have an increasingly large impact on the Peruvian security situation. In the period between 1978 and 1990 tens of thousands of people were killed, although government repression is likely to have been responsible for a larger number of these casualties than the actions of SP.

Rapoport also shows that terrorism became a much more international phenomenon, as organisations sometimes accepted support from third-party actors. This could include other militant organisations and, at times, terrorist organisations met each other abroad to train together. For example, members of the (German) Red Army Faction went to Jordan where they trained together with Palestinian terrorist organisations. The involvement of states in terrorism is considered to be another distinctive characteristic of the third wave, according to Rapoport. The RAND Corporation (1999) defines state-sponsored terrorism as 'the active involvement of a foreign government in training, arming, and providing other logistical and intelligence assistance as well as sanctuary to an otherwise autonomous terrorist group for the purpose of carrying out violent acts on behalf of that government against its enemies'. Naturally, state sponsorship is not a dichotomy, as there are different levels of state engagement in terrorist activity. Edward Mickolus (1989) has developed a scale that identifies the degree of government support or attitude towards terrorism: (1) intimidated governments (governments that succumb to terrorist demands, refuse to sign or ratify international treaties, etc.); (2) ideologically supportive regimes (governments that provide rhetorical support to terrorist groups, refuse to extradite terrorists, etc.); (3) generally facilitative regimes (governments that permit terrorist safe houses/safe havens, terrorist training facilities, etc.); (4) governments that provide incident-specific support (providing documents/passports/aliases/cover stories/direct financing/training for specific operations, etc.); and (5) governments that take part in joint operations (which includes the involvement of government personnel in terrorist attacks, incarceration of hostages, etc.). One of the prime examples of state-sponsored terrorism was Libya under the reign of Muammar Gaddafi. The Libyan dictator was notorious for his support of anti-western terrorism all over the world and was accused of direct involvement in the 1986 La Belle Disco bombing in Berlin and the 1988 Pan Am Lockerbie bombing over Scotland. Additionally, the field of operation of terrorist organisations became more international as well. According to Rapoport, terrorists were no longer bound by national borders. Within this process of internationalisation, US targets became increasingly popular among terrorist organisations because of alleged US government support for undemocratic and oppressive regimes in Latin America and the Arab world.

Another element of the new left wave of terrorism was the return of high-profile assassinations. Despite their relative lack of political success in the first wave, terrorist organisations adopted the strategy of targeting public figures, such as ambassadors, prime ministers and members of royal families. In 1984, former UK Prime Minister Margaret Thatcher narrowly escaped death when the Provisional IRA bombed the Brighton hotel where the members of the Conservative Party stayed during its annual meeting. The bombing ultimately resulted in the deaths of four people and injured over 30 others. Rapoport explains that the rationale behind some of these assassinations was often punishment. While terrorists from the first wave would often target a public figure based on his or her symbolic value, third-wave victims were often chosen because they were considered to be personally responsible for certain policies. Thatcher, along with her fellow Conservative Party members, was held accountable for the death of nine members of the IRA, as they died of the consequences of a hunger strike in response to the loss of their special status as political prisoners.

Typical forms of action employed by third-wave terrorism were hijackings, hostage takings and kidnappings. Passenger planes were often targeted. Rapoport explains that 700 hijackings occurred already in the first three decades of this wave. There were also many victims of hostage takings on the ground. Rapoport shows how, eventually, hostage taking became a lucrative business, as companies could insure their employees, which turned the practice into a multi-million dollar industry. Its victims included high-ranking officials and politicians. Some of the most infamous cases were the kidnappings of the Italian politician Aldo Moro and the German executive, employer and industry representative Hanns-Martin Schleyer (see box 2.03).

Hostage takings and hijackings in the 1970s

The 1970s witnessed a number of high-profile hostage takings and hijackings. In 1978, Aldo Moro, former prime minister and leader of the Christian Democrats, was kidnapped by the Red Brigades. When negotiations failed (they demanded the immediate release of a number of Red Brigades prisoners), Moro was executed after being held in captivity for 55 days. Other high-profile hostage takings of that decade include the 1974 attack on the French Embassy in The Hague by members of the Japanese Red Army, the 1975 West German embassy occupation in Stockholm by the Red Army Faction and the 1977 kidnapping of Hanns-Martin Schleyer, a German business executive and industry representative, also by the RAF. The 1970s also saw a number of hijackings, such as the simultaneous 1970 Dawson's Field hijackings of three western aircraft by the Popular Front for the Liberation of Palestine in Jordan and the 1977 hijacking by the Palestinian hijackers of Lufthansa Flight 181 which ended in Somalia.

Recommended movies

- Barreto, B. (1997). *Four Days in September*. 110 min
- Bellocchio, M. (2003). *Buongiorno, notte*. 106 min
- Edel, U. (2008). *The Baader Meinhof Complex*. 150 min
- MacDonald, K. (1999). *One day in September*. 91 min
- Spielberg, S. (2005). *Munich*. 164 min
- Taravrelli, G.M. (2008). *Aldo Moro- Il Presidente*. 173 min

BOX 2.03   HOSTAGE TAKINGS AND HIJACKINGS IN THE 1970S

In most cases, the hostage takings and hijackings did not lead to the desired results for the terrorists, especially when they included policy changes or the release of terrorists from jail. In response to their demands not being met, terrorists sometimes decided to kill their hostages, as happened in the cases of Moro and Schleyer. Other endings included attempts by the authorities to liberate the hostages: sometimes they were successful, but often they were not, leading to several fatalities. As example of the latter is the attack on the Israeli team during the 1972 Summer Olympics in Munich. An ill-prepared attempt by the German police force to free the members of this team ended with the death of all the athletes and five of the eight Palestinian terrorists (see box 2.04).

The attack on the 1972 Summer Olympics in Munich

Roughly a week after the grand opening of the 1972 Summer Olympics in Munich, members of the Black September organisation attacked the Israeli Olympic team. The terrorists initially killed two athletes, before they took nine others hostage. Their demands included the immediate release of 234 prisoners in Israel, including a member of the Japanese Red Army and partaker in the 1972 terrorist attack on Lod Airport in Tel Aviv, Israel. When initial negotiations failed – Israel refused to give in to the demands of the hostage takers – both the terrorists and their hostages were taken to an aeroplane that would take them to Cairo. After snipers botched an attempt to shoot the terrorists, they returned fire and killed the remaining hostages. The German police force killed five of the terrorists and captured three others. In retaliation for the death of eleven members of the Israeli Olympic team, the Israeli intelligence organisation, Mossad, set up Operation Wrath of God, which successfully targeted many of the members of Black September held responsible for the Munich Massacre in the following years.

Recommended reading and movie
- Klein, A. (2005). *Striking back: The 1972 Munich Olympics Massacre and Israel's Deadly Response.* New York: Random House
- The movie *Munich*, directed by Steven Spielberg (2005)

BOX 2.04   THE ATTACK ON THE 1972 SUMMER OLYMPICS IN MUNICH

The new left wave started to lose its significance in the 1980s. In those years, states that sponsored terrorism were increasingly facing sanctions, varying from boycotts and embargoes to military strikes. Think of Libya under the regime of Muammar Gaddafi, who was believed to be behind the Lockerbie incident. Additionally, national police forces coordinated efforts which resulted in the creation of more or less formal intergovernmental cooperation networks, such as TREVI and, later, Europol. As a result, Rapoport notes that left-wing terrorist organisations were defeated in many countries. Furthermore, the collapse of the Soviet Union and the reduced attractiveness of communism contributed to their demise. Around the same time, a new wave of terrorism emerged: the so-called 'religious wave'.

Key points
- The 'new left wave' commenced in the late 1960s and dissipated largely in the 1990s.
- Terrorists were no longer bound by national borders and cooperation between different militants from various countries was not uncommon.
- US targets became increasingly popular because of alleged US government support for undemocratic and oppressive regimes and its actions in the Vietnam War.
- Hijackings and hostage takings were frequently used modus operandi.
- Another element of the new left wave of terrorism was the return of high-profile assassinations.

2.5 The fourth wave of terrorism: the 'religious wave'

We are currently facing the religious wave which, according to Rapoport, started in 1979. Although religion had played an important role in the previous waves as well, think of terrorist organisations that fought for a community whose ethnicity or identity was linked to a particular religion, the religious wave differs from earlier waves. Fourth-wave terrorist organisations tend to aim at the establishment of a religious state, rather than a secular one. Three key events in the Islamic world have been catalytic for the start of the fourth wave, according to Rapoport: (1) the 1979 Iranian Revolution; (2) the 1979 Soviet invasion of Afghanistan; and (3) the new Islamic century.

First, from 1979 onwards Ayatollah Khomeini, leader of the Iranian Revolution, not only alienated Iran from the western world, but also further divided the global Sunni and Shi'ite Muslim communities. Inspired by his theory of Islamic fundamentalism, Shi'ites turned against Sunni populations in nearby states, such as Iraq, Saudi Arabia, Kuwait and Lebanon, where a terrorist group perpetrated one of the first suicide attacks in 1983. The second event was the Soviet invasion of Afghanistan in 1979, which united much of the Sunni world, as volunteers from all over the world joined the local Afghan fighters. The Soviet Union eventually withdrew its forces from Afghanistan in 1989. Around the same time, some foreign fighters who had come to Afghanistan formed al-Qaeda, literally meaning 'the base' to make plans for terrorist activity elsewhere. The collapse of the Soviet Union also created new conflict zones, such as in Chechnya, Kyrgyzstan and Tajikistan. The third 'event' mentioned by Rapoport is related to the fact that the year 1979 marked the beginning of a new Islamic century. An Islamic tradition suggested that at the beginning of a new century a redeemer would come. Within the first minutes of this so-called new century, Muslim rebels stormed and occupied the Grand Mosque in Mecca, which resulted in the deaths of 10,000 people. Similar events, though on a lesser scale, occurred in other countries such as Egypt, Syria, Algeria, and Indonesia.

Despite the connection of these three events with Islam, terrorism during the religious wave is not exclusively Islamic. In 1995, Aum Shinrikyo, a Japanese doomsday cult, carried out an attack on Tokyo's subway system, using sarin gas (see box 2.05). In 1994, Jewish extremist Baruch Goldstein, an American-born Israeli, killed 29 Muslims and injured another 125 in the Ibrahimi Mosque, before he was killed by bystanders. Historically the most notorious terrorist organisation linked to Christianity is probably the Ku Klux Klan, which follows a racist interpretation of the Bible. A more recent example is right-wing extremist Anders Breivik, who killed 77 people in Norway in 2011, who considered himself to be one of the Knights Templar, an international Christian military order, and claimed he had to defend Europe against Muslims.

The 1995 sarin attack in Tokyo

During the rush hour of 20 March 1995, members of the Aum Shinrikyo cult left a number of small plastic bags containing sarin liquids on five different subway cars and stations near the political centre of Tokyo. The perpetrators punctured the packages with umbrellas with sharpened tips, which caused them to leak while they could get away. The toxic vapours coming off the thick sarin liquid killed 13 people and injured hundreds more. According to witnesses, the subway entrances resembled battlefields as commuters were gushing blood from their noses and mouths, and people in panic were gasping for air. The consequences could be felt far outside Japan, as experts and analysts worldwide feared that the attack indicated a new era of terrorism in which terrorist groups would advance towards more complex tactics and weaponry, including unconventional chemical and biological ones.

BOX 2.05   THE 1995 SARIN ATTACK IN TOKYO

The strategies of fourth-wave terrorists have shown a certain degree of similarity to those of the previous waves. Assassinations, hostage-takings and hijackings were common operational tools for religious-inspired terrorist organisations. One of the more deadly hostage crises of modern times was the Beslan school massacre, in which Chechen separatist- and Islamic-fundamentalist terrorists held over 1,100 people hostage for three days. Footage of the incident was broadcast all over the world. Eventually, at least 331 people – mostly children – were killed and well over 700 people injured.

A new feature of the fourth wave was the introduction of suicide terrorism. Although this form of terrorism is often linked to Islamic fundamentalism, there are also examples of non-Islamic terrorist organisations which apply this strategy. Impressed by the efficacy of Lebanese suicide terrorism, which led to the withdrawal of French and American troops in 1983, the Liberation Tigers of Tamil Eelam (LTTE) in Sri Lanka for a while deployed more suicide bombers than all Islamic groups added together. This challenges the rather widespread idea that suicide terrorists are religious fanatics who have fallen for the prospect of paradise or eternal life, given the Marxist roots of the nationalist/separatist LTTE. Pape (2012) has analysed suicide terrorism and suggested that suicide terrorist acts follow a certain strategic logic, as suicide terrorism is successful in terms of being capable of producing a desired effect and being an efficient act.

Al-Qaeda: origins and evolution

Al-Qaeda means 'the base' in Arabic. The organisation was founded by veterans of the Soviet invasion of Afghanistan. During this period, from 1979 to 1989, religiously motivated fighters fought to oust the Soviet armed forces from Afghanistan. Chief amongst them was a Saudi citizen called Osama Bin Laden. Bin Laden would go on to serve as a figurehead for the organisation until he was killed in May 2011. Initially, al-Qaeda had its base in Afghanistan and trained and supported fighters and groups that participated in the global jihad against various regimes in the Islamic world and against the West. After the US intervention in Afghanistan following the 9/11 attacks, al-Qaeda was decimated. However, the network reinvented itself as a transnational resistance network. Having lost its base in Afghanistan, al-Qaeda became a rallying point around which other groups affiliated. Consequently, it became more difficult to define and target the organisation. According to one interpretation, in its new form al-Qaeda resembled a dune. As a 'dune organisation' it would move across territorial borders. More than 20 years after 9/11, it still has a presence in dozens of countries in- and outside the Islamic world.

BOX 2.06   AL-QAEDA: ORIGINS AND EVOLUTION

Until the rise of Islamic State (IS) – formerly known as Islamic State of Iraq and the Levant (ISIL) – the most notorious terrorist organisation of our era was al-Qaeda (see box 2.06), formerly led by Osama bin Laden. Prior to the '9/11 attacks', terrorists associated with al-Qaeda were responsible for, amongst other acts of terrorism, the 1993 World Trade Center bombing (six fatalities; over 1,000 injured), the 1996 Khobar Towers bombing in Dhahran, Saudi Arabia (19 fatalities; some 500 injured) and the simultaneous 1998 Nairobi and Dar es Salaam US embassy attacks (301 fatalities; over 5,000 injured). The most devastating al-Qaeda attack took place on 11 September 2001, when nearly 3,000 people died after two aeroplanes crashed into both towers of the World Trade Center in New York, a third hit the Pentagon in Washington D.C. and a fourth crashed in Shanksville, Pennsylvania, when passengers tried to wrestle control from the terrorists (see box 2.07). Many people around the world watched the live broadcasts of the collapse of the South Tower, followed by the North Tower half an hour later. The attacks are, in terms of casualties, the worst in history carried out by a non-state actor. In the years that followed, and despite the attempts by the US to counter those responsible for the attacks in its 'Global War on Terror', al-Qaeda-linked groups have managed to perpetrate attacks across the world. Its affiliates in

Iraq and the Arabian peninsula added hundreds, if not more, of victims to the list of al-Qaeda casualties, and so did its affiliates operating in Syria, the al-Nusra Front and its successor Tahrir al-Sham.

'9/11': the attacks on the US
On Tuesday, 11 September 2001, 19 terrorists hijacked four US commercial airliners with the aim of simultaneously crashing them into several targets. The terrorists successfully gained control of three out of the four planes. At 8:46 a.m. the hijackers crashed 'American 11' into the North Tower of the World Trade Center (WTC), in the centre of New York city, followed by the 'United 175' crash into the South Tower at 9:03 a.m. Just over half an hour later, the third hijacked plane, 'American Airlines flight 77', was flown into the Pentagon, the headquarters of the US Department of Defense. The fourth flight, 'United 93', came down in an empty field near the small town of Shanksville, Pennsylvania, around 10:00 a.m. The last plane failed to reach its intended target as passengers tried to retake the cockpit from the hijackers. The planes that hit the WTC caused both towers to collapse. In total the 9/11 attacks cost almost 3,000 lives and injured and permanently traumatised countless others. Some basic information can be found at the site of the US-based National September 11th Memorial & Museum: see 911memorial.org.
BOX 2.07   '9/11': THE ATTACKS ON THE US

The group that is now known as Islamic State (IS) is an offshoot of al-Qaeda. The organisation was established by Abu Musab al-Zarqawi in 1999. In 2004 he joined al-Qaeda and pledged allegiance to Bin Laden. The organisation became known as al-Qaeda in Iraq or al-Qaeda in the Land of Two Rivers. It took part in the insurgency that followed the US-led invasion of Iraq in 2003 and became an organisation that operated more and more independently of al-Qaeda. It also participated in the civil war in Syria that started in 2012, leading to violent confrontations with affiliates of al-Qaeda in that country. In April 2013, it changed its name to Islamic State of Iraq and the Levant (ISIL). In June 2014, under the leadership of Abu Baqr al-Baghdadi, the organisation announced the formation of a caliphate and renamed the group Islamic State.

Today, al-Qaeda and IS are both still engaged in the global jihad, regional military campaigns and local politics. The two differ on religious interpretations and on ideas about a caliphate or an Islamic state. IS's primary goal has been to capture and govern territory, while al-Qaeda's goal is to convert people to extremist ideology in order to gradually build a global caliphate. Most other jihadist groups have sided with either al-Qaeda or IS since the discord between these two main jihadist groups developed.

Key points

· The fourth or 'religious wave' began in 1979.
· Islam is the most important religion in this wave, but terrorists also act in the name of other religions.
· Assassinations and hostage taking, common features of the third wave, persisted, but suicide bombing was the most striking and deadly tactical innovation.
· Fourth-wave groups have perpetrated large-scale attacks against military and government installations as well as against ordinary citizens.

2.6   A fifth wave of terrorism?

Rapoport's analysis of modern terrorism demonstrates that terrorism is neither new nor static. He distinguishes four different waves, each with its own set of characteristics in terms of strategies, targets and audiences. Generally, these waves last a few decades before they gradually peter out. It should be emphasised that Rapoport does not necessarily mean that these waves and the terrorist organisations that are part of a wave will completely dissolve or cease to exist within a time frame of about 40 years. For instance, there are still a number of anarchist groups and left-wing extremist organisations that have 'outlived' their wave, but they are simply not attracting as many sympathisers or followers as they used to. This means that it might be difficult always to draw clear boundaries between waves, which some scholars see as a point of criticism of Rapoport's ideas. Trying to separate history into distinct waves might indeed be a form of simplification, as Rapoport himself also noted. For instance, some argue that extreme right-wing terrorism or eco-terrorism should be considered to have had waves as well. The division into four categories does not mean that all developments within the history of terrorism are accurately captured.

Another point of reflection on the waves pertains to the prediction of when they end. As noted, each wave usually lasts around a generation. When Rapoport wrote his article in 2004, he explained that the fourth wave would be likely to be over in two decades from that moment, but only if it were to follow the patterns of the other waves. He also noted, however, that the life cycles of its predecessors might 'mislead us' and this religious wave might last longer. Whether this prediction will come true is yet to be seen. It does seem likely that the religious wave will last longer than the previous ones, but at some point it, too, is likely to fade out.

This leaves us with an interesting and important question: what would a fifth wave look like? Terrorism is a constantly changing phenomenon and counterterrorism professionals and policy-makers try to discern important trends in order to be prepared for what might come next or to prevent new types of terrorism. However, the issues and events that initiated new waves of terrorism were unexpected to most and anticipated by only a few. We will further elaborate in chapter 7 on the track record of terrorism experts in forecasting the future.

What we do know for sure is that terrorism is unlikely to disappear and that as long as there are conflicts on earth there will be terrorism. What we also know is that terrorism is a generational phenomenon that recurs in new forms. Terrorists will adopt new strategies and use new tactics and weaponry in their fight. Although Aum Shinrikyo has been the only case to date in which a terrorist organisation successfully used a chemical agent (sarin) that is classified as a weapon of mass destruction, we cannot rule out the possibility of such an attack in the future (see also box 1.13). At the same time, history has taught us that weapons do not have to be expensive, difficult to obtain or highly advanced to cause death and despair. After all, some plastic knives and box cutters were enough for 19 hijackers to carry out on 11 September 2001 the single most devastating terrorist attack in modern history.

Key points

- The concept of waves is a useful tool for understanding history, but it is also a form of simplification.
- Not all terrorist organisations that are part of a wave will completely dissolve or cease to exist.
- The four waves do not capture every single important development in the history of terrorism.
- Based on the length of the previous three waves, the religious wave could possibly come to an end around the year 2025.
- Terrorism is a generational phenomenon that recurs in new forms, meaning that we may expect a fifth wave with groups adopting new strategies and using new tactics and weaponry in their fight.
- As long as there is conflict in the world, there is no reason to expect the disappearance of terrorism.

2.7 Conclusion

In this chapter we looked into the history of terrorism and important trends regarding this worldwide phenomenon. Many authors have shown how terrorism as a phenomenon has changed significantly throughout time. According to Rapoport, terrorism can be categorised into four different 'waves', each with its own specific mechanisms, audience and supporters. These different waves, however, also have something in common. For instance, actors who adopt terrorist tactics do not necessarily consider themselves to be terrorists: they are fighting, in their own perception, a just war or for a just cause. The anarchists tried to topple autocratic regimes, while the terrorists of the anti-colonial wave fought for freedom and the right to self-determination. This illustrates the subjective elements in assessing terrorism, as it is often a matter of perspective whether the rebels or insurgents should be labelled terrorists or whether they should be granted the higher status of 'freedom fighters'. How we will look at terrorism in the future and what specific mechanisms, audience and supporters of terrorism we may expect in the years to come we cannot know for sure. But we know that terrorism is a generational phenomenon, recurring in new forms or waves, each with its own specific mechanisms, audience and supporters. Finally, following Laqueur (2007), there is no good reason to expect the disappearance of terrorism in our time. He argues that 'as long as there are conflicts on Earth, there will be terrorism'.

Bibliography

Bakker, E., & Boer, L. (2007). *The evolution of Al-Qaedaism*. The Hague: Netherlands Institute of International Relations Clingendael.

Bergen, P. (2011). *The Longest War: the enduring conflict between America and Al-Qaeda*. New York: Free Press.

Bergen, P. (2013). *Manhunt: The Ten Year Search for Bin Laden: from 9/11 to Abbottabad*. London: Vintage Books.

Bhatia, M. (2005). Fighting words: naming terrorists, bandits, rebels and other violent actors. *Third world quarterly, 26*(1), 5-22.

Burke, J. (2007). *Al-Qaeda* (third ed.). London: Penguin Books.

Carr, M. (2006). *The Infernal Machine: A History of Terrorism: From the assasination of Tsar Alexander II to Al-Qaeda*. New York: The New Press.

Jensen, R. (2004). Daggers, Rifles, and Dynamite: Anarchism Terrorism in 19th Century Europe. *Terrorism and Political Violence, 16*(1), 116-153.

Klein, A. (2005). *Striking back: The 1972 Munich Olympics Massacre and Israel's Deadly Response*. New York: Random House.

Laqueur, W. (1977, revised edition 2001). *A History of Terrorism*. Boston/New Brunswick: Little Brown/Transaction Publishers.

Laqueur, W. (2007). Terrorism: a Brief History. *Countering the Terrorism Mentality, in Non-violent Paths to Social Change*. US Department of State, EJournal.

Laqueur, W. (2016). *A History of Terrorism. Expanded edition*. Abingdon/New York: Routledge.

McGurn, W. (1987). *Terrorist or Freedom Fighter? The Cost of Confusion*. London: Alliance Publishers Ltd.

Merari, A. (1997). Terrorism as a Strategy of Insurgency. *Terrorism and Political Violence, 5*(4), 213-257.

Mickolus, E. (1989). What Constitutes State Support to Terrorists. *Terrorism and Political Violence, 1*(3), 287-293.

Murakami, H. (2000). *Underground. The Tokyo gas attack and the Japanese psyche*. New York: Vintage Books.

National Commission on Terrorist Attacks upon the United States. (2004). *The 9/11 Commission Report: Final Report of the National Commission on Terrorist Attacks upon the United States*. Washington DC.: National Commission on Terrorist Attacks upon the United States.

Pape, R. (2003). The Strategic Logic of Suicide Terrorism. *American Political Science Review, 97*(3), 343-361.

RAND Corporation. (1999). *First Annual Report to The President and The Congress of the Advisory Panel to Assess Domestic Response Capabilities for Terrorism Involving Weapons of Mass Destruction*. Santa Monica: RAND Corporation.

Rapoport, D. (2004). Four Waves of Modern Terrorism. In Cronin, A. K. *Attacking terrorism: Elements of a Grand Strategy* (46-73). Washington DC: Georgetown University Press.

Reader, I. (2010). Spectres and Shadows: Aum Shinrikyo and the Road to Megiddo. *Terrorism and Political Violence, 14*(1), 145-186.

Rendon, S. (2019). Capturing correctly: A reanalysis of the indirect capture-recapture methods in the Peruvian Truth and Reconciliation Commission. *Research and Politics*, 1-8.

Ulam, A. B. (1977). *In the Name of the People. Prophets and Conspirators in Prerevolutionary Russia*. New York: The Viking Press.

3

3.1   Introduction

In this chapter we will look into the field of terrorism studies and introduce different authors, centres, disciplines and approaches. What have academia and think tanks come up with since 9/11? We will also focus on why conducting research in the field of terrorism is so difficult. What are the particular challenges when investigating this phenomenon and the attempts to counter or to manage it? Finally, we will have a critical look at the results of research on terrorism and counterterrorism and discuss the state of the art of this multidisciplinary field of study.

3.2   The history of terrorism studies

As shown in the previous chapter, terrorism is not new, and this also holds for the study of this phenomenon. In this section we will look at research into modern-day terrorism, meaning the terrorism that emerged in the late 1950s and early 1960s.

Terrorism studies pre-9/11

In the late 1950s and the 1960s relatively few scholars looked into the political violence and so-called 'revolutionary terrorism' of that age. They focused on a number of the fundamental questions: Why do people fight? Why do they use violence? Why do they rebel? Scholars tried to answer these questions, amongst others, with the help of conflict theories. These theories were partly derived from the work of sociologists and political scientists who emphasised the social, political or material inequality of groups in society. Relatively many scholars were influenced by the works of Karl Marx, who is regarded as the father of the social conflict theory. They were particularly interested in the phenomenon of violence related to the decolonisation process in Africa and Asia, but also in riots and political violence in Western European and North American cities and university campuses. These types of political violence were studied under the name of either terrorism studies or political violence studies. The groups they studied included revolutionary terrorist groups and anti-colonial or anti-imperialist groups. These particular groups were active in the era of what Rapoport called the third wave of terrorism or the new left wave. In the 1970s, some of the organisations of that wave received a fair amount of scholarly attention, in particular the Red Army Faction (RAF) in Germany (see box 3.01), the Red Brigades in Italy, the Weathermen in the US and the Tupamaros in Uruguay (see box 3.02). The last were regarded as the archetypes of urban guerrillas as analysed by, amongst others, Arturo Porzecanski in his book *Uruguay's Tupamaros: the urban guerrilla* (1973). Additionally, investigative journalists published valuable and detailed studies of these groups. A good example is the work of journalist and editor Stefan Aust on the RAF (see box 3.01).

The Red Army Faction

One of the most extensively studied groups of the new left wave of terrorism is the Red Army Faction in Germany. The RAF emerged in 1970 from a core group composed of Andreas Baader, Gudrun Ensslin, Horst Mahler and Ulrike Meinhof. It saw itself as a communist and anti-imperialist group resisting what it regarded as a fascist West-German state. The group was responsible for a few dozen violent attacks and hostage takings, especially in the second half of the 1970s. In total, more than 30 people were killed by the RAF, among them bankers, public prosecutors and businessmen, and their chauffeurs and bodyguards. One of the best-selling books on the RAF is the one by the journalist Stefan Aust, *The Baader Meinhof Complex* (1985), on which Bernd Eichinger and Uli Edel based their 2008 film of the same name. Both the book and the movie give a picture of the context in which the group was operating in those days and the motivations of some of the individual members to join what they called the 'city guerrilla'.

BOX 3.01   THE RED ARMY FACTION

Compared to the previous decade, the 1970s and 1980s saw much more scholarly attention focusing on the modus operandi of terrorist groups: the methods they used, the way they organised themselves and how they selected their targets. As already mentioned in the previous chapter, the strategies and the modus operandi of those days included hijackings, hostage takings and hit-and-run operations as part of urban guerrilla. Examples of scholars and publications that looked into the way terrorist organisations operated include David Rapoport's *Assassination and Terrorism* (1971), Richard Clutterbuck's *Protest and the Urban Guerrilla* (1974), and the book by Yonah Alexander, David Carlton, and Paul Wilkinson (1979), *Terrorism: Theory and Practice*.

The Tupamaros

Tupamaros, or Tupamaros National Liberation Movement, was a left-wing urban guerrilla group in Uruguay in the 1960s and 1970s. The movement was named after a revolutionary, Túpac Amaru II, who resisted the Spaniards in the 18th century. The movement started as a Robin Hood-like organisation, robbing banks and other businesses and distributing the stolen money among the poor. After a government crackdown, Tupamaros engaged in political kidnappings, what it called 'armed propaganda' and assassinations. The Uruguayan regime unleashed a repressive campaign in which many were arrested or disappeared, which severely weakened the movement. Its principal leaders spent years in jail, among them José Alberto 'Pepe' Mujica Cordano, who continued his political activities after his release in 1985 and who was elected president of Uruguay in 2010.

BOX 3.02   THE TUPAMAROS

Increasingly, terrorism scholars were also interested in the international or transnational nature of terrorism. This was partly spurred on by joint attacks and joint training camps of, for instance, the RAF, the Palestinian Liberation Organisation (PLO) and the Japanese Red Army (JRA). Many books on the transnational nature of terrorism were published in the mid-1970s. Examples are Yonah Alexander's edited volume, *International Terrorism* (1976) and Mahmoud Cherif Bassiouni's *International Terrorism and Political Crimes* (1975).

In the late 1970s and the 1980s there was less interest in counterterrorism. In fact, that term was not often used or not used in a neutral way. Instead, many authors focused on state repression in relation to terrorism and political violence. The fight against terrorism or what was labelled as such was a rather sensitive topic. Scholars who looked into it and who produced studies that are still of interest today include Christopher Hewitt with *The Effectiveness of Anti-Terrorism Policies* (1984), Richard Clutterbuck with *Kidnap, Hijack and Extortion: The Response* (1987), and Jerrold Post who wrote the article

'Rewarding Fire With Fire: Effects of Retaliation on Terrorist Group Dynamics' (1987).

In the 1990s, as in previous decades, scholars focused mainly on the topics of those days, the type of groups that were active, the way they staged attacks and the way governments reacted to them. In the 1990s these were mainly nationalist or separatist groups. Specific groups that received much scholarly attention included the Provisional Irish Republican Army (IRA; PIRA), fighting for an independent and united Ireland, and several other (northern) Irish militant groups. There was also a fair amount of attention given to nationalist and separatist groups in Spain (such as ETA, the acronym for Euskadi Ta Askatasuna, the Basque Fatherland and Freedom) and groups in India and Sri Lanka (such as a number of Sikh terrorist organisations and the LTTE). A relatively new type of terrorism that was attracting more and more attention was what we call Islamist or jihadist terrorism (see box 3.03). Initially, academics and investigative journalists were mainly looking at groups such as the Palestinian Hamas and the Lebanese organisation Hezbollah. The German journalist Andrea Nüsse, for instance, studied the fundamentalist ideology in *Muslim Palestine: The Ideology of Hamas* (1999). The Israeli scholar Etani Azani was one of several scholars who analysed the Lebanese organisation Hezbollah. In his book, *Hezbollah: The Story of the Party of God from Revolution to Institutionalization* (2009), he reflects on the changes the organisation underwent.

Jihadist terrorism and global jihad

Describing terrorist violence that, according to its perpetrators, is conducted in the name of Islam is difficult and a very sensitive exercise. Terms that are used include 'Islamic terrorism', 'Islamist terrorism' or 'jihadist terrorism'. The first two terms should be avoided as the perpetrators represent only a fraction of the world of Islam and that of Islamists, those who believe Islam should guide social and political as well as personal life. Instead, we use the term 'jihadist terrorism'. This could be regarded as a combination of Islamist ideology and the notion of jihad. The jihad is understood as a fight or a quest that has two distinct forms. The first is the so-called 'greater jihad', the effort of every Muslim to become a better human being, a struggle and test of every Muslim's obedience to God and being a good Muslim. The second form is the 'lesser jihad'. It sanctions the use of violence against an unjust ruler, whether Muslim or not. In the context of this textbook, by jihad we mean the violent form of jihad: a fight or a quest that is claimed by its supporters and fighters to be in furtherance of the goals of Islam as they interpret it. These goals may pertain to a national political agenda or an international one, the establishment of a (pan-)Islamic theocracy and the restoration of the caliphate. If the goal and agenda also includes armed conflict to expand the Islamic world, we speak of a global jihad.

Scholars devoted considerable attention to a relatively new type of attack that has been associated with these groups ever since: the suicide attack. The first of this type of attack shocked the world and raised many questions such as, why do people become suicide terrorists? Perhaps one of the most applauded works on suicide terrorism is the book *Dying to Win: The Strategic Logic of Suicide Terrorism* by Robert Pape (2005), in which he reflects on this phenomenon and the logic behind it. Although suicide terrorism seems irrational to some, the author asserts that its logic involves a strategic and coercive element. As we learned in the previous chapter, suicide terrorism is not exclusively an Islamic fundamentalist strategy, but was also adopted by the LTTE and other secular groups.

Especially in Israel, researchers looked into possible ways to deal with the threat posed by Islamist groups in general and suicide attacks in particular. In his book, *Terror in the Mind of God*, Mark Juergensmeyer (2003) argues that religion provides a moral justification for such attacks, as it suggests a battle between good and evil. Other notable publications with regard to Islamist suicide terrorism are Anne Speckhard's book, *Talking to Terrorists: Understanding the Psycho-social Motivations of Militant Jihadi Terrorists, Mass Hostage Takers, Suicide Bombers & "Martyrs"* (2012) and Anat Berko's *The Path to Paradise: The Inner World of Suicide Bombers and Their Dispatchers* (2007) in which she looks into Palestinian suicide bombers and the cult of death and martyrdom.

From the mid-1990s onwards there was also some academic interest in a new transnational phenomenon and terrorist network, one that had received the attention of the Central Intelligence Agency (CIA). In 1995 this agency 'noticed a recent stream of reports about Bin Ladin and something called al Qaeda'. This quotation also appears in final report of the 'National Commission on Terrorist Attacks upon the United States' (2004). A few years later the authorities paid a great deal more attention to this 'new' terrorist organisation, especially after its attacks on the US Embassies in Dar-es-Salaam and Nairobi in East Africa in 1998 and the attack on the USS Cole in the port of Aden in 2000. However, scholarly interest in this particular group and the phenomenon which we now call the global jihad remained rather low. According to Andrew Silke (2009), in the 1990s and around the turn of the century al-Qaeda did not manage to make the top twenty list of terrorist groups that received most attention from terrorism researchers.

In fact, the 1990s saw a gradual decline in academic interest in terrorism and counterterrorism in general. This decline, in terms of the number of both involved academics and publications, can be explained by the intertwined developments of a decline in terrorist incidents in the West, the subsequent devaluation of terrorism as a policy and security concern, and the reduction in financial support for research into terrorism. The terrorism research community which remained was a small and closed group of scholars. That group of experts did not and could not foresee that their area of study would receive so much attention in the new millennium. Of course, in hindsight it is hard to believe that in the years before the attacks on 9/11 fewer and fewer scholars were focusing on terrorism as an interesting and important subject to study.

Terrorism studies post-9/11

Al-Qaeda, the phenomenon of the global jihad and terrorism in general received an enormous amount of attention after the most deadly terrorist attacks the world had ever witnessed. The 9/11 attacks were the starting point of a new era in the field of terrorism and counterterrorism studies. The number of scholars and experts looking into terrorism and counterterrorism increased rapidly in the years after these attacks. The same holds for the number of academic or governmental research centres in the field of terrorism studies. Examples of these newcomers are the National Consortium for the Study of Terrorism and Responses to Terrorism, better known by its acronym START, at the University of Maryland (2005), the International Centre for the Study of Radicalisation and Political Violence (ICSR) at King's College in London (2008), the African Centre for the Study and Research on Terrorism in Algeria (2004), the Global Terrorism Research Centre at Monash University in Melbourne (2006), and the Centre for Terrorism and Counterterrorism of Leiden University (2007) and the International Centre for Counter-Terrorism (2010) both located in The Hague, the Netherlands.

The attacks on 9/11 also sparked an enormous increase in training, policy advice and consultancy as governments wanted answers to all kinds of questions. How large is the threat? Who or what poses a threat? Why? What to do about it? A typical example of a post-9/11 initiative that was directly linked to these kinds of questions was the Nine Eleven Finding Answers Foundation (NEFA Foundation), a non-profit-making, charitable organisation that was engaged in terrorism research and analysis. Its stated goal was 'to help prevent future tragedies in the US and abroad by exposing those responsible for planning, funding, and executing terrorist activities, with a particular emphasis on Islamic militant organizations'. Scholars and consultants tried to answer these and other questions and provided their services to local, national and international organisations and the private sector. This resulted in an enormous growth in the number of reports, papers, articles and books on terrorism and counterterrorism, generating a vast amount of literature. Silke found that articles on terrorism were also published in other than the usual journals on international relations or political science. New articles on terrorists and terrorism started appearing even in periodicals on aeronautics and engineering.

Below you can find a graph (figure 3.01) depicting the number of publications with 'terrorism' or 'terrorist' in the title. A quick look at it teaches us that the number of titles more than doubled in the first decade after 9/11 in comparison to the number of titles published in the decades before it. This number continues to increase, as multiple terrorism-related books and articles are published every single day. A quick scan of Google Scholar shows us that the number of articles with 'terrorism' or 'terrorist' in the title has increased almost five-fold in 12 years. The avalanche of new academic books, articles, reports and PhD theses is testimony to the fact that the majority of all terrorism studies were published after the events of 9/11. Finally, in addition to published books and articles, numerous academic conferences have been held throughout the world in an effort to bring experts together and increase our understanding of the subject. These events have also contributed to the scholarly debate on terrorism and counterterrorism and produced many working papers and reports. Given the continuing stream of scholarly output it is safe to say that, as of today, a clear majority of all terrorism studies literature is 'post-9/11'.

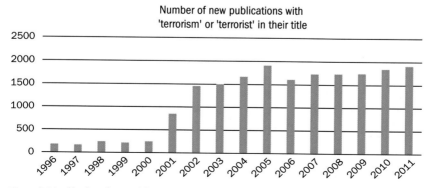

Figure 3.01   Number of new publications with 'terrorism' or 'terrorist' in their title

One of the key issues in the debate about terrorism after the attacks on the United States in 2001 revolved around whether or not the world was facing a new type of terrorism, one more lethal than ever before, also referred to as 'catastrophic' terrorism. The debate focused on the question whether this 'new' terrorism, which emerged in the 1990s and the development of which culminated in the disaster of 9/11, was fundamentally different from earlier terrorism. This also raised the question to what extent knowledge of 'old' or traditional terrorism was still relevant. One proponent of the new terrorism school, Walter Laqueur (2000), argued that terrorism had become fanatical and catastrophic, and that the new terrorists had no inhibitions about using weapons of mass destruction. With regard to the organisational structure, new terrorists are described as more decentralised, flat or diffuse, as opposed to old terrorist groups. Peter Neumann, in his book *Old & New Terrorism* (2009), shows how the structures of the 'new terrorism' are indeed difficult to grasp, more so than in the past, explaining why they are often described as networks rather than as organisations.

Martha Crenshaw also analyses why the idea of a fundamentally new terrorism has been so attractive among certain groups of academics. Her somewhat cynical answer to this question is that 'terrorism "experts," especially newcomers to the field, might find it convenient not to have to take the time to study the long and complicated history of the terrorist phenomenon' (2007, p. 30). Crenshaw and others have challenged the logical and empirical foundations of the 'new terrorism' argument and concluded that it is weak. Isabelle Duyvesteyn and Leena Malkki (2012) even speak of a fallacy of the new terrorism thesis.

Today, more than two decades after the catastrophic terrorist attacks on 9/11, many seem to agree that the distinction between 'new' and 'old' terrorism is not as fundamental as the proponents of 'new' terrorism believed it to be in the aftermath of the mass-casualty attacks by al-Qaeda and other new terrorist networks.

Key points

- The development of terrorism and counterterrorism studies started in the early 1960s with just a handful of scholars.
- The number of scholars and the academic output grew in the 1970s and 1980s, followed by a decline in the 1990s.
- The terrorist attacks of 9/11 sparked an enormous and unprecedented growth in terrorism studies, more than doubling its output compared to that of the whole of the pre-9/11 era.

· Some scholars argued that the 1990s saw the rise of 'new' terrorism which is fundamentally different from terrorism in the past; others challenge the logical and empirical foundations of this idea.

3.3 Disciplines and approaches

In the last section we discussed the history of terrorism studies. Below we will explore the approaches and disciplines behind that term. These disciplines are as manifold as the study of terrorism is multidisciplinary. In figure 3.02 you see just a few examples of scholarly disciplines that have contributed to terrorism studies. One of them is political science. Scholars in that field are very much interested in the question of how and where terrorism fits into political systems, and if or to what extent it is the product of political systems. They also want to know how terrorism has an impact on political processes, on decision making and on how governments act or react to terrorist incidents. Some of these questions are also of interest to scholars in the field of public administration.

There are also other disciplines with different research interests. Take, for instance, military science or war studies. Academics in this field focus on the possibilities and limitations of the use of military force as part of the struggle against terrorism. Scholars in the field of international relations want to know how the international political system deals with this threat; they want to understand who puts terrorism on the international agenda and why, or are interested in the possibilities and challenges of international cooperation in countering terrorism. The aim is, among other things, to offer insights into how states can tackle global issues of terrorism within the international system and its norms, procedures and institutions, such as the UN.

Terrorism studies

Another interesting example of a discipline that provides important insights into terrorism and counterterrorism is communication studies. In the previous chapter we mentioned the fact that terrorism is, amongst others, a tool for terrorists to spread a message, to create fear, to have an impact on society. Scholars in the field of communication studies want to understand how that works. What is the role of the media? What circumstances influence whether or not a country is shaken up by a terrorist attack, and how can authorities limit the impact of terrorism on societies? In addition, the issue of terrorists' narratives has been an important object of study in recent years. The same holds true for the use of social media.

Finally, (social) psychology needs to be mentioned. Scholars of this discipline have looked into terrorism since the 1960s and even before that. This interest from the start of modern-day terrorism can be linked in part to the fascination among the general public and policy-makers about why people engage in political violence and the characteristics of those people, in particular how the thoughts, feelings and behaviour of individuals are influenced by others. In fact, there are several books that have in their titles 'the mind of the terrorist' or 'the terrorist mind'. Perhaps one of the most well-known books that looks into the psychological side of terrorism is Post's book, *The Mind of the Terrorist: The Psychology of Terrorism from the IRA to Al-Qaeda* (2007). Apparently, we are curious about what goes on inside the heads of terrorists. How do they think? Why do they do the things they do? Who radicalises under what circumstances, and (how) can these individuals be deradicalised? And we are very interested in the fundamental question: are terrorists different from you and me? Are they crazy or not? We will discuss the latter question also in the next chapter. These are not only fascinating questions, but also important ones for the struggle against terrorism. Brian Philips wrote an article entitled 'How Did 9/11 Affect Terrorism Research?', mapping the field of terrorism studies. He observed that psychologists in fact became the most numerous group of terrorism researchers for several years after 9/11, displacing political scientists, who used the be the largest group, for about ten years.

Criminology **History**
Criminal **Law** Sociology
Economics Intelligence Studies
Police Studies **Public Administration**
International Law Conflict Studies
Anthropology *Philosophy*
Political Geography

Figure 3.02   Examples of disciplines involved in studying terrorism

As you can see in figure 3.02, there are many other disciplines that study the phenomena of terrorism and counterterrorism or closely related issues. There are too many disciplines to mention them all; the list in the figure is not exhaustive. It should also be mentioned that there is no single dominant discipline, although there are relatively many scholars who have a background in political science and psychology.

Approaches

How does one study and understand terrorism and counterterrorism? Where do we start approaching these phenomena? There are many different options at different levels of abstraction. Will we look at the behaviour of individuals or do we try to understand the larger picture, the world political system and how terrorism and counterterrorism fit in? Or, in other words, do we start with a very concrete case at the individual level or with more abstract developments at the global level? There are also differences in approach regarding the way in which we can study terrorism and counterterrorism. Are we going to talk to people? Try to interview terrorists or the people who fight terrorism? Or will we analyse statistical data or define and explore theoretical concepts? Finally, especially with regard to the societal relevance of research, one could be confronted with the choice between a more policy-oriented study or a study into how terrorism or counterterrorism affects human rights and societies in general. These are just a few basic questions related to the many different possible approaches to studying terrorism and counterterrorism, each with its own challenges and dilemmas, which we will explore later in this chapter.

Besides these different concrete and practical approaches to studying terrorism and counterterrorism, there are also different theoretical approaches in researching these phenomena. Unfortunately, the general consensus is that if we look at theories on terrorism there is a lack of common ground, and that there is no general theory of terrorism. There are many different explanations for this. In the *Routledge Handbook of Terrorism Research* (2011), the editor, Alex Schmid, gives several explanations, ranging from the absence of a generally accepted definition of terrorism to the politicised discourse on terrorism. According to Schmid, the scattered thinking on terrorism is most visible when one looks at the root causes debate, which is at the heart of the theoretical discussion on terrorism. This also means that there are no established theoretical schools in terrorism research. However, despite the divergence of considerations on the root causes of terrorism and the lack of schools, it is possible to gather together some of the more generally accepted views on how to study terrorism and what should be high on the research agenda.

We distinguish three main approaches to the study of terrorism:

1. the rational or instrumental approach
2. the (socio-)psychological approach
3. the multi-causal approach

The first cluster is that of the rational and instrumental approach. This approach tries to understand terrorism as rational actions by individuals and groups who want to achieve certain political goals. Their terrorist activities are regarded as the result of a cost-benefit analysis. Terrorism is a tool or an instrument – therefore this approach is also described as the instrumental approach.

Among the scholars whose work can be linked to this cluster is Crenshaw. She was one of the early scholars who looked at terrorism as a rational act and considered terrorists to be rational actors. She argued that terrorism was not necessarily the product of individual decisions and experiences, but rather the result of collective rational decisions that take place within a social system with its various social dysfunctions and conflictive trends. Those who have criticised this approach have pointed to the fact that there are hardly any empirical studies providing evidence of how decisions are reached collectively in terrorist groups. Max Abrahms has highlighted the social dynamics of terrorist groups and suggested that these organisations also function as a social unit (see box 3.04). For example, in his article, 'What Terrorists Really Want: Terrorist Motives and Counterterrorism Strategy', Abrahms (2008) concludes that 'friendship' is a more common motive for joining a terrorist organisation than ideology or concrete political goals. In other words, the rational and instrumental approach might miss the point of non-political goals, motivations and choices of terrorist organisations.

What do terrorists want?

What exactly do terrorists really want? According to Max Abrahms (2008), no question is more fundamental for devising an effective counterterrorism strategy. In an attempt to understand the incentives of terrorists, the model commonly adopted is the strategic one, which treats terrorist actors as pure utility maximisers. However, as Abrahms argues, this model does not accurately reflect the motives of terrorist organisations in the past. He draws a distinction between the official goals of the organisation and those of its lower-ranked members. In her book, *What Terrorists Want: Understanding the Enemy, Containing the Threat* (2006), Louise Richardson also looks into the motives of terrorists and terrorist organisations. She differentiates between the primary (e.g. political) and secondary motives, which she refers to as the 'three Rs': (1) revenge; (2) renown; and (3) reaction. This cycle allows terrorists to garner support for their cause, while it may not necessarily help them to achieve their political motives. The poor track-record of counterterrorism policies of the past is partly due to policy-makers neglecting the differentiations stipulated by scholars such as Abrahms and Richardson.

BOX 3.04   WHAT DO TERRORISTS WANT?

The second main theoretical approach is that of (social) psychologists. The earlier mentioned Post is one of the leading authors who have contributed to this approach, together with the forensic and legal psychologist, Max Taylor, and John Horgan, author of *The Psychology of Terrorism* (2005). They and their colleagues focus on the thinking and behaviour of individuals and those of smaller groups. This approach has been described by the research consortium 'Transnational Terrorism, Security and the Rule of Law' (2008), as being '[c]oncerned with the personalities, beliefs and attitudes of terrorists … this approach focuses primarily on the features and characteristics of the individual perpetrator or terrorist group; examining the behaviour, recruitment methods, individual profiles, and "careers" of terrorists'. Like the rational approach, the (socio-)psychological approach takes into account the motivation of individuals who resort to terrorism.

The third main theoretical approach is the multi-causal approach. One could argue whether or not this is a separate approach. It is certainly not a well-defined one, as many studies and most academics would fit into this category as there is widespread understanding that terrorism is highly complex, and that there is not one single explanation for it. Moreover, according to Wilkinson (2007), from its earliest stages the study of terror and terrorism has been, out of necessity, a multidisciplinary endeavour. Already back in the 1970s he viewed the causes of political violence, including ethnic, religious and ideological conflicts, as also the causes of terrorism. Emphasising multiple causal variables, this approach incorporates psychological considerations, economic, political, religious and sociological factors as contributors to understanding the causes of terrorism.

Finally, critical studies in terrorism can be regarded as a distinct approach in terrorism studies. In general, a critical approach in a certain domain of science refers to a school of thought that stresses the need for reflective assessment and critique of politics, society and culture. In the domain of terrorism studies, the critical approach developed as a reaction to the political, legal, cultural and academic context in which, after 9/11, thousands of new books and articles on terrorism were published every year. Dissatisfied with some of the biases and practices present in the field, a group of scholars, mainly from the UK, felt the need for a different approach.

According to Marie Breen-Smyth, Jeroen Gunning and Richard Jackson, and as formulated in the first issue of *Critical Studies in Terrorism*, the critical approach is understood as 'a research orientation that is willing to challenge dominant knowledge and understandings of terrorism, is sensitive to the politics of labelling in the terrorism field, is transparent about its own values and political standpoints, adheres to a set of responsible research ethics, and is committed to a broadly defined notion of emancipation' (Breen-Smyth et al., 2008, p. 1). It should be stressed that this 'orientation' or attitude is also adopted by many scholars who are not associated with, or self-proclaimed adherents to, the critical approach. Of course, as Breen-Smyth and others also noted, there is no sharp divide between 'traditional' or 'orthodox' and 'critical' terrorism studies. All research on terrorism and counterterrorism requires greater self-reflexivity, as we will further explore in section 3.6.

Key points
- There are many different ways to study terrorism and counterterrorism.
- There are also many different disciplines that look into these phenomena, ranging from political science and war studies to social psychology and communication studies.
- The three main academic approaches are the following: the rational/instrumental approach, the (socio)psychological approach and the multi-causal approach.
- Critical terrorism studies can also be seen as a distinct approach that emphasises reflective assessment and critique of politics, society and culture.

3.4   Key authors and centres

In the previous section we mentioned some of the leading authors in the field of terrorism and counterterrorism studies. In this section we will look at other examples of key authors, very important centres and key journals in the field of terrorism studies.

Authors
Below you will see a figure (figure 3.03) containing some of the most well-known, influential and most often-quoted authors in the field of terrorism and counterterrorism studies before 9/11. Among the founding fathers of

this multidisciplinary field who published influential books and articles in the 1970s are the political scientist David Rapoport, author of *Assassination and Terrorism* (1971), *The Rationalization of Terrorism* (1982) (with Yonah Alexander) and the earlier discussed publication, 'Four Waves of Modern Terrorism' (2004); the historian Paul Wilkinson, the former chairman of the St Andrews Handa Centre for the Study of Terrorism (CSTVP) and author of *Political Terrorism* (1974) and *Terrorism versus Liberal Democracy: the Problems of Response* (1976); Brian Jenkins, author of the RAND report, 'International Terrorism: A new kind of warfare?' (1974) and known for his insights such as 'terrorism is theatre' (1974) and 'terrorists want a lot of people watching, not a lot of people dead' (1975); and the historian Walter Laqueur, author of *Terrorism* (1977). Other early examples of scholars who contributed to a better understanding of terrorism are the political scientist Martha Crenshaw, author of the article, 'Causes of Terrorism' (1981) which has been quoted over 2,500 times; the historian Alex Schmid, also a former director of CSTVP, currently editor-in-chief of the online journal, *Perspectives on Terrorism,* and principal author of *Violence as communication: insurgent terrorism and the Western news media* (written together with Janny de Graaf) (1982); the political psychologist and psychiatrist Jerrold Post, the author of one of the first (social) psychological publications on terrorism, 'Notes on psychodynamic theory of terrorist behaviour' (1984); and Bruce Hoffman, who became the first director of CSTVP in St Andrews 1994 and who wrote *Inside Terrorism* (1998).

Paul Wilkinson

Walter Laqueur Alex Schmid

Max Taylor Brian Jenkins Clark McCauley

Bruce Hoffman Martha Crenshaw Leonard Weinberg

Todd Sandler **John Mueller** Yonah Alexander

Robert Pape Rohan *Gunaratna*

David Rapoport

Figure 3.03   Examples of pre-9/11 authors in the field of terrorism studies

The list of key scholars in the field of terrorism studies is primarily composed of scholars who work in the Anglo-Saxon world and most of them are men. If we look at a list of influential authors who published a lot after 9/11, we see more women. In terms of geographical variety not much has changed, as most scholars are still based in the US or Europe (see figure 3.04).

Andrew Silke Tahir Abbas

Thomas Hegghammer Magnus Ranstorp

Jessica Stern Daniel Byman Bart Schuurman

Marc Sageman Maura Conway Peter Neumann

Richard Jackson Audrey Kurth Cronin Frank Furedi

Richard English Joseph Young James Piazza

Ann Speckhard Paul Gill Beatrice de Graaf

Peter Bergen John Horgan

Mia Bloom Tore Bjørgo

Figure 3.04   Examples of post-9/11 authors in the field of terrorism studies

Centres

The attacks on the US in September 2001 led not only to an enormous growth in publications and other academic output in the field of terrorism studies, but also to a growth in the number of research centres studying terrorism. These centres include many academic institutes, but also think tanks, and non-governmental organisations (NGOs) that look into terrorism and counterterrorism-related issues. As is the case with most of the scholars in this field, most of these centres are located in the Anglo-Saxon world and a number of other western countries. There is not a single one that clearly sticks out, but some locations stand out as places with the most prestigious or well-known centres.

The Washington D.C. area is perhaps the place with most institutes, think tanks and governmental and non-governmental organisations that study terrorism and counterterrorism. This is of course related to the presence of the US federal government and its executive branches that deal with terrorism that are also located in the D.C. area. Examples include the University of Maryland and the START consortium just outside the beltway, and the RAND Corporation in Arlington, next to the Pentagon. Other important academic centres include the GW Program on Extremism at George Washington University and many non-governmental organisations that work in the field of counterterrorism or counter-radicalisation, such as the Foundation for Defense of Democracies or the Washington offices of the Global Center for Cooperative Security, Human Rights Watch and the RESOLVE network linked to the United States Institute of Peace.

Outside Washington you find important research institutions in and around Boston, for instance, Harvard University and the Belfer Center for Science and International Affairs, or the Center of Terrorism and Security Studies at University of Massachusetts Lowell. In New York you can find the headquarters of the Soufan Group, a global intelligence and security consultancy with many experts who used to work in the intelligence sector, military and law enforcement. The National Counterterrorism, Innovation, Technology and Education Center launched its activities at the University of Nebraska in Omaha in 2020. There is one specific centre in the US that needs mentioning: the Memorial Institute for the Prevention of Terrorism (MIPT), which conducted research into the causes of terrorism and maintained the MIPT Terrorism Knowledge Base, but which today mainly focuses on training US police officers in terrorism and crime reporting. The institute was established after the attack by Timothy McVeigh in 1995. McVeigh blew up a federal building in Oklahoma City, killing 150 people.

In Europe, London is the location of several important centres in the field of terrorism studies, among them the International Centre for the Study of Radicalisation (ICSR) at King's College London and the Institute for Strategic Dialogue (ISD). There are also various think tanks that focus more broadly on security and global affairs, including terrorism-related issues, such as Chatham House and The Royal United Services Institute. Perhaps the most important and most prestigious research centre on terrorism is based in St Andrews, all the way up in Scotland. The Centre for the Study of Terrorism and Political Violence (CSTPV) was founded in 1994 and is Europe's oldest for the study of terrorism.

Earlier we mentioned the enormous increase in terrorism studies and the establishment of many new centres after the attacks on the US on 9/11. The Centre for Terrorism and Counterterrorism of Leiden University, now called the Institute of Security and Global Affairs, is one of them. It is based in The Hague, as is the International Centre for Counter-Terrorism, the T.M.C. Asser Institute and the Netherlands Institute of International Relations Clingendael, which makes this Dutch city one of the new and emerging locations for terrorism studies. The same holds true for a number of locations and institutes in Scandinavia, such as the Terrorism Research Group at the Norwegian Defence Research Establishment, the Centre for Research on Extremism at the University of Oslo and the Consortium for Research on Terrorism and International Crime at the Norwegian Police University College in Oslo, and the Centre for Asymmetric Threat Studies at the Swedish Defence University in Stockholm. In Spain you can find the Royal Institute Elcano which studies terrorism-related issues.

Outside Europe and America, you find important centres of knowledge on terrorism and counterterrorism in Herzliya, Israel, the International Institute for Counterterrorism (ICT) and in Singapore, the International Centre for Political Violence and Terrorism Research (ICPVTR). The Hedayah organization is an important centre of expertise which is based in Abu Dhabi in the United Arab Emirates. In Turkey, NATO's Centre of Excellence - Defence Against Terrorism in Ankara deserves to be mentioned. This centre was accredited by NATO in 2006 with the aim of providing expertise on terrorism and counterterrorism matters through training and education. Further to the east, in India, there are research institutes, such as the Institute of Peace and Conflict Studies and the Manohar Parrikar Institute for Defence Studies and Analyses, both based in New Delhi.

In other parts of the world there are only a few institutes or centres that specifically focus on terrorism. In Australia, the most prominent academic research institute is the Global Terrorism Research Centre (GTReC), established in 2006 by Monash University in Melbourne. In Africa you find the Algiers-based African Centre for the Study and Research on Terrorism (ACSRT). This centre was founded by the African Union (AU) in order to help AU member states with developing strategies for the prevention and combating of terrorism. The Institute of Security Studies (ISS), with offices in Pretoria, Dakar, Addis Ababa and Nairobi, also conducts important studies into terrorism in Africa. For more information on terrorism studies in Africa see box 3.05.

Terrorism research in Africa
Although there are relatively few terrorism scholars from Africa, there are several who have studied terrorism or terrorism-related topics that should be mentioned. A selection of more recent publications follows:
* Ehiane, S. O. (2018). Strengthening the African Union (AU) Counterterrorism Strategy in Africa: a re-awakened order. *Journal of African Union Studies* 7(2), 109-126
* Okoli, A. O. & Ogayi, C.O. (2018). Herdsmen militancy and humanitarian crisis in Nigeria: A theoretical briefing. *African Security Review* 27(2), 129-143
* Olojo, A. & Mahdi, M. (2022). Transitional Justice: Testing the Waters in Lake Chad Basin. *ISS West Africa Report* 39
* Ajide, K. B. (2021). Democracy, Regime Durability and Terrorism in Africa. *Defence and Peace Economics* 32(5), 550-571

BOX 3.05 TERRORISM RESEARCH IN AFRICA

Journals

Where do you find the main academic output and experts' reports of these research centres and think tanks, and those of individual scholars and experts? Today, much of the output is disseminated freely by way of the internet through websites, web logs or in webinars. However, (closed access) academic journals are still very important, especially in the academic world. The six leaders in the field of terrorism and counterterrorism studies, from the oldest to the newest, are the following: *Terrorism and Political Violence* (founded by David Rapoport and Paul Wilkinson in 1989), *Studies in Conflict and Terrorism* (founded by Bruce Hoffman in 1992, after it merged with *Terrorism: An International Journal* which was edited by Yonah Alexander), *Intelligence and National Security* (founded by Christopher Andrew and Michael Handel in 1986) and the more recently founded journals, *Critical Studies on Terrorism* (founded by Richard Jackson in 2008), *Behavioral Sciences of Terrorism and Political Aggression* (founded by Samuel Justin Sinclair and Daniel Antonius in 2009) and *Perspectives on Terrorism* (founded by Alex Schmid, Robert Wesley and James Forest in 2007). The last is the only free open online journal in the field. This journal offers a platform to many authors who can write and publish, but also to a lot of readers inside and outside academia who can freely access all the interesting studies that are published in that journal.

Diversity issues

When we project the lists of the 'location' of authors in the field of terrorism studies and that of the centres and journals on a map, it becomes very clear that the study of terrorism and counterterrorism is a discipline dominated by western scholars. This raises the question if or to what extent this is problematic. As part of the Coursera course titled 'Terrorism and Counterterrorism: Comparing Theory and Practice', we asked the participants – including students and practitioners in the field of counterterrorism – what they thought of this question. About 80 per cent of almost 6,000 respondents to the questionnaire regarded the study of terrorism and counterterrorism to be a western-dominated discipline and believed this to be problematic. There are indeed too few scholars from Africa, Asia and Latin America. The American and European dominance in the field of terrorism studies has resulted in much attention being paid to terrorism in those parts of the world and the West in general. Far less attention is being paid to terrorism elsewhere. This does not correspond with the geographical distribution of terrorism-related incidents. The overwhelming majority of terrorist attacks take place outside the western world, as discussed in chapter 1. Moreover, academic studies that explore terrorism in Africa or Asia often focus on the impact or consequences of this phenomenon in the West or on western interests and less on the effects on the society and politics within those countries. Against this backdrop it is important to note that the western bias has some negative implications for the research agenda, resulting in relatively limited attention being paid to the consequences of terrorism and counterterrorism in non-western countries.

We also noted that the field of terrorism studies has been dominated by men, especially in the years prior to 9/11. Philips, in his previously mentioned investigation of the field, noted that the diversity in terms of gender is increasing. Before 9/11, around 10 per cent of authors were women. After 9/11, these figures changed rapidly. By 2015, around 30 per cent of scholars publishing on terrorism were female. This increase is partly explained by the fact that more psychologists started to investigate terrorism-related issues, as we discussed in the section on academic disciplines.

This observation corresponds to another positive development with regard to diversity in terrorism studies. The academic diversity in terms of the disciplinary background of authors has increased considerably. As we noted in the beginning of this chapter, terrorism studies is a multidisciplinary field of study. The fact that terrorism scholars adopt a wide variety of disciplinary angles and concepts to study the phenomenon leads to a richer and more nuanced understanding of the topic. Moreover, the emergence of critical terrorism studies contributed to an additional focus on terrorism and counterterrorism and the societal and academic responsibilities of scholars.

We can conclude that since 9/11 an ever more diverse body of scholars has been investigating terrorism- and counterterrorism-related issues. However, particularly in terms of geographical focus and diversity, there is still a lot of room for improvement.

Key points

- The 'founding fathers' of terrorism studies include Yonah Alexander, Martha Crenshaw, Walter Laqueur, David Rapoport, Bruce Hoffman and Paul Wilkinson.
- Most scholars in the field of terrorism studies are from the Anglo-Saxon world and most of them are men.
- As is the case with most of the scholars in this field, most of the terrorism knowledge centres are also located in the Anglo-Saxon world and a number of other western countries.
- The six leading academic journals are *Terrorism and Political Violence*, *Studies in Conflict and Terrorism*, *Intelligence and National Security*, *Critical Studies*

on Terrorism, *Behavioral Sciences of Terrorism and Political Aggression* and *Perspectives on Terrorism*.

- Western dominance in the field of terrorism studies has resulted in much attention being paid to terrorism in that part of the world and far less attention to terrorism elsewhere, which does not correspond to the geographic distribution of terrorism-related incidents.
- The field of terrorism studies has become more diverse in terms of the gender and academic backgrounds of scholars.

3.5 Challenges and dilemmas

By now the reader will know more about the history of terrorism studies, the main disciplines feeding in to it and the different approaches to it. We have also mentioned a number of names of centres and people involved in researching terrorism and counterterrorism. In this section we would like to show why and how all these scholars and experts find it difficult to study these phenomena. What challenges and dilemmas are they confronted with? Below you will find an overview of the main difficulties:

- No generally accepted definition
- Subjective and politicised
- Small numbers
- Complex and ever-changing
- Secrecy
- Ethical issues
- Reliability and validation

In the previous chapter we discussed the problem of defining terrorism and observed the lack of a generally accepted legal definition of the term. The absence of such a definition and the conceptual stretching of 'terrorism' into many other forms of political violence and conflict waging are widely regarded as an obstacle to conducting research. It is a challenge when, for instance, doing comparative research on the growth or decline in the number of terrorist incidents in a number of countries if the data of organisation X in country A are based on a different definition from those of organisation Y in country B. If you look at the reports of international organisations such as Europol, the EU's law enforcement agency, the challenge is very clear. Despite an EU definition of terrorism, the data in its annual 'EU Terrorism Situation and Trend Report' (TE-SAT) include examples of terrorism-related incidents that in different EU member states would probably have been defined rather differently. Think of the many incidents linked to the National Liberation Front of Corsica (FLNC) which included not only arson attacks and the occasional bombing of buildings, but also bank robberies and extortion through so-called 'revolutionary taxes'. Such incidents might in other countries be labelled violent activism or simply registered as criminal acts. The French, however, insist that these are acts of terrorism and, as a result, if we stick to the data provided in the TE-SAT report, the FLNC should be regarded as one of Europe's most active terrorist organisation in recent years, responsible for more terrorist incidents than, for instance, ETA, Northern Irish groups or jihadist terrorists. For more information on the TE-SAT report, see box 3.06.

Europol's TE-SAT report

According to the Europol website (europol.europa.eu) where you can find the reports, 'The TE-SAT offers law enforcement officials, policymakers and the general public facts and figures regarding terrorism in the EU while, at the same time, seeking to identify developing trends in this phenomenon. It is a public document produced annually and is based on information provided and verified by the competent authorities of the EU Member States'. The report provides an overall analysis based on facts about terrorist attacks (completed, failed and foiled), arrests, convictions and penalties, and the types of terrorism (jihadist, right-wing, left-wing and anarchist, and ethno-nationalist and separatist and single-issue terrorism).

BOX 3.06   EUROPOL'S TE-SAT REPORT

The second difficulty is the fact that the concept of terrorism is subjective and politicised, making it difficult to obtain accurate and unbiased information. When researching counterterrorism for example, researchers often have to rely on governmental reports. Such reports may be influenced by inter- and intra-agency rivalries or political interests. The subjectivity and political sensitivity of terrorism is something to be aware of, and the same holds for the lack of transparency of what agencies in the field of counterterrorism are doing and why. For all sorts of reasons, agencies might want to present the numbers in their reports or choose the wording of their descriptions of events and developments in a way that is in line with the policies and interests of their political leaders. While this may often make sense and is legitimate, scholars have to be aware of it. It might of course affect the usability of these reports.

In addition, there is the problem of small numbers. How can small numbers in terms of terrorism constitute a problem? We should first emphasise that, of course, we should be happy about the fact that in many parts of the world there are not that many terrorists or terrorist incidents. To researchers, however, this poses a challenge. In general, the 'small n' problem in social scientific analysis holds that it is difficult to arrive at a reliable picture of the relations between variables if there are only a limited number of observations. It is easier to arrive at reliable descriptive and causal inferences from empirical research if the numbers are high. When there are many terrorists and terrorist incidents, researchers can say more precisely how and why terrorism develops in a certain way, why people join terrorist groups, or why they use a certain tactic.

Number four on the list of main difficulties and dilemmas in doing research on terrorism and counterterrorism is the fact that these are very complex phenomena and that they are changing all the time. The terrorism and counterterrorism of today, in many ways, are quite different from those of a number of decades ago. In chapter 2 we discussed the history of the phenomenon and the various waves with different manifestations of terrorism.

The most challenging problem and most important barrier to overcome when doing research on terrorism and counterterrorism is secrecy. How should researchers deal with the secrecy that surrounds both terrorism and counterterrorism? This characteristic is reflected in the names of some terrorist organisations or networks. Examples are the Weather Underground and the Armenian Secret Army for the Liberation of Armenia. Even more so, it is reflected in the names of organisations that try to counter the threat posed by terrorism, the many secret and intelligence services around the world that work with 'secret agents' or 'undercover agents'. Think of the South African Secret Service (SASS) or the Secret Intelligence Service (SIS), often known as MI6, which collects the UK's foreign intelligence. The secrecy attached to or underground nature of key actors in the field of terrorism and counterterrorism is a serious obstacle when doing research. For instance, how do you get to interview the people who represent these actors? Traditionally in social science research, there are some easy steps to take if you want to know more about people. You send them an e-mail or a carefully drafted letter, or simply knock on their doors and ask if you can interview them or have them fill out a survey. Obviously, this is not so easy in the case of terrorism and counterterrorism studies. It could also be dangerous (for two main types of danger see box 3.07). There are, however, new opportunities with the rise in the use of social media, even by terrorist organisations. For instance, interviewing people who joined groups like Jabhat al-Nusra or Islamic State in Syria and Iraq – currently on the UN list of designated terrorist organisations – was actually quite easy for a number of years. Conducting research by way of participant observation, meaning that you gain a close and intimate familiarity with a given group of individuals for a while, is and probably will remain quite difficult. The likelihood that you will be allowed to do that, within either a terrorist organisation or a counterterrorism agency, is very small, although it must be stressed that it is not impossible to do this. There are numerous examples of scholars who have done so in Northern Ireland and in Spain.

Facing these difficulties, researchers have often shied away from action- and actor-based research. Secrecy is and will probably remain a formidable barrier. It even limits getting information from relatively open organisations such as police forces and local authorities dealing with less legally or politically sensitive issues such as radicalisation or counter-radicalisation. Of course, even higher is the barrier to gaining access to the files and archives of secret services and intelligence agencies, especially those on sensitive or current operations. In fact the chance of being given access to such sources is close to zero, and often (but not always) for good reasons.

Two types of danger

According to Raymond Lee in his book *Dangerous Fieldwork* (1995), there are two types of danger when doing field research into terrorism and counterterrorism: the ambient and the situational. Ambient danger arises from being in a dangerous setting. Think of trying to interview top leaders of a terrorist organisation who are also targeted by way of drone attacks, or being a participant observer among potential victims of terrorism, for instance a religious minority that is often targeted by terrorists. Situational danger arises when the presence of a researcher provokes aggression from others in the setting, for instance from an interviewee who does not like a certain question or who starts to doubt the researcher's motives or accuses him or her of being a secret agent. As Horgan (2004, p. 34) states, 'obviously, it is wise not to attempt to engage in discussion on what might be seen as sensitive or dangerous issues'. Horgan also mentions that the risks of conducting fieldwork are sometimes exaggerated.

BOX 3.07   TWO TYPES OF DANGER

Research into terrorism also has several ethical challenges and dilemmas. Terrorism is a very politically sensitive and sometimes polarised and politicised topic. Researchers who manage to talk to terrorists or representatives of police and intelligence organisations might run the risk of being blamed for being one-sided, or being too understanding. This mainly holds for interviews with terrorists or alleged terrorists, but also for working with those in the counterterrorism field. Moreover, researchers who manage to get access to 'secret' or sensitive information have to be aware of the consequences of releasing that information, for legal and ethical reasons, as they might, for instance, jeopardise the privacy of individuals or compromise national security.

The seventh challenge of terrorism studies is the reliability and validation problem. If a researcher has managed to gain entry to a terrorist organisation and interview individual terrorists, several new problems emerge that he or she needs to overcome. Given the subjective, sensitive and politicised nature of terrorism and the fact that terrorists want to communicate their message to the world or frighten people, interviewers have to be aware of the possibility that they might be used to spread wrong messages or contribute to myths or a false picture of a situation or development. Or, in simpler terms, the interviewer might be fooled. Terrorists, or those who fight them, also simply give them their (preferred) version of the truth. To researchers it is very difficult, with all that secrecy involved, to validate statements, to check whether the information they receive is factual or not. Terrorists might want to exploit academic research for their own purposes and might want to influence its outcome. Furthermore, the people you interview might have a hindsight bias or suffer from distorted memory, so they might not always be aware of the fact that they are giving a different version of the truth. So in terrorism studies, as in other social sciences, reliability and validity are important issues, which are also linked to the problem of secrecy and ethical challenges and dilemmas.

One scholar who managed to overcome the secrecy problem and dealt with the ethical issues and the challenge of reliability and validation is Jessica Stern. This leading scholar tried to answer the question why religious militants kill. She believed that the only way to answer this question was to talk to them directly. She interviewed a number of people around the globe who, at one point in time, wanted to kill others in the name of God. She managed to gain the trust of prison authorities and several power brokers and got access to these people. Moreover, she managed to gain the trust of several terrorists and extremists and interviewed them. Thus, Stern showed that it is possible to overcome many challenges in terrorism studies, although it took a lot of effort, time and energy. The result was an outstanding book, one of the most successful attempts to understand the motivations of terrorists who claimed to act in the name of God.

More recent challenges in doing research pertain to the use of online data and research into social media. These sources have enormous potential for the study of terrorism, extremism and radicalisation, as well as the impact of terrorist attacks. However, there are also a number of difficulties in using these sources. For instance: authorship: how can one verify who wrote something? But also issues of privacy, ethics, data storage and – increasingly – the spread of fake news. Many of these are linked to many of the earlier mentioned challenges such as secrecy, reliability and validity, but they take new forms in the digital domain.

Key points

· There are many challenges and dilemmas when doing research into terrorism and counterterrorism.
· Secrecy is possibly the most important challenge, next to reliability and validity, and ethical challenges and dilemmas.
· Some scholars have shown the importance of talking to terrorists and have managed to interview (former or imprisoned) terrorists.
· Online data and social media offer new possibilities, but also pose new challenges to researchers.

3.6   The current state of the art

In the previous section we discussed the challenges and dilemmas encountered when doing research on terrorism and counterterrorism. And in the first sections of this chapter we pointed to the enormous increase in studies, centres and researchers in the field of terrorism studies after 9/11. But what insights has this boom in scholarly interest in terrorism produced? And what about the most important question: do we now know much more about terrorism and counterterrorism than we did before 9/11 or has the result been relatively meagre?

The answers to these questions by some of the leading scholars in the field showed a relatively critical or even downright negative attitude to the products of the study of terrorism, especially when referring to the 1990s and the immediate aftermath of 9/11. Often heard forms of criticism are that the field is ahistorical, alarmist, event-driven and has a tendency to over-generalise. Schmid and Jongman wrote in 1988 that terrorism studies is probably one of the fields where 'so much is written on the basis of so little research' (p. 179). With regard to the quality of terrorism research in years before 9/11, there has been a lot of criticism regarding the fact that academics had not seen coming the attacks, and the wider developments they reflected (see box 3.08). This criticism was, however, aimed not only at an alleged failure of imagination, but also at general flaws in the field of terrorism studies.

Academic failures and intellectual myopia

In his foreword to Silke's edited volume, *Research on Terrorism. Trends, Achievements and Failures*, Bruce Hoffman (2004, p. xvii) is very critical of the state of the art of terrorism studies in the years before 9/11. He notes, '[m]uch attention has been focused on the intelligence failures that led to the tragic events of 11th September 2001. Surprisingly little attention, however, has been devoted to the academic failures. Although these were patently less consequential, they were no less significant: calling into question the relevance of much of the scholarship on terrorism during the years leading up to 9/11'. He regarded the fact that al-Qaeda figured so unnoticeably in terrorism research as a reflection not just of a failure to anticipate or interpret emerging trends in terrorism but of an intellectual myopia that characterised the field. Hoffman shows how, until 9/11, the conventional wisdom was that terrorists would not carry out mass casualty attacks, as killing a handful of people often sufficed. However, by the mid-1990s the appearance of new adversaries, with new motivations and new rationales, began to challenge this logic with a number of attacks that were intended to kill hundreds of people, such as the sarin nerve gas attack on the Tokyo subway, the Oklahoma City bombing, and the bombing of US embassies in Kenya and Tanzania.

BOX 3.08   ACADEMIC FAILURES AND INTELLECTUAL MYOPIA

Post-9/11 research

As explained earlier, the tragic attacks on the US in 2001 completely changed the context for terrorism research. There was an incredible increase in investment in research into terrorism and counterterrorism. Therefore, one might expect that many, if not most, of the shortcomings in this field of study were quickly overcome in the years after these attacks. The reviews of the state of the art of terrorism studies indicate that, unfortunately, this did not happen or happened only at a slow rate, and that the increase in interest also created its own problems.

Three years after 9/11, Silke (2004) stressed the need for high-quality research, as it can provide powerful tools for insight into and guidance of what he considered to be one of the most challenging problems of the modern age. He also stressed that in the years up to 9/11 and its immediate aftermath, such high quality research had often been desperately lacking. Magnus Ranstorp in his edited volume, *Mapping Terrorism Research: State of the Art, Gaps and Future Direction* (2007), expressed the need for vigorous debates, critical self-reflexivity and alternative analytical assumptions and approaches. And Horgan (2004) pointed to the still limited conceptual development in the field of terrorism studies and its almost total reliance on secondary and tertiary source material. He also stressed the need for first-hand research, quoting Crenshaw who also noted that terrorism research efforts still lacked an empirical foundation of primary data based on interviews and the life histories of those engaged in terrorism.

Fortunately, researchers have been more positive about the state of the art of terrorism studies since 2010. Schmid looked back at four decades of terrorism research in 2011, observing that, next to much pretentious nonsense, a fairly solid body of consolidated knowledge has emerged. He concluded that terrorism studies 'has never been in better shape than now' (p. 470). There were several dedicated researchers who were engaged in high-quality research and there were great improvements regarding the collection and use of primary data. Just before, Silke had written that 'the field overall appears to be showing signs of beginning to stabilise from the biases in focus in the immediate aftermath of 9/11 and a war on terror' (2009, p. 49) In addition, Silke observed more detailed data analysis and trends that can improve the reliability and validity of the conclusions reached by researchers.

This is not to say that we can relax and lean back, as not everyone agreed with these more positive assessments. Marc Sageman, a forensic psychiatrist and former CIA officer, wrote an article in 2014 about what he considered to be the stagnation in terrorism research. He was very critical about the effects of 9/11, writing that 'the post-9/11 money surge into terrorism studies and the rush of newcomers into the field had a deleterious effect on research' (p. 569). We are no closer today to answering the basic question, 'what leads a person to political violence?', he also claimed. Schmid replied to this piece, saying that such a broad and simple question can never be adequately answered, just as it is impossible to give one answer to the question why someone commits another type of crime. Bart Schuurman tried to approach this question on a more meta-level by analysing research on terrorism published between 2007 and 2016. He noted that terrorism studies had improved considerably on a number of well-known challenges, such as the use of primary sources. Yet, articles were still frequently written by people who wrote about terrorism only once: about 75 per cent of the authors in main terrorism journals were one-time authors.

Philips adopted a broader approach in his study from 2021 which looked at all articles on terrorism published between 1970 and 2019, so not only in the main terrorism journals. Interestingly, he noted that the steep rise of scholars who focused on terrorism after 9/11 had remained stable: in other words, it was not so much a one-time boom, but led to more sustained effort. He also found that more than 1,500 authors wrote more than one article on the topic, which sheds a different light on the idea that scholars only briefly engage with this subject. Philips' study raises an interesting question: are terrorism scholars perhaps focusing too much on these so-called 'key terrorism journals' and therefore failing to engage with other findings? Terrorism studies remains a relatively small field, so perhaps we should look more closely at what else is going on in other disciplines.

Characteristics of terrorism research today

Looking at these statements and having studied other works that look into the current state of the art in terrorism studies, we observe strong and weak points. Below we discuss five characteristics that stand out:
1. Focus on niches and event-driven nature
2. Alarmist nature
3. Selection bias to western interests
4. Policy-oriented nature
5. Lack of theory testing

The first characteristic is that terrorism studies remains focused on niches and is often very event-driven. Terrorism is a constantly changing phenomenon and there are still a lot of issues that remain on the 'to do list'. A lot of terrorism researchers have a tendency to look into very specific types of terrorism or modus operandi. A good example of this is the interest in terrorism and weapons of mass destruction (WMD), also referred to as CBRN terrorism involving chemical, biological, radiological or nuclear weapons, materials or targets. A lot of books, articles and reports have been published on this specific topic. However, fortunately, it is not the type of terrorism that constitutes a clear or present danger. It is a very worrying idea or potential threat, but it constitutes a typical high impact/low probability risk. Compared to other very deadly attacks, the threat of WMD terrorism is massively over-inflated. According to Silke (2009), of the 300 most deadly terror attacks in the 20 years before he wrote the article, not one involved the use of WMDs. Against this backdrop it could be argued that too much attention has been devoted to this terrorist threat and that many studies are quite alarmist but often lack the data or sound arguments to support their assertions. This is not to say that we should not study WMD terrorism. The incredible impact of a nuclear or other WMD attack justifies in-depth research into this possibility, especially if it aims to come up with policy recommendations on how to prevent this ultimate threat or *Sum of All Fears*, as a well-known book by Tom Clancy and Hollywood movie on the threat of nuclear weapons are entitled. Probably the most well-known example of this is the work of Graham Allison who is both a scholar and a former US Assistant Secretary of Defense responsible for the strategy and policy towards the states of the former Soviet Union (see box 3.09).

Graham Allison on nuclear terrorism

Since the collapse of the Soviet Union, the scholar and politician Graham Allison has sounded the alarm bell on nuclear terrorism, alerting citizens and lawmakers to this threat and promoting ways to prevent it. In his book, *Nuclear Terrorism: The Ultimate Preventable Catastrophe*, Allison (2004) argues that terrorists are working to acquire and use nuclear weapons and shows that the materials to make those nuclear weapons continue to be vulnerable to theft or sale through the nuclear black market. Allison is, however, not just alarmist. He also spells out the doctrine of the 'Three No's', three priorities for preventing nuclear terrorism: no unsecured nuclear weapons; no new countries capable of enriching uranium or reprocessing plutonium; and no more states with nuclear weapons. Although much has been achieved in these three domains, there is still much work to be done, which means that the main point in Allison's book is still relevant today.

BOX 3.09   GRAHAM ALLISON ON NUCLEAR TERRORISM

Another example of a niche in terrorism that received a lot of attention after a major attack, also indicating the event-driven nature of terrorism studies, is the phenomenon of lone-actor terrorism. This indeed is a fascinating and in some cases worrying phenomenon, as became clear because of the attacks in Norway by Anders Breivik. Terrorism scholars want to know who these people are, what motivates them and how they might differ from terrorists who act in groups. The authors of this handbook were involved in the 'Countering Lone-Actor Terrorism Project', together with researchers from RUSI, ISD and Chatham House, publishing several articles and reports on this topic (see box. 3.10). If we look at all terrorism-related incidents, we have to conclude that lone-actor terrorism remains a small phenomenon. The event-driven nature of terrorism studies means that there is often a lot of funding available for conducting research into the latest developments. This might motivate scholars to jump on the bandwagon of trying to get funding to study these most recent trends. As explained above, these topics are often niches, meaning that more fundamental issues could receive less attention.

Countering Lone-Actor Terrorism Project

The International Centre for Counter-Terrorism (ICCT), Leiden University, Chatham House, the Royal United Services Institute (RUSI) and the Institute for Strategic Dialogue (ISD) joined forces in 2014 to study lone-actor terrorism in Europe. The project started with a two-day expert consultation with 30 academics and practitioners to develop a working definition of lone-actor terrorism. In the 18 months that followed, the team built a database of 120 perpetrators of lone-actor terrorism in Europe between 2000 and 2014. The consortium focused on various angles, including 1) the personal characteristics of the perpetrators, 2) attack methodology and logistics, 3) motivations, political engagement and online activity and 4) leakage and interaction with the authorities.

For the analysis report see: Ellis, C. et al. (2016). Lone-Actor Terrorism: Analysis Paper. *Countering Lone-Actor Terrorism Series* (4).

BOX 3.10   COUNTERING LONE-ACTOR TERRORISM PROJECT

A second characteristic of the state of the art of terrorism and counterterrorism studies that needs mentioning is the fact that it is often still quite alarmist. It is based on the assumption that terrorism is a very big threat and that it consists of major attacks that are increasing and increasingly lethal, as we will also discuss in the next chapter. However, if we look at the facts, we see that, with the exception of a few countries, it is not a huge physical threat, compared to civil war, earthquakes, tsunamis or a wide range of diseases that annually kill a lot more people around the globe. Moreover, most terrorist attacks are not of the scale of 9/11 or the tragedies in Bali, Beslan or Bombay that claimed hundreds of lives. At the same time, of course it should be stressed that every victim is one too many. However, making the terrorist threat bigger than it is not a good thing, for several reasons. As Jackson (2009, p. 176) puts it, 'At the very least, the media and politicians who play the fear card actually empower terrorism and amplify its impact far beyond its objective capabilities to cause material harm'. In other words, we do the terrorists a favour as they want to appear bigger than they are and want to spread fear, something we will discuss in more detail in chapter 6 on dealing with terrorism. Another negative consequence of inflating the terrorist threat is that it tends to justify any means necessary to deal with it. We have seen examples of this in many countries around the globe, especially in the wake of lethal terrorist attacks, most notably after the attacks on 9/11 that set off the 'Global War on Terror' (see box 3.11) which resulted in much support for not only restrictions on human rights and the use of military force, but extreme measures such as torture and targeted killings.

The 'Global War on Terror'

After the terrorist attacks of 11 September 2001, the Bush administration declared a 'Global War on Terror'. It was the label under which the US started a military campaign to fight al-Qaeda and other terrorist or militant organisations, in particular the Taliban in Afghanistan. It also involved new security legislation and efforts to block the financing of terrorism. Warning the rest of the world that 'either you are with us, or you are with the terrorists', the US administration called on other states to join in the fight against terrorism. Many NATO member states and non-NATO countries such as Pakistan joined this worldwide coalition against terrorism, sending troops to Afghanistan, adopting new terrorism laws and stepping up domestic policing and intelligence work. The strong focus on a military and repressive approach soon led to criticism regarding its proportionality, legality and efficiency, and increased resentment against the West in large parts of the Islamic world. Many also called the notion of a 'war' against 'terrorism' a misnomer, as terrorism is not an enemy but a tactic.

BOX 3.11   THE 'GLOBAL WAR ON TERROR'

A third issue that needs attention when discussing the state of the art of terrorism studies is the selection bias to western interests. If we look at the map of terrorist incidents worldwide, we see that most terrorism takes place outside the western world. And what about the study of counterterrorism? We have also mentioned the fact that most scholars and institutes in the field of terrorism studies are based in North America, Europe or a few other western countries. Obviously there is a discrepancy between the location of most attacks and the location of the study of terrorism, which is also reflected in the issues and developments that are studied. This not only constitutes a limitation to our insight into the phenomenon of terrorism in general, it has also contributed to the idea that the term 'terrorism' is often too strongly associated with enemies of the West.

Another, fourth, characteristic or issue that needs mentioning when discussing the state of the art of terrorism studies is the policy-oriented nature of research. There are many ways to look at this. To a large extent, it is a positive aspect of a study into a phenomenon that poses a threat to security and peaceful relationships in societies. Especially after 9/11, there has been an incredible amount of research into questions that authorities have on how to deal with this threat. The fact that scholars study topics that are relevant should be seen as a positive characteristic of the field. However, its policy-oriented nature may also have a number of negative side effects. According to Jackson (2009, p. 78), 'when virtually the entire academic field collectively adopts state priorities and aims, and when it tailors its research towards assisting state agencies in fighting terrorism (as defined by state institutions), it means that terrorism studies functions ideologically as an intellectual arm of the state and is aligned with its broader hegemonic project'. It is good to be aware of this possible risk and to foster a more independent academic attitude in the field of terrorism studies. However, it also means that scholars are likely to follow the political agenda: we study what the funders think is important to study as we are dependent on funding. This means that there is a risk of going along with the overly alarmist rhetoric by studying the latest threats and developments, leaving more fundamental questions unanswered. Nonetheless, there is nothing wrong with policy-oriented research as such, and it is good to note that there have been numerous studies that have helped authorities to formulate and execute coherent, proportional and ethically just counterterrorism policies.

A fifth and final characteristic of the state of the art of terrorism studies is that there is a lack of theory testing. Conceptual discussions are scarce, there is limited theory development and the field lacks comparative studies. Partly as a result of this, many of the key assumptions in the field have not been properly tested. This observation is not particularly new and is also related to the earlier mentioned challenges and particularities of conducting research on terrorism and counterterrorism.

This brings us to the final and fundamental question: do we know much more about terrorism and counterterrorism today than in the past, before the attacks on 9/11? No doubt the answer is yes, we do know much more. But of course, there are still quite a few issues on the 'to do list' and the 'to improve list'. In chapter 7 we will discuss several un- and under-researched topics and provide some ideas for the future research agenda in terrorism studies.

Key points

- Since 9/11, the academic output regarding terrorism has grown tremendously.
- Nonetheless, there has been a lack of empirical research and of conceptual and theoretical development. Moreover, many of the key assumptions in the field of terrorism studies still need to be tested and compared with empirical evidence.
- In recent years, scholars have been more positive about the state of the art in terrorism studies.
- Terrorism research today is still characterised by a focus on niches and latest developments, a selection bias to western interests, a policy-oriented nature and lack of theory testing.
- Despite these flaws, it is safe to say that we do know much more about terrorism than we did before 9/11.

3.7   Conclusion

In this chapter we looked into the field of terrorism studies and its different authors, centres, disciplines and approaches. This field started to emerge in the early 1960s, initially with just a handful of scholars. Their numbers and the academic output grew in the 1970s and 1980s, followed by a decline in the 1990s. The attacks on the US in 9/11 sparked an enormous and unprecedented growth in terrorism studies, more than doubling the academic output compared to that of the whole pre-9/11 era. Most of the scholars and knowledge centres, both before and after 9/11, have been located in the Anglo-Saxon world and a number of other western countries. This western dominance has resulted in much attention being paid to terrorism in that part of the world and far less attention to terrorism elsewhere, which does not correspond with the geographic distribution of terrorism-related incidents.

The field of terrorism studies is also characterised by a wide variety of disciplines that look into terrorism and counterterrorism, ranging from political science and war studies to social psychology and communication studies. Moreover, there are several distinct approaches to studying these phenomena. The three main academic approaches are the following: the rational/instrumental approach, the (socio-)psychological approach and a multi-causal approach.

We also explored the results of the study of terrorism and counterterrorism, answering the question 'what have academia and think tanks come up with since 9/11?'. The answer to this question is twofold: in recent years the body of knowledge regarding terrorism has grown tremendously. At the same time, there has been a lack of empirical research and of conceptual and theoretical development. Moreover, many of the key assumptions in the field of terrorism studies have not been properly tested. Fortunately, we noted a number of positive developments that have moved terrorism research forward, for instance the increase in the collection and use of primary sources such as police files, court records and interviews with (former or imprisoned) terrorists. Therefore, we concluded that despite many shortcomings the field, it is safe to say that we do know more about terrorism than before 9/11.

The chapter has also tried to explain the reasons behind the many shortcomings. We looked into the difficulties of conducting research on terrorism and counterterrorism. Several challenges and dilemmas were mentioned, among them the problem of secrecy. This particular challenge is perhaps the most important one. At the same time we showed that this and other difficulties are no excuse for not trying to overcome them. Some scholars have, for instance, managed to talk to terrorists or gain access to files and archives after lengthy procedures and gaining the trust of the authorities, terrorist organisations or individual terrorists. In other words, conducting research on terrorism, especially empirical research, is difficult but it is not impossible, as an increasing number of scholars have shown.

This brings us to the final part of this chapter in which we assessed the current state of the art of terrorism studies. Despite progress, there are still a number of characteristics of the field that need our attention: its focus on niches and latest developments, a selection bias to western interests, its policy-oriented nature and lack of theory testing. We also observed that academia and think tanks have produced interesting assumptions about causes, mechanisms and processes regarding terrorism and counterterrorism, but that many of the key assumptions have not been properly tested. This is a serious flaw, as these assumptions are very often the basis of counterterrorism policies. If the assumptions are right, there is no problem, but what if the assumptions are wrong? Therefore we need to test these assumptions, which we will do in the next two chapters.

Bibliography

Abrahms, M. (2008). What Terrorists Really Want: Terrorist Motives and Counterterrorism Strategy. *International security, 32*(4), 78-105.

Ajide, K. B. (2021). Democracy, Regime Durability and Terrorism in Africa. *Defence and Peace Economics 32*(5), 550-571.

Alexander, Y. (ed.). (1976). *International terrorism: national, regional, and global perspectives*. New York: Praeger.

Alexander, Y., & Rapoport, D. (eds.). (1982). *The Rationalization of Terrorism*. Los Angeles: University Publications of America.

Alexander, Y., Carlton, D., & Wilkinson, P. (1979). *Terrorism: Theory and Practice*. Boulder: Westview Press.

Allison, G. (2004). *Research on Terrorism: The Ultimate Preventable Catastrophe*. New York: Times Books.

Anat, B. (2007). *The Path to Paradise: The Inner World of Suicide Bombers and Their Dispatchers*. West Port: Praeger Security International.

Aust, S. (1985). *The Baader Meinhof Complex*. Hamburg: Hofmann & Campe Verlag.

Azani, E. (2009). *Hezbollah: The Story of the Party of God from Revolution to Institutionalization*. New York: Palgrave MacMillan.

Bakker, E., & Roy van Zuijdewijn, J. de. (2015). Lone-Actor Terrorism: Definitional Workshop. *Countering Lone-Actor Terrorism Series, 2*. London: RUSI.

Bassiouni, M. (1975). *International terrorism and political crimes.* Springfield: Charles C. Thomas.

Berko, A. (2009). *The Path to Paradise: The Inner World of Suicide Bombers and Their Dispatchers.* Herndon: Potomac Books.

Breen-Smyth, M. et al. (2008). Critical Terrorism Studies-an introduction. *Critical Studies on Terrorism, 1*(1), 1-4.

Clancy, T. (1991). *Sum of all Fears.* New York: Putnam.

Clutterbuck, R. (1974). *Protest and the urban guerilla.* New York: Abelard & Schumann.

Clutterbuck, R. (1987). *Kidnap, Hijack and Extortion: The Response.* London: MacMillan.

Crenshaw, M. (1981). The Causes of Terrorism. *Comparative Politics, 13*(4), 379-399.

Crenshaw, M. (1995). *Terrorism in Context.* University Park: Penn State University Press.

Crenshaw, M. (2007). *The Debate over "New" vs. "Old" Terrorism.* Presented at the Annual Meeting of the American Political Science Association, Chicago.

Duyvesteyn, I., & Malkki, L. (2012). No: The Fallacy of the New Terrorism Thesis. In Jackson, R., & Sinclair. J. (eds.), *Contemporary Debates on Terrorism* (35-41). London: Routledge.

Ehiane, S. O. (2018). Strengthening the African Union (AU) Counterterrorism Strategy in Africa: a re-awakened order. *Journal of African Union Studies 7*(2), 109-126.

Ellis, C. et al. (2016). Lone-Actor Terrorism: Analysis Paper. *Countering Lone-Actor Terrorism Series 4.* London: RUSI.

Gurr, T. (1970). *Why men rebel.* Princeton: Princeton University Press.

Hewitt, C. (1984). *The Effectiveness of Anti-Terrorist Policies.* Lanham: University Press of America.

Hoffman, B. (1998, 2006). *Inside Terrorism.* New York, Columbia University Press.

Horgan, J. (2004). The case for firsthand research. In Silke, A. (ed.), *Research on Terrorism, trends, achievements and failures* (30-57). New York: Frank Cass.

Horgan, J. (2005). *The Psychology of Terrorism.* London: Routledge.

Jackson, R. (2009). The Study of Terrorism after 11 September 2001: Problems, Challenges and Future Developments. *Political Studies Review, 7*(2), 171-184.

Jackson, R., Breen-Smyth, M., & Gunning, J. (2009). *Critical Terrorism Studies: A New Research Agenda.* New York: Routledge.

Jenkins, B. M. (1974). *International Terrorism: A new kind of warfare?* Santa Monica: The RAND Corporation.

Jenkins, B. M. (1975). *Will Terrorists Go Nuclear?* Santa Monica: The RAND Corporation.

Juergensmeyer, M. (2003). *Terror in the mind of God: the global rise of religious violence* (3rd ed.). Berkeley: University of California Press.

Laqueur, W. (1977). *Terrorism*. Boston: Little, Brown.

Laqueur, W. (2000). *The New Terrorism: Fanaticism and the Arms of Mass Destruction*. Oxford: Oxford University Press.

Lee, R. (1995). *Dangerous Fieldwork*. London: Sage.

National Commission on Terrorist Attacks upon the United States. (2004). *The 9/11 Commission report: final report of the National Commission on Terrorist Attacks upon the United States*. Washington D.C.: National Commission on Terrorist Attacks upon the United States.

Neumann, P. (2009). *Old & New Terrorism. Late Modernity, Globalization and the Transformation of Political Violence*. Cambridge: Polity.

Nüsse, A. (1999). *Muslim Palestine: The Ideology of Hamas*. Abingdon: Routledge.

Okoli, A. O., & Ogayi, C. O. (2018). Herdsmen militancy and humanitarian crisis in Nigeria: A theoretical briefing. *African Security Review, 27*(2), 129-143.

Olojo, A., & Mahdi, M. (2022). Transitional Justice: Testing the Waters in Lake Chad Basin. *ISS West Africa Report 39*.

Pape, R. (2005). *Dying to Win: The Strategic Logic of Suicide Bombing*. New York: Random House.

Philips, B. (2021). How Did 9/11 Affect Terrorism Research? Examining Articles and Authors, 1970-2019. *Terrorism and Political Violence* [online first].

Porzecanski, A. (1973). *Uruguay's Tupamaros: the urban guerrilla*. New York: Praeger.

Post, J. (1984). Notes on a psychodynamic theory of terrorist behavior. *Terrorism, 7*(2), 241-256.

Post, J. (1987). Rewarding Fire With Fire: Effects of Retaliation on Terrorist Group Dynamics. *Terrorism, 10*(1), 23–36.

Post, J. (2007). *The Mind of the Terrorist: The Psychology of Terrorism from the IRA to Al-Qaeda*. New York: Palgrave McMillan.

Ranstorp, M. (ed.). (2007). *Mapping Terrorism Research: State of the Art, Gaps and Future Direction*. New York: Routledge.

Rapoport, D. (1971). *Assassination and Terrorism*. Toronto: Canadian Broadcasting Corporation.

Rapoport, D. (2004). Four Waves of Modern Terrorism. In Cronin, A. K. and Ludes, J. M. (eds.). *Attacking terrorism: Elements of a Grand Strategy* (46-73). Washington: Georgetown University Press.

Richardson, L. (2006). *What Terrorists Want: Understanding the Enemy, Containing the Threat*. New York: Random House.

Sageman, M. (2014). The Stagnation in Terrorism Research. *Terrorism and Political Violence, 26*(4), 565-580.

Schmid, A. P., & Graaf, J. de. (1982). *Violence as communication: insurgent terrorism and the Western news media*. London and Beverly Hills: Sage.

Terrorism studies

Schmid, A. P., & Jongman, A. J. (1988). *Political Terrorism: A New Guide to Actors, Concepts, Data Bases, Theories & Literature.* New Brunswick: Transaction Publishers Inc.

Schmid, A. P. (2011). *The Routledge Handbook of Terrorism Research.* London: Routledge.

Schuurman, B. (2020). Research on Terrorism, 2007-2016: A Review of Data, Methods, and Authorship. *Terrorism and Political Violence, 32*(5), 1011-1026.

Silke, A. (ed.). (2004). *Research on Terrorism, trends, achievements and failures.* London: Frank Cass.

Silke, A. (ed.). (2009). *Research on Terrorism: Trends, Achievements, and Failures.* London: Routledge.

Speckhard, A. (2012). *Talking to Terrorists: Understanding the Psycho-Social Motivations of Militant Jihadi Terrorists, Mass Hostage Takers, Suicide Bombers & Martyrs.* McClean: Advance Press.

Stern, J. (2003). *Terror in the name of God: why religious militants kill.* New York: Ecco.

Taylor, M., & Horgan, J. (2006). A Conceptual Framework for Addressing Psychological Process in the Development of the Terrorist. *Terrorism and Political Violence, 18*(4), 585-601.

Transnational Terrorism, Security, and the Rule of Law. (2008). *Exploring Root and Trigger Causes of Terrorism.*

Weimann, G. (1983). The Theatre of Terror: Effects of Press Coverage. *Journal of Communication, 1*(33), 38-45.

Wilkinson, P. (1974). *Political Terrorism.* London: MacMillan.

Wilkinson, P. (1976). *Terrorism versus liberal democracy: the problems of response.* London: Institute for the Study of Conflict.

Wilkinson, P. (2007). Research into terrorism studies: achievements and failures. In Ranstorp. M. (ed.), *Mapping Terrorism Research* (316-328). New York: Routledge.

4

Assumptions about terrorism

4.1 Introduction

In the previous chapter we looked into the field of terrorism studies and its different authors, centres, disciplines and approaches. We explored the results of the study of terrorism and counterterrorism and looked at the difficulties of doing terrorism research. In this chapter we are going to investigate some of the assumptions about terrorism that have often been put forward by scholars, practitioners, politicians or journalists. These assumptions are frequently repeated in the public debate on terrorism, or even constitute the basis of policy-making. Therefore, it is important to test these assumptions to see whether they are true, partly true or false. The five assumptions we are going to explore and analyse are the following:

1. Terrorism is caused by poverty.
2. Terrorists are crazy.
3. Terrorism is becoming increasingly lethal.
4. Terrorism is predominantly anti-western.
5. Terrorism is successful.

4.2 Assumption one: Terrorism is caused by poverty

One of the most frequently repeated assumptions about terrorism is that it is caused by poverty. The basic idea behind this assumption is that poverty leads to a lack of opportunities to improve the quality of someone's life. This could result in antagonism towards people who are better off and could lead to blaming others, such as the government, for this lack of chances in life. These kinds of grievances are believed to be an important cause of terrorism. In combination with the idea that terrorists are rational actors, it is argued by some that violence might be the last resort of the downtrodden to put grievances on the political agenda. Others point to the fact that many poor countries seem to suffer from terrorism and that there are many examples of terrorists from the lower ranks of society. Then they assume that a correlation between poverty and terrorism exists. Lastly, it has to be mentioned that some terrorist organisations, specifically left-wing-oriented ones, have claimed to fight for or on behalf of the poor. Think of the earlier example given in chapter 3 of the Tupamaros who initially were mainly involved in robberies, distributing the stolen money among the poor (see box 4.01).

Terrorists claiming to act on behalf of the poor

In an interview with Al Jazeera at a checkpoint in Cauca, Colombia, in 2010, local commander of the Fuerzas Armadas Revolucionarias de Colombia (FARC) Duber explained why they continue to fight. 'A new Colombia is where the poor have jobs, social equality', he said. 'Free health care, free education. Not like now. There is no equality here. There is no health, no education for the poor, only for the rich'.

Al Jazeera, 21 June 2010. See, http://www.youtube.com/watch?v=U9KwI67wZf8.

BOX 4.01   TERRORISTS CLAIMING TO ACT ON BEHALF OF THE POOR

Why does it matter to know whether or not terrorism is caused by poverty?

If the assumption that terrorism is caused by poverty is true, this should have implications for counterterrorism. If poverty is indeed a root cause of terrorism, then counterterrorism efforts should include policies aimed at reducing (the causes of) poverty. Of course, policies to reduce poverty are also welcome if there is no link to terrorism, simply from a humanitarian perspective. However, we have to test whether or not it is also useful to fight poverty in relation to terrorism. Because, just like in other policy areas, counterterrorism policy-makers are confronted with the problem of allocating scarce resources. There is only a finite amount of resources, such as money, people and political will, that could be spent on formulating strategies, translating them into concrete measures and implementing them. Hence, if these scarce resources are spent on reducing poverty, they cannot be used on other counterterrorism measures. That is why we need to investigate if and how poverty is linked to terrorism. If there is no causal relationship, at least from a counterterrorism perspective, it might be more useful to focus counterterrorism efforts on something else.

Interestingly, many of those who claim that terrorism and poverty are linked are politicians. This group of people includes world leaders who are responsible for developing strategies and policies on important global issues, including terrorism. In their paper, 'Is Terrorism the "Poor Man's Patent"?: Evaluating the Causal Connection between Education, Poverty, and Political Violence', Mia Bloom and Cale Horne (2009) provide a number of examples of political leaders who assume that terrorism is by and large a by-product of poverty and a lack of education. They quote US Secretary of State Colin Powell, who wrote that 'I fully believe that the root cause of terrorism does come from situations where there is poverty, where there is ignorance, where people see no hope in their lives'. Archbishop Desmond Tutu from South Africa also pointed to this cause during the start of the World Social Forum in Nairobi in 2007: 'you can never win a war against terror as long as there are conditions in the world that make people desperate. Poverty, diseases, ignorance'. More recently, France's justice minister, Christiane Taubira, stressed the importance of targeting poverty and injustice as major factors that contribute to terrorism. She did so at a meeting of the UN's Counterterrorism Committee in February 2015.

There are numerous other examples of well-known politicians and leaders of public opinion who have contributed to the popular notion of a causal relationship between poverty and terrorism and who have stressed the need to eradicate this assumed root of terrorism. While eradicating poverty is important for a wide variety of reasons, we need to establish whether the popular assumption is true or just a myth.

Is terrorism caused by poverty or not?

When we compare the assumption of a causal link between terrorism and poverty with empirical data and bring in academic evidence, we find that there are reasons to doubt any relationship, let alone a causal one. Most terrorists are not extremely poor or that much poorer than others who do not engage in terrorism. In fact, some terrorists are extremely rich. Examples of terrorists who defy the terrorism-poverty link include Osama bin Laden, who came from a wealthy Saudi Arabian family (see box 4.02). There are many examples of terrorists from middle or upper middle classes. Abimael Guzmán, the leader of the Shining Path in Peru, was a professor of philosophy before he turned his theoretical ideas about revolution into violent practice. Anders Breivik, who killed almost 80 people in Norway, came from a middle class family, as did Ulrike Meinhof, a left-wing terrorist and one of the key people of the Red Army Faction (RAF) which had its roots in West Germany in the 1960s. A more recent example is so-called Jihadi John, the British-Kuwaiti man who featured in several IS videos beheading captives in 2014 and 2015.

Before joining IS he went to study business management and information systems in the UK and worked for an IT company in Kuwait. Such examples are useful as anecdotal evidence, but they do not have any explanatory value regarding the (lack of) existence of a link between poverty and terrorism. Before we move to academic studies that have explored this link, we will first look at what we can conclude when we look at the world map: what countries are most often targeted by terrorists and how do they rank in terms of economic development?

Osama bin Laden's family background

Osama bin Laden's father, Mohammed bin Awad bin Laden, immigrated from Yemen to Saudi Arabia. He worked his way up from being a porter for pilgrims in Jeddah to being the owner of the Binladin Group – a billion-dollar oil, equity management and construction company with offices all over the world. Osama bin Laden was the son of his tenth wife and one of dozens of (half-)brothers and (half-)sisters. He grew up in wealth and privilege and was given a good education, attending elite high schools and earning a degree in civil engineering from King Abdulaziz University in Saudi Arabia. Journalist Peter Bergen interviewed Bin Laden and several people who worked with him and wrote about these interviews in the book, *The Osama bin Laden I know. An oral history of Al Qaeda's leader* (2006).

BOX 4.02   OSAMA BIN LADEN'S FAMILY BACKGROUND

While the above-mentioned examples pertain to poverty on the individual or group level, it is also possible to analyse the link between poverty and terrorism by studying the world map of terrorist attacks. If we take, for instance, the 2020 Global Terrorism Index by the Institute of Economics and Peace, we see that Afghanistan, Iraq, Nigeria, Syria and Somalia are most often confronted with terrorism. The rest of the ten most impacted countries are Yemen, Pakistan, India, the Democratic Republic of the Congo (DRC) and the Philippines. How do these countries perform in economic terms? According to data of the World Bank, which ranks states on various economic indicators including Gross Domestic Product (GDP), Iraq is considered an upper middle income country and Pakistan, Nigeria, the Philippines and India are regarded as lower middle income countries. Some of the countries that are hit hardest by terrorism are on the bottom part of the list: Afghanistan, Yemen, DRC, Syria and Somalia. This thus provides a mixed picture in terms of the economic development of these countries: some are middle income countries, others low income countries. However, many of those countries that are very low on the list of the World Bank, such as Burundi, Malawi, Madagascar, Sierra Leone and Togo, do not experience high or even moderate levels of terrorism.

Moreover, highly developed countries with high GDPs have also been confronted with terrorism. In the 1960s and 1970s, left-wing terrorism affected a number of them: Germany, Italy and Japan were frequently confronted with this type of terrorism. And the UK and Spain have been confronted with separatist-nationalist terrorism for many decades. These countries were, at that time and today, some of the richest countries in the world. Looking both at the general picture of individuals and that of countries, there seems to be little support for the idea that poverty causes terrorism.

Various scholars have tried to investigate this assumption more systematically in recent years. For instance, James Piazza (2006) explored the relationship between poverty and terrorism from different angles. He included many indicators of poverty, such as low levels of per capita income, illiteracy, low life expectancy and lack of employment opportunities. Comparing this with statistical data, Piazza concluded that these poverty-related factors could not be linked to higher levels of terrorism (see also box 4.03).

James Piazza on poverty and terrorism

A study by Piazza (2006) titled 'Rooted in Poverty?' evaluates the assumption that poverty, inequality and poor economic development are root causes of terrorism. 'Employing a series of multiple regression analyses on terrorist incidents and casualties in ninety-six countries from 1986 to 2002, the study considers the significance of poverty, malnutrition, inequality, unemployment, inflation, and poor economic growth as predictors of terrorism, along with a variety of political and demographic control variables. The findings are that, contrary to popular opinion, no significant relationship between any of the measures of economic development and terrorism can be determined.' Instead, Piazza points to variables such as ethno-religious diversity, increased state repression and, most significantly, the structure of party politics as significant predictors of terrorism.

BOX 4.03   JAMES PIAZZA ON POVERTY AND TERRORISM

An example of scholars who looked at the link between poverty and terrorism at the individual level were Alan Krueger and Jitka Malečková. Their study from 2003 is still widely used 20 years later. In their article, 'Education, Poverty and Terrorism: Is There a Causal Connection?', the authors focused specifically on the militant wing of Hezbollah – a Shi'a Islamist group and political party in Lebanon – , Palestinian suicide bombers and Israeli Jewish settlers attacking Palestinians. Using an extensive statistical dataset, they analysed the determinants of participation in Hezbollah militant activities. Their conclusion was that having a living standard above the poverty line or

Terrorism and Counterterrorism Studies

113

Assumptions about terrorism

secondary or higher education was positively associated with participation in Hezbollah. Krueger and Malečková also found that Israeli Jewish settlers who attacked Palestinians in the West Bank in the early 1980s were overwhelmingly from high-paying occupations. Based on these findings, their general conclusion was straightforward: '[a]ny connection between poverty, education and terrorism is indirect, complicated and probably quite weak' (p. 119). They also concluded that terrorism is more likely caused by a 'response to political conditions and long-standing feelings of indignity and frustration that have little to do with economics'.

A third and more recent study is the 2021 article, 'Poverty and terrorism in Africa: Understanding the nexus based on existing levels of terrorism', by Chimere Iheonu and Hyacinth Ichoku. They explored the relationship in the African context. In their quantitative study they argued that poverty is not a determining factor for terrorism in Africa. They pointed to other economic indicators such as economic growth, income inequality and unemployment which affect terrorism on the continent. As such, their study invites researchers to look at more specific indicators than just poverty when trying to understand what causes terrorism.

Conclusion

So is the assumption that terrorism is caused by terrorism true, partly true or false? We have provided various examples of politicians and other important global figures who mention poverty as a root cause. Looking at individual cases, we can find various examples of terrorists who do not originate from lower economic backgrounds. The map of terrorism shows that some of the countries most often targeted by terrorists are poor, but others are not. Yet, such anecdotal evidence that might show the existence or absence of a correlation is not sufficient to determine whether or not a causal relationship exists. Academics who have studied the relationship between poverty and terrorism and performed quantitative analyses concluded that there is no evidence for such a link. As a result, we label this assumption false. We would even go as far as to call it a myth – an assumption that is a fictitious and unscientific conclusion that is nevertheless widely believed to be true. At the same time, the link between economics and terrorism is a complicated one, and more research is needed to understand to what extent other economic indicators might play a role in the emergence of radicalisation and terrorism.

Key points

· The idea of a causal relationship between poverty and terrorism has often been mentioned by politicians and public figures.

- Looking at statistics and studying the academic literature on terrorism, there is no support for the idea of a direct link between poverty and terrorism.
- The assumption that terrorism is caused by poverty can be labelled as false.
- Some scholars observe that other economic indicators might affect the emergence of terrorism, providing new angles for future research.

4.3 Assumption two: Terrorists are crazy

A second often-heard assumption is that terrorists are crazy, insane, psychotic or suffering from another form of mental illness. The logic behind the assumption is simple: how could a sane person commit such violent acts, target innocent people and sometimes even kill him- or herself in the act? Around the world, people find it difficult to answer these questions. To many, if not most, of us it is hard to imagine why someone would send bomb letters, try to blow up a plane, shoot people in a mosque, or kill hundreds of innocent office workers in a building in New York. We might find it even more difficult to comprehend the behaviour and thoughts of suicide terrorists. It is easy and perhaps even comforting to think that people who commit such horrible acts must be insane. But are they? Do they suffer from any kind of abnormal behavioural patterns or psychological disorders that can explain their behaviour? While it is important to dive into this assumption, we need to be aware of many inherent biases or the problematic use of language when we speak about such questions. Mental health issues are, in fact, normal and common. Many people need to deal with those at some point in their lives. Most mental health issues may have no link to violence at all.

Ted Kaczynski, the 'Unabomber'

The mugshot of Theodore Kaczynski after his arrest in 1996 shows a bewildered man just arrested at his remote cabin in Montana, where he was found in an unkempt state. The picture seems to show the stereotypical crazy lone wolf terrorist. However, he was (also) a very intelligent and talented man who was accepted into Harvard at the age of 16. He holds a PhD in mathematics and worked at the University of California, Berkeley. At the age of 25 he left university and after a few years moved to his remote cabin, where he lived in seclusion from society. From there, he sent 16 bombs to targets including universities and airlines – hence the name 'Unabom' (UNiversity & Airline BOMber). He killed three people and injured 23. In a manifesto, which ironically would lead to his arrest, he called for a worldwide revolution against the effects of modern society's 'industrial-technological system'. In court Kaczynski rejected an insanity defence. A court-appointed psychiatrist, however, diagnosed him as suffering from paranoid schizophrenia, but also declared him competent to stand trial.

BOX 4.04   TED KACZYNSKI, THE 'UNABOMBER'

The popular idea that terrorists are crazy or that there are many insane people among terrorists is partly inspired by (media reports of) the behaviour of a number of well-known terrorists or their physical appearance, for instance captured in pictures or other footage. Think of Ted Kaczynski (see box 4.04), the so called 'Unabomber', who sent bomb letters to universities and companies. His mugshot after his arrest portrays a man most people would describe as deranged and bewildered. This also holds true for Richard Reid, the so-called 'Shoe Bomber', who tried to blow up a plane with a bomb that was hidden in his shoes. Another example that feeds the idea that (many) terrorists are insane is the behaviour in court of Anders Breivik, the man who killed 77 people in Norway in 2011. According to one of the psychiatric evaluations conducted, the perpetrator suffered from narcissistic and anti-social personality disorders (see box 4.05). In the eyes of many non-experts in the field of psychiatry, his performance during the trial was 'proof' of this assessment. A final case that should be mentioned is that of Nidal Malik Hasan, who worked for the US Armed Forces as a psychiatrist and who killed 13 of his colleagues in Fort Hood, Texas. This case of a psychiatrist turning into a mass murderer raises questions about not only the mental state of this particular person, but also that of terrorists in general.

Breivik: two psychiatric assessments, two outcomes

Breivik underwent two examinations by court-appointed psychiatrists. The first group of experts diagnosed him as having paranoid schizophrenia. He displayed a severe lack of empathy and acted compulsively based on grandiose and delusional thoughts and ideas. They also believed him to be psychotic when he set off the bomb in Oslo and killed dozens on the island of Utøya. The psychiatrists consequently argued Breivik to be criminally insane.

Breivik himself seems to have been surprised by these findings and felt insulted by the conclusions in the diagnosis. He was not the only one who was upset. The diagnosis was fiercely debated in Norway by mental health experts, legal experts and the public. If the diagnosis were to have been accepted by the court, he could not have been sentenced to prison, but would have gone to a psychiatric hospital instead.

The controversy led to a second psychiatric evaluation which concluded that the perpetrator was not psychotic when he carried out the attacks. The second group of experts diagnosed antisocial and narcissistic personality disorders. A psychiatrist testified in court that Breivik also suffered from Asperger's

Syndrome, after having observed, among other things, that he showed a lack of emotion when talking about his victims. In the end, Breivik was adjudged competent to stand trial and sentenced to 21 years in prison, the maximum penalty in Norway.

BOX 4.05   BREIVIK: TWO PSYCHIATRIC ASSESSMENTS, TWO OUTCOMES

Moreover, to many the acts committed by terrorists evoke moral outrage. This moral outrage sometimes clouds our ability to form an objective judgement of the rationale or mental state of terrorists. Additionally, because such acts are generally strongly condemned, there is a tendency to regard these people as fundamentally different from the rest of society. Terrorists are also often discussed in the same breath as mass murderers and school shooters, quite a few of whom have been diagnosed with mental illnesses. While terrorists are often put in the same category as people who use indiscriminate, random violence, important differences exist. The main difference between mass murderers and terrorists is that the former, generally speaking, are not politically motivated and the latter are, if we at least agree on the nature of terrorism as an instrument to achieve certain political goals, as discussed in chapter 1. In other words, there seems to be a difference in terms of the rationality behind their actions. If there is rationality in the act and if the act is regarded as a political instrument, can one still call this a crazy act or the behaviour of an insane person?

Some might consider this question unethical as it might imply some kind of justification. However, understanding the rationale behind certain attacks does not mean that one agrees with the perpetrators, nor does it mean that one cannot condemn it at the same time. Finally, it should be stressed that it is important to be careful when using the term crazy, insane or mentally disturbed in the debate on terrorism. These terms have many different connotations and meanings and often do not reflect specific abnormal mental or behavioural patterns. Instead, these words often reflect only violations of societal norms.

Why does it matter to know whether or not terrorists are crazy?

If most or many terrorists are indeed insane or suffer from mental illnesses, that has several consequences for counterterrorism policies. It would require a more important role for the (mental) healthcare sector to better understand why people commit such acts. At the same time, a confirmation of this assumption might lead to the conclusion that there is little we can do to prevent terrorism, as in every society people display abnormal mental or behavioural patterns, or are clinically psychotic. Moreover, we cannot jail people simply for being mentally ill, although this is still a horrible widespread practice in various countries. If the assumption is true, another consequence would be that there is little use in investigating the motivations and rationale of some terrorists or terrorist organisations as there might not be a motivation or rationale … they are simply crazy.

Are terrorists crazy or not?

The two most common approaches to studying terrorism and counterterrorism are the rational or instrumental approach and the (socio-)psychological approach. As discussed in chapter 3, the rational approach clearly rejects the assumption that terrorists are crazy. Proponents of this approach see terrorism as a deliberate strategy of coercing an opponent to agree to one's aims, making terrorists rational actors who kill to gain political results. Within the second approach in terrorism studies, the (socio-)psychological approach, there is more or less consensus that terrorists are not mentally disturbed. Jerrold Post, one of the most important scholars on the psychology of terrorists and author of *The Mind of the Terrorist: The Psychology of Terrorism from the IRA to Al Qaeda,* is very clear on the question whether or not terrorists are different from us. Post (2005, p. 195) stated, '[i]t is not going too far to assert that terrorists are psychologically normal – that is, not clinically psychotic'. He also noted, '[t]hey are neither depressed, severely emotionally disturbed, nor are they crazed fanatics. Indeed, terrorist groups and organizations regularly weed out emotionally unstable individuals. They represent, after all, a security risk' (p. 196). According to Louise Richardson (2006, p. 3), there is no empirical evidence that supports the idea of crazy terrorists. She states that '[a]t the level of the individual, psychologists have long argued that there is no particular terrorist personality and that the notion of terrorists as crazed fanatics is not consistent with the plentiful empirical evidence available'. Israeli scholar Ehud Sprinzak (2000) would regard them as fanatics, but used the term 'rational fanatics' to describe suicide terrorists.

This is not to say that there are no terrorists who are suffering from mental illness. This seems to be especially relevant for the small category of so-called lone actor terrorists or, in more popular terms, lone wolves. Christopher Hewitt's (2003) study of what he labels 'unaffiliated terrorists' in the US found that psychological disturbance among this group of terrorists was relatively high. The attacks by Breivik in 2011 led to a rise of studies into this phenomenon and the link with mental health issues.

The evidence on the prevalence of mental health issues among lone actor terrorists is mixed. Some authors, such as Gruenewald, Chermak and Freilich

(2013) found that lone actors indeed suffered from elevated rates of mental health issues. Gill et al. (2014) found that 32% the lone actors they studied had a history of mental illness. Others, such as Moskalenko and McCauley (2011), for instance, concluded that the individuals that they had studied were psychologically stable with no signs of psychopathology. A study conducted by the Countering Lone-Actor Terrorism Project consortium, which included the authors of this book (see box 3.10), found that 35% of the lone actor terrorists might have suffered from some form of mental health issue. As such, these studies show that there is no consensus among academics on this issue.

More problematic, however, are the difficulties associated with interpreting figures on mental health issues. What does a rate of 35% mean? We can only make sense of this data if we have a useful benchmark, or in other words: how many of the 'non-terrorists' actually suffer from such issues? Organisations such as the World Health Organization (WHO) provide data on these topics. For instance, they estimated that about 12 per cent of the European population is confronted with a mental health disorder at any one time. This figure would increase to 15 per cent if substance disorders were included. The Johns Hopkins Medicine Institute provided a higher estimate: it estimated that about 26 per cent of the adult population in the United States suffers from a mental illness in any given year. Kessler et al. (2005) adopted a longer timespan, looking at someone's whole lifetime. Using the data of the WHO, they found that around half of Americans will face a mental health disorder in their lifetime.

So, again, these figures vary, but they raise the important question whether or not a rate of approximately 30-35 per cent of lone actors who suffer from mental health disorders indeed is much higher than the average population. We should perhaps approach the issue of mental health more carefully. Yes, terrorists can and sometimes do suffer from mental health issues. But perhaps no more or less than you or me. Moving beyond just these figures, a more relevant question might be where to draw the line between political motives and mental health issues: if someone is delusional, has hallucinations and cannot distinguish real from imagined, then perhaps we could say they can no longer be a terrorist, because they perhaps cannot understand the consequences of their actions. Other mental health issues might have little explanatory value. More research is thus needed into what type of mental health issues someone is suffering from to know if this could be a relevant factor.

Conclusion

Fortunately, as we observed in chapter 3, important progress has been made regarding empirically based studies, but in this particular field academics have experienced many difficulties in 'diagnosing' terrorists. Talking to terrorists is not sufficient to enable one to understand mental health issues: psychiatric expertise and analysis are needed. Related to this challenge, most studies look at only a relatively small numbers of cases they have managed to gain access to. Moreover, very few scholars have actually had the opportunity to interview and observe terrorists in a way psychiatrists normally can. Many of the scholars who had this opportunity, such as Jessica Stern, talked to terrorists who were in jail, which is not really a normal environment in which to study potentially abnormal mental or behavioural patterns. Nonetheless, most academics and experts who did look terrorists in the eye agree on their rationality and the 'normality' of their behaviour and mental state of health. In his book, *The Psychology of Terrorism* (2005), John Horgan states that evidence-based research does not just illustrate the lack of any identifiable psychopathology in terrorists. He also concludes that they are rather unremarkable in psychological terms. Against this background, we label the assumption that terrorists are crazy as false. At the same time, more empirically based research is needed to look at this intriguing and important assumption.

Key points

- Many people find it difficult to comprehend terrorist violence, in particular the phenomenon of suicide terrorists.
- Academic research shows that most terrorists are rational actors and that they are, clinically speaking, normal.
- The assumption that terrorists are crazy can be labelled as false.

4.4 Assumption three: Terrorism is becoming increasingly lethal

As has been mentioned several times before, terrorism is making headlines worldwide, on almost a daily basis. Older generations would say that things were not very different in the 1970s, 1980s and 1990s, recalling the attack on the 1972 Summer Olympics in Munich and other terrorist actions by Palestinians, the violence by left-wing terrorists in Europe and Latin America, or separatist and nationalist attacks in the UK, India, Sri Lanka and other parts of the world. Although this violence cost the lives of thousands, many of the most notorious attacks were much less lethal than the attacks on the US on 9/11 and some of the subsequent mass casualty attacks. Moreover, around the world, even younger people remember the images of the attacks on 9/11, the attacks in Paris or near Oslo, and recall the headlines about bloody attacks in Iraq, Afghanistan and Pakistan. This has provided the background for the popular belief that terrorism has become more lethal, with the attacks on 9/11 as a turning point after which terrorists want to have not only a lot of people watching, but also a lot of people dead. Connected to the use of new technologies and fear of terrorists using Weapons of Mass Destruction (WMD), many scholars, experts and politicians have expressed worries about a continued increase in lethality or have described terrorism as the biggest threat the world is facing. They state that we can only expect even more and more deadly terrorism, with a nuclear terrorist attack being what Tom Clancy (1991) called 'the sum of all fears'.

Former Vice President of the US Dick Cheney, for instance, noted in the years after 9/11, '[t]he biggest threat we face now as a nation is the possibility of terrorists ending up in the middle of one of our cities with deadlier weapons than have ever before been used against us – biological agents or a nuclear weapon or a chemical weapon of some kind to be able to threaten the lives of hundreds of thousands of Americans' (2004). These worries can also be found in official governmental documents, such as the 'Transnational Terrorism: The Threat to Australia' report of the Australian Government Department of Foreign Affairs and Trade (2004). The report is also quite alarmist, stating, '[a]dvances in weapons technology are making them more lethal than ever before. The range of weapons at the terrorists' disposal is wide and increasing'. Also many scholars speak of a new era. According to Peter Neumann (2009), '[i]n the era of the new terrorism, the two considerations – violence and symbolic value – seem to have merged, with mass-casualty attacks against civilian populations being routine and intentional'. Also more recently, 20 years after 9/11, such discourse has been omnipresent. The website of the French Ministry for Europe and Foreign Affairs stated that '[i]nternational terrorism is one of the most serious threats to international peace and security. [And] this threat has never been so strong'. That terrorism has changed is an observation that few people would disagree with. But the question is, has it changed fundamentally so as to speak of a new era, a post-9/11 era, and new terrorism?

In chapter 1 we quoted Brian Jenkins who, in 1975, wrote that 'terrorists want a lot of people watching …, and not a lot of people dead' (p. 4). So having high casualty figures was not a main goal of terrorists. More than 30 years later, in 2006, Jenkins explained that terrorism had changed, as it had become bloodier. In his 1975 publication he also wrote that terrorists were limited not only by access to weapons but also by self-constraint such as a sense of morality, a self-image, operational codes and practical concerns. In 2006 (pp. 118-119), he noted that 'these constraints gave way to large-scale indiscriminate violence' and rephrased his famous quotation of 1975 into 'many of today's terrorists want a lot of people watching *and* a lot of people dead'. Is Jenkins right in assuming that terrorists want more people dead? Has terrorism indeed become more lethal in recent decades?

Why does it matter to know whether or not terrorism is becoming increasingly lethal?

If terrorism has indeed become more lethal and if this trend is continuing, it must have several political and policy implications. First, it would make sense to keep it high on the political agenda as one of the most important security concerns of our time and for the years to come. Second, it would require more means and efforts to counter this very serious physical threat that might lead to terrorists using much-feared chemical, biological, radiological or nuclear weapons. However, if it is not a trend and if terrorism has not become much more lethal in recent years, while we think it is, we may have invested too much in dealing with this particular threat. Perhaps we have to conclude that governments have wasted scarce resources that could have been used to make our world safer, such as improving health care or dealing with organised crime. Moreover, we might need to reconsider the proportionality of the current counterterrorism measures and evaluate whether or not we have overreacted after 9/11 and other very deadly attacks which have given us the impression that today's 'new terrorism' is more deadly than the terrorism of the past.

Are terrorist attacks becoming increasingly lethal?

The assumption that terrorism is increasingly lethal can be interpreted in two ways: first, it could mean that there are more fatalities each year: more people killed in terrorists acts around the world or in certain regions. Second, it could also mean that individual terrorist attacks are becoming more deadly, meaning that the number of people killed per attack is increasing. These are two different sides of the assumption that we will discuss below.

First, we will investigate the idea that the total number of people killed by terrorists worldwide has increased in recent decades and that this trend is continuing. In order to do so, we will compare the assumption with empirical data, for which we will use the GTD database made available by the National Consortium for the Study of Terrorism and Responses to Terrorism, better known as START. This is an open-source database containing information about terrorism-related incidents since 1970.

After downloading and processing the data, we were able to plot the total number of fatalities per year in the 1990-2020 period. This graph includes perpetrator fatalities and 'ambiguous cases' where it was not absolutely certain that it was a terrorism incident. It does not include data from 1993 because of the loss of the set of cards for that year in the pre-digital age. The resulting graph offers a reliable indication of the long-term development of fatalities in terrorist incidents (see figure 4.01).

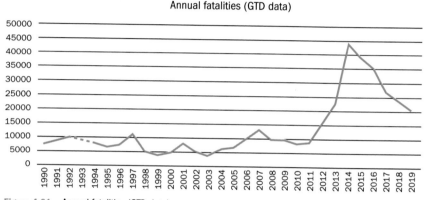

Figure 4.01   Annual fatalities (GTD data)

We see that the number of fatalities was high in the early 1990s with 7,000 to 10,000 people being killed in terrorist incidents. After 1992 the number drops, until 1996, when it rose to what was then an all-time high in 1997. After that year, it drops to a much lower level at the turn of the century. It remains low until 9/11. The magnitude of this single attack which killed 3,000 people caused a spike in the number of fatalities. However, in the next two years the numbers return to pre-9/11 levels of about 3,000 to 4,000 people killed annually worldwide. From 2003 onwards, we again witness a rise in the number of fatalities, with a death toll of about 13,000 in 2007. In the years between 2007 and 2011 the numbers are somewhat lower, but still relatively high at 8,000 to 9,000 a year. After 2011, the rise is much steeper and more enduring than before, reaching nearly 45,000 people killed in 2014: the year that IS proclaimed the caliphate in Syria and Iraq. To a large extent, this peak is caused by the civil wars in those countries. After that year, aligning with the decline of IS and other developments in the Islamic world, we fortunately observe a steep decline: the number of people killed in 2019 because of terrorism was less than half the number in 2014. Yet, with more than 20,000 people killed in attacks, this figure is still much higher than in the 1990s and 2000s. In the first years of the 2020s, the numbers still seem to be going down.

Hence, what do we make of these numbers; is there a consistent upward trend? Clearly, the development of the number of fatalities can best be described as one with ups and downs. The enormous peak in 2014 was primarily caused by the civil wars in Syria and Iraq. Not everyone would agree to have these casualties labelled casualties of terrorism. If you take those two countries out of the statistics, the picture looks very different. Against this backdrop, it is difficult to speak of a general trend, but the figures seem to be affected primarily by (unexpected) geopolitical developments. The trend line shows no indications of where it will go next: it could go up again, or it could go down even further. Statistical evidence does not as such support the assumption that the total number of people killed in terrorist attacks is consistently increasing.

The second side of this assumption that has to be investigated pertains to the number of people killed per attack. Many would argue that the number of fatalties per incident has increased, simply by following the news and being confronted with one devastating mass-casualty attack after another. Indeed, the attacks on 9/11 and major attacks in Madrid, Bombay, Beslan, Bali, Baghdad and Paris resulted in large numbers of casualties. They made headlines all over the world, sometimes for several days or longer. Also the threats by some terrorist groups to use WMD or other unconventional weapons have contributed to the popular notion that terrorism has become more lethal. Although there were only a few concrete attempts to use these types of weapons, which either failed or had only a limited impact, attacks using conventional weapons were devastating with high numbers of casualties. In Iraq, Pakistan and elsewhere, terrorists have shown that they are able and willing to make use of all kinds of weapons to kill many people in a single attack. We also witnessed an enormous increase in the number of suicide attacks using very sophisticated explosives in belts, backpacks, cars, etc. In other words, there is a worrying combination of techniques and tactics, and a change in ethics or operational codes, which makes it possible and acceptable to kill more people and to do so in an instant.

This idea is supported by the work of Piazza (2009), who in a quantitative study observed that the number of victims per 'international terrorist attack' has indeed gone up. In order for it to be counted as an 'international' incident an element of the attack had to involve a foreign perpetrator or target. His data show that in the 1968-1979 period there were on average 2.08 victims (fatalities and injured) per attack. In the 1980s, this number had increased to

3.83. In the 1990s, it increased again quite markedly to more than ten victims per attack (10.38), after which it only slightly increased in the first five years of the new millennium to 10.89. (p. 62). In Piazza's eyes, 'it is particularly striking that the average number of annual international terrorist attacks actually decreased from a high point of 339.6 annually in the 1980s to 262.5 annually for the 1990s, demonstrating that while the frequency of attacks declined, the intensity of attacks increased' (p. 62).

However, if we focus only on those killed – so not injured – which corresponds more closely to our assumption on lethality, and also look at non-international attacks, a different picture emerges. If we plot the fatalities per attack from 1990 to 2019 we see no upward trend (see figure 4.02). On the contrary: the number of victims per attack went down. In the year 2014, the peak of the number of both attacks and victims, there were on average 2.6 fatalities and 2.4 injured per attack, which is comparable to the situation in the early 1990s.

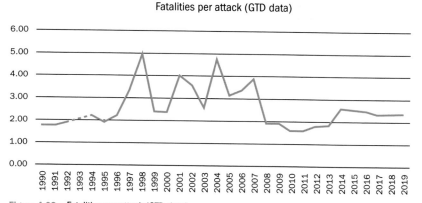

Figure 4.02   Fatalities per attack (GTD data)

Conclusion

Back to the central question of this section: are terrorist attacks becoming increasingly lethal? We falsified the part of the assumption that says that terrorism kills more and more people each year. The part of the assumption that says that the number of victims per attack is increasing also provides a mixed picture, one with ups and downs. If we focus exclusively on those killed, we see no upward trend. Combining the two, we can conclude that the assumption that terrorism is increasingly lethal is false, although it is important to stress that the overall number of fatalities has significantly increased if we compare the current situation with that of the 1990s or earlier periods.

Key points

- The idea that terrorism has become a more deadly threat has been very popular among the media, public officials and scholars, especially since 9/11.
- The total number of fatalities has gone up and down over the past decades and defied any clear pattern.
- The number of fatalities per attack also shows no clear pattern.
- The assumption that terrorism is increasingly lethal can be labelled as false.

4.5 Assumption four: Terrorism is predominantly anti-western

As with the previous assumption, the assumption that today's terrorism is predominantly anti-western can also be interpreted in two different ways. First, are the attacks predominantly taking place in the western world and against western targets or not? Second, is the rhetoric behind the attacks, meaning the slogans and language used by terrorist organisations, predominantly anti-western? In this discussion we use the contested term 'the West'. Although it has many different interpretations, it is commonly used to refer to Europe, the Americas, Australia and New Zealand. So let us first see where this assumption comes from. What is the origin of the claim?

There is no single origin of the claim that terrorism is predominantly anti-western, but an important example of the claim can be found in the speech by US president George W. Bush. About a week after the 9/11 attacks, he addressed the nation and said, 'Americans are asking "Why do they hate us?" They hate what they see right here in this chamber: a democratically elected government. Their leaders are self-appointed. They hate our freedoms: our freedom of religion, our freedom of speech, our freedom to vote and assemble and disagree with each other'. With these statements, he clearly hinted at an anti-western idea or agenda among certain groups of terrorists.

President Bush referred to al-Qaeda, and in particular Osama bin Laden, who was the leader of the group. Several statements that the terrorist leader made are clear proof of an anti-western agenda. Most notable is his 1998 fatwa entitled, 'Jihad Against Jews and Crusaders', which he signed as part of the so-called 'World Islamic Front'. He explained to all Muslims that '[t]he ruling to kill the Americans and their allies, civilian and military, is an individual duty for every Muslim who can do it in any country in which it is possible to do it'. Another example of terrorists that are explicitly anti-western is the group called the Congregation of the People of Tradition for Proselytism and Jihad, also known under the name Boko Haram which can best be translated as 'Western education is sin' (see box 4.06). This Nigerian organisation seeks to establish a 'pure' Islamic state ruled by sharia law and wants to put an end to westernisation by forbidding interaction with the western world.

But it is not just a US President and terrorist leaders and organisations that have contributed to the popular notion that today's terrorism is predominantly anti-western. Scholars and experts have also discussed a possible increase in anti-western talk and terrorist attacks against the West or western targets. For instance Walid Phares, who wrote several books about jihadists, points to the many examples of terrorist groups and individuals that wage an ideological war against western civilisation and democracy. This sounds reminiscent of Samuel Huntington's famous *Clash of Civilizations* book from 1996, where he argued that the prime reasons for conflict in the post-Cold War world would be located along civilisational lines.

Boko Haram

According to Andrew Walker (2012) in a report of the United States Institute of Peace, 'Boko Haram is an Islamic sect that believes northern politics has been seized by a group of corrupt, false Muslims. It wants to wage a war against them, and the Federal Republic of Nigeria generally, to create a "pure" Islamic state ruled by sharia law. Since 2009 it has been driven by a desire for vengeance against politicians, police, and Islamic authorities for their role in a brutal suppression of the group that year. But the group has proved itself to be very adaptable, evolving its tactics swiftly and changing its targets at the behest of a charismatic leadership. The group leapt onto the world's agenda in August 2011, when it bombed the United Nations compound in Abuja, killing twenty-three people'. Today, two decades after it was founded, Boko Haram still constitutes a major threat to the northern part of Nigeria.

BOX 4.06 BOKO HARAM

Even before 9/11, some scholars argued that this anti-western jihadist terrorism should be regarded as a new type of terrorism. Martha Crenshaw discussed the emergence of this idea of a 'new terrorism' in 2000. She noted that scholars see this new terrorism as one that is 'motivated by religious belief and is more fanatical, deadly and pervasive than the forms of terrorism the world had grown accustomed to'. She also showed that a large part of this new terrorism is described as 'anti-Western terrorism originating in the Middle East that is linked to radical or "fundamentalist" Islam'. In the same article, Crenshaw (p. 412) also noted that the increased worries were caused by new tactics such as suicide bombings, mass casualty attacks and anti-American and anti-western targeting patterns. She is herself rather critical of the new terrorism thesis, which she again emphasised in a chapter of a book written 8 years later, challenging the 'soundness of the definition and its applicability to empirical data' (2008, p. 27).

Why does it matter to know whether or not terrorism is predominantly anti-western?

If we believe and continue to say that terrorism is anti-western, we strengthen that notion or narrative. If true, this could help us to focus primarily on counterterrorism measures and on groups with that particular agenda and their specific cultural and political grievances against the west. But if the anti-western focus of terrorists is a myth and most terrorist acts are in fact not aimed against the west, this might mean that counterterrorism measures and policies are too much focused on one particular type of terrorist threat, the one posed by violent Islamist or jihadist groups. Moreover, it might draw attention away from other groups, causes and origins of terrorism. Additionally, if terrorism is not predominantly anti-western and we continue to think it is and act upon it, we might actually help those who would like to threaten the West and make these groups more important than they really are. Finally, we might contribute to the idea of a struggle between Christianity and Islam or a 'clash of civilisations', the concept used by Huntington, while there might not be factual support for such a clash or struggle. We have to be careful with such ideas or narratives, as they might influence the way people around the world look at different cultures, different countries, or neighbours with a different background or religion. This can lead to generalisations, stereotyping and, as a worst case scenario, it could contribute to religious or cultural conflict. So there are legitimate and ample reasons to check the factual basis of the assumption that terrorism is predominantly anti-western.

Is terrorism predominantly anti-western?

As can be derived from the example of Osama bin Laden's 1998 fatwa and the name and goals of Boko Haram, there are quite a number of groups that are calling for terrorist action against the west. The organisation and network of al-Qaeda were for a long time perhaps the prime example, but in recent years more attention has been devoted to the so-called Islamic State. And there are many other groups with anti-western agendas. The question remains whether or not the facts on the ground support the assumption. What about the attacks by these (mainly jihadist) groups? Do they predominantly target the west?

There are many different way to investigate the anti-western question. From a geographical perspective the question whether terrorism is mainly anti-western can be rephrased into the question whether terrorist attacks mainly take place in the western world. The answer is a plain and simple no. The countries that suffer most from terrorist attacks are located in the wider Middle East, South Asia and Africa, not in the West. Think of Syria, Iraq, Afghanistan, Pakistan, Yemen, Somalia or the north of Nigeria. Moreover, the overwhelming majority of the victims of these attacks are citizens who live in these countries, not westerners. Even in Iraq, with large contingents of western troops present in the years after the US-led invasion of the country in 2003, the majority of the attacks by al-Qaeda-affiliated groups targeted Iraqis, according to Piazza (2009). They also killed many western soldiers and a number of civilians, including aid workers and journalists, but most victims were Iraqi nationals who died waiting in line at police recruitment offices, at pilgrim sites or in local markets. Moreover, the overwhelming majority were Muslims (see box 4.07). The same holds for the victims of Islamic State in Syria and Iraq, or for al-Shabaab in Somalia and Boko Haram in Nigeria.

Main targets of attacks by al-Qaeda-affiliated groups in Iraq

According to Piazza (2009) in his study titled 'Is Islamist Terrorism More Dangerous?', al-Qaeda-affiliated groups were responsible for most of the attacks by Islamists in the 1998-2005 period. They were behind 277 of a total of 327 attacks, killing almost 6,000 people. Strikingly, 83.6 per cent of attacks were aimed against Muslims, most of them (58.3 per cent) Iraqis. Other Islamist groups targeted mainly non-Muslims (53.5 per cent) and non-Iraqis (62.5 per cent). Apparently, al-Qaeda groups are uninhibited about attacking Iraqi nationals and other Muslims (pp. 75-76).

BOX 4.07   MAIN TARGETS OF ATTACKS BY AL-QAEDA-AFFILIATED GROUPS IN IRAQ

According to the often quoted United States National Counter Terrorism Center, in its 'Report on Terrorism 2011' (2012, p. 14), in general, most victims of terrorism were Muslims. It states, '[i]n cases where the religious affiliation of terrorism casualties could be determined, Muslims suffered between 82 and 97 percent of terrorism related fatalities over the past five years'. Hence, even though the rhetoric behind attacks may be predominantly anti-western, most victims are not westerners.

What do we see when we look at the relatively limited number of attacks executed in the West? Are they perhaps predominantly anti-western? According to the Global Terrorism Index 2020 (GTI), the deadliest form of terrorism in the West over the past two decades has been jihadist terrorism. Jihadist terrorists have been responsible for about 800 fatalities in the West since 2002. The most notable surge occurred between 2015 and 2017, with almost 100 attacks and almost 500 fatalities. Although jihadist terrorism has been the deadliest form of terrorism in the West over the past two decades, it has not been the most common form. Most attacks have been what GTI calls political: left-wing, right-wing and ethno-nationalist, but they resulted in smaller numbers of fatalities. In the years since 2014 the number of politically motivated attacks has increased steadily. Between 2015 and 2019, there were about 350 political terrorist incidents, resulting in almost 200 people being killed (2021, p. 62).

Zooming in on the US, the picture is somewhat different. Of the 409 people killed in terrorist attacks post-9/11, 124 were killed by jihadists. Around a similar number were killed by individuals and groups that could be categorised as right-wing extremist. So in the US jihadists have not been responsible for most fatalities since 9/11, in contrast to in Europe.

Conclusion

What do we make of the assumption that today's terrorism is mainly aimed against the West? If we were to look only at the rhetoric or the narrative of individual jihadist terrorists and that of al-Qaeda or Islamic State, the answer might be yes. Their propaganda efforts strongly suggest an anti-western agenda. These jihadist groups dominate the current wave of terrorism and are responsible for many victims. However, the picture changes entirely if we look at the targeting patterns. Most people killed by these groups are not located in the western or westerners, but the overwhelming majority of attacks take place in the Muslim world and target the local, often Muslim population. In the West, the majority of the attacks are linked to ethno-nationalist, right-wing and left-wing groups next to relatively few, but much more deadly, attacks by jihadist terrorists. The US is an exception as the number of people killed by right-wing extremists since 9/11 is almost the same as the number killed by jihadists.

Combining the observations above, the assumption that terrorism is predominantly anti-western is partly true if we attach the same weight to rhetoric and attacks. However, we would argue that actions speak louder than words. Therefore, we think it is more appropriate to label this assumption false.

Key points

- Much rhetoric of today's terrorism is anti-western.
- The overwhelming majority of terrorist attacks take place outside the western world.

- Most people killed in terrorist attacks are not westerners.
- In the West the picture is more mixed, but attacks there constitute only a small percentage of the overall number of attacks.
- Combining these observations, we label the assumption that terrorism is predominantly anti-western as false.

4.6 Assumption five: Terrorism is successful

A fifth, often-repeated assumption pertaining to terrorism is that it is successful. It ranks high on political agendas, receives a lot of attention from the media, and the fact that there are successive waves of terrorism suggests that new groups keep thinking that terrorism is an effective tool for reaching their goals. If this were not the case, why would we still be confronted with this phenomenon more than a century after the anarchist attacks in tsarist Russia or half a century after the bombings and armed assaults in Algeria or Israel in the early 1960s?

The notion of successful terrorists is partly the product of the media. Journalists have knowingly or unwittingly promoted the idea that terrorism is successful by making terrorist attacks front page news. Add to that the reactions by governments and individual politicians which include many examples of inflating the threat. One which, according to US President George W. Bush, required nothing less than a global war to deal with it. But scholars have also contributed to the perception of success. The authors of this handbook, for instance, by repeatedly mentioning how terrorism is making headlines worldwide and that it ranks high on political agendas. These kinds of statements, reactions and ways of communicating terrorist incidents to the general public have, directly or indirectly, contributed to making terrorists appear successful, at least at first glance. But are they really?

Why does it matter to know whether or not terrorism is successful?

If we believe and continue to say that terrorism is successful and it is not, that might lead to fatalism about efforts to counter this threat. The many counterterrorism measures have apparently failed if terrorists manage to be successful nonetheless. Moreover, it might give terrorists the feeling that their threat and attacks actually work and stimulate them to continue their violent activities and attract new recruits. If it is true that terrorists succeed, authorities need to alter counterterrorism strategies.

Is terrorism successful or not?

To answer the question whether or not terrorism is successful, we first need to examine what constitutes success for terrorists. Is it just getting worldwide attention and being talked about in political fora, or can terrorists be labelled successful only if they achieve certain other quantifiable goals? The various definitions of terrorism often include the words 'fear' and 'political goals'. If you regard terrorism as an instrument to achieve certain political goals by the use of violence and intimidation, the criteria for success should be twofold: first, does terrorism create attention and cause intimidation or fear and, second, do terrorists achieve their political goals? These are relatively simple criteria for measuring success that can be analysed with the help of empirical data such as public opinion polls, by analysing written or vocal language (discourse analysis) and videos, or by studying the academic literature on this topic.

Of course, one could explore the assumption that terrorists are successful from several other angles. For instance, terrorists may be called successful if they cause a high number of fatalities, or when they are perceived as powerful actors with whom a government (or other actor) has to talk or negotiate. Success for terrorists could also simply mean avoiding being killed or captured, or the survival of the terrorist organisation itself (for an example see box 4.08). Another yardstick would be the level of public support these groups or individuals manage to gain among the general public or those they claim to fight for.

The (lack of) success of the Shining Path

The Communist Party of Peru, also known as the Shining Path (Sendero Luminoso; SL), is a Maoist guerrilla insurgent group that appears on the lists of terrorist organisations of several countries around the world. When it launched its violent activities in 1980, its stated goal was to replace Peru's 'bourgeois democracy', induce a cultural revolution, and eventually spark a world revolution in order to arrive at pure communism. Was it successful in achieving these goals? While the SL quickly seized control of much of the countryside of the centre and south of Peru and had a large presence in parts of Lima, it soon faced serious problems. It never had the support of a large section of the Peruvian people. This was partly because it used much violence against peasants, popularly elected officials and the civilian population in general. As mentioned earlier, the leader of SL, Abimael Guzmán, was captured in 1992. His arrest left a huge leadership vacuum. The organisation rapidly went into a decline.

BOX 4.08   THE (LACK OF) SUCCESS OF THE SHINING PATH

Most academics have taken a rather one-dimensional approach to measuring the success of terrorists. They have measured that of a terrorist organisation primarily by looking at the stated aims of terrorist organisations and to what extent these have been accomplished. We would argue that this approach is too narrow and too rational. As discussed in chapter 3, there are other approaches explaining terrorism that for instance focus on socio-psychological causes and effects, and communication aspects of terrorism. Therefore, we also need to take into account levels of fear and media coverage, as they are considered key components of how terrorism works. Fear and media exposure may perhaps not be the end goals of terrorists, but they definitely are important intermediate goals. Furthermore, one could add that being feared and being listened to might be an important goal in itself to some terrorist groups or individual terrorists.

We will look at the fear and media dimension later in this section. First, we will explore the level of success of terrorism in terms of achieving political goals. The focus on the definition of success by reaching political goals when trying to determine whether or not terrorism is successful stems from the rational or instrumental approach to studying terrorism. As discussed in chapter 3, according to this approach terrorism is an instrument for achieving certain goals employed by rational individuals who are making some sort of cost-benefit analysis to decide on their tactics and strategy. According to this line of thought it can be assumed that terrorists believe there is at least a small chance of achieving some of their political goals.

One important author who has argued that the success of terrorists is relatively limited if we look at political goals is Max Abrahms (2006). He has repeatedly challenged the rational or instrumental approach. In his publication, 'Why terrorism does not work', he analysed 28 terrorist groups that were on the US Department of State's list of designated foreign terrorist organisations. His analysis yielded two distinct findings. First, the groups accomplished their stated policy objectives only 7 per cent of the time. Second, the level of success depended on tactical choices, in particular in target selection. Groups whose attacks on civilian targets outnumbered attacks on military ones systematically failed to achieve their policy objectives.

These findings suggest that terrorist groups rarely achieve their policy objectives and that the poor success rate is inherent in the tactic of terrorism itself. According to Abrahms (2006), the outcome of his study challenges the dominant scholarly opinion that terrorism is strategically rational behaviour, as terrorism obviously provides very little political return for the terrorists.

Other authors like Wilkinson and Jenkins have reached similar conclusions regarding terrorism's lack of success, which raises the question why terrorists continue their activities if they do not lead to achieving their political goals. Wilkinson (2006, p. 6), for instance, notes that '[s]ome terrorists appear to believe that terrorism will always "work" for them in the end, by intimidating their opponents into submitting to the terrorists "demands"'. He also observes that terrorists only very rarely succeeded in achieving their strategic goals. Wilkinson also states that in recent history there have been only a few exceptions to this which occurred in the period of anti-colonial struggles against the British and the French after the Second World War. An example is the earlier-mentioned National Liberation Front (FLN) in Algeria. Furthermore, Hoffman (2006) explained that terrorism succeeds only in very particular circumstances, such as colonial situations where national liberation movements struggling for independence often have high levels of popular support, unlike most other terrorist groups (for some examples of successful terrorists see box 4.09).

For the post-colonial era, there is not a single case of a terrorist organisation that has managed to gain political control over an independent state. One could argue that the Afghan Taliban, both in the 1990s and now in the 2020s, are an exception to this rule. After the US withdrew its remaining troops from Afghanistan in 2021, the organisation seized large swathes of territory and exercised control over many key cities such as the capital, Kabul. Yet, the group itself then aimed to get international recognition, and some countries, such as Russia, have announced that they would consider removing the group from their list of designated terrorist organisations. So it very much depends on the definition of terrorism whether one wants to regard the Afghan Taliban as the exception to the rule. Another difficult case is that of Hamas. Some might argue that this Palestinian organisation has won control over the Gaza Strip by the use of violence against both Israel and other Palestinian factions, but it should be stressed that it is not an independent state, but only a part of the territory of the Palestinian Authority.

Terrorists turning into politicians

Not many terrorist organisations have managed to achieve their stated goals. However, a number of individuals who were regarded as terrorists in the past have had successful political careers. Some even made it to become Prime Ministers or even Presidents. Often, they also managed to achieve some of the goals without the use of violence. Well-known examples include Nelson Mandela, once jailed as a terrorist of the ANC, later President of South Africa; Yasser Arafat, leader of the Palestine Liberation Organisation, later the first

President of the Palestinian National Authority; José 'Pepe' Mujica, once jailed as member of the Tupamaros, later President of Uruguay; Menachem Begin, once the leader of The National Military Organisation in the Land of Israel 'Irgun', later Prime Minister of Israel; and Gustavo Petro, former member of the Colombian terrorist organisation M-19 and later President of Colombia.

BOX 4.09 TERRORISTS TURNING INTO POLITICIANS

One of the reasons for a lack of success for terrorists is that the use of terrorist violence can backfire and alienate them from the general public or even those they claim to represent: see also the example of the SL in Peru. Jenkins (2006) also noted this dynamic. He expressed worries over the increase in bloodshed caused by terrorism and is therefore also sceptical about the success of terrorists. He stated that terrorism is focused primarily not on a military battle, but on 'making the enemy's life unbearable' or, rather, engaging in a psychological battle (p. 127). He observed that terrorists have escalated their violence and developed, amongst others, new methods of financing their operations and exploited new communications technologies, but none of them have achieved their own stated long-range objectives. He calls this the paradox of terrorism: '[t]errorists often succeed tactically and thereby gain attention, cause alarm, and attract recruits. But their struggle has brought them no success measured against their own stated goals. In that sense, terrorism has failed, but the phenomenon of terrorism continues' (p. 129).

Using the yardstick of 'own stated goals' or strategic demands, several scholars have managed to calculate the success of terrorist organisations. Seth Jones and Martin Libicki (2008) examined a large sample of terrorist groups between 1968 and 2006. Of the 648 groups in their database, only 10 per cent accomplished their goals in some way or another, but this holds mainly for groups that had narrow goals, such as policy change or the release of a fellow terrorist. Jones and Libicki (2008, p. 33) also state that no terrorist group that sought empire or social revolution has achieved victory since 1968. Audrey Kurth Cronin (2009) in her book, *How Terrorism Ends: Understanding the Decline and Demise of Terrorist Campaigns,* re-examined the success rate of these groups and found that less than 5 per cent of them prevailed over governments.

How do these findings relate to the case of the group that caused most fatalities in one attack in history: al-Qaeda? Has this group succeeded in achieving its stated goals? The first problem in answering this question is that it is difficult to define al-Qaeda as it is a network rather than an organisation. According to Jason Burke (2007) and Edwin Bakker and Leen Boer (2007), the organisational structure has changed during the course of time and continues to do so. It consists of many different 'presences': from the core al-Qaeda leadership and recognised affiliates of 'franchises', to self-proclaimed affiliates and groups and individuals that are merely inspired by al-Qaeda. If we limit the question to the core of the group and its recognised affiliates, such as al-Qaeda in the Islamic Maghreb, we run into a second difficulty. What are their political goals? The problem is that they are rather vague and have changed over time. They include the establishment of a pan-Islamic caliphate, the overthrow of what they label 'non-Islamic' regimes, the expulsion of all foreigners from Muslim countries, and the killing of Jews, Americans and their allies.

The same questions pertain to Islamic State, an offspring of al-Qaeda. This raises the question of how successful al-Qaeda and Islamic State have been when one looks at these goals and possible other indicators of success (see box 4.10)?

The (lack of) success of al-Qaeda and Islamic State
Using the yardsticks mentioned in the text above, how would you answer the questions regarding the success of core al-Qaeda and its recognised affiliates, such as al-Qaeda in the Islamic Maghreb, al-Qaeda in Iraq and al-Qaeda in the Arabian Peninsula and Islamic State and its affiliates?
• Did they achieve their political goals?
• Did they create attention and cause fear?
• Did they cause a high number of fatalities?
• Are they perceived as powerful actors with whom governments have to talk or negotiate?
• Did they force governments to refrain from certain policies?
• Did their leaders manage to avoid being killed or captured?
• Did they manage to overthrow governments?
• Did they attain high levels of public support?
• Did the organisation survive?

BOX 4.10   THE (LACK OF) SUCCESS OF AL-QAEDA AND ISLAMIC STATE

If we look at the stated political goals, it seems that they have not been reached, nor are they within reach. Despite some spectacular successes on the battlefields of Mali, Syria and Iraq, resulting in the conquest of large parts of these countries, there is no pan-Islamic caliphate. In fact, today jihadist groups have lost almost all the territories they controlled in the past decade. Moreover, al-Qaeda and Islamic State have not managed to overthrow what they labelled 'non-Islamic' regimes. In Tunisia, Libya and Egypt regimes were overthrown, but thanks to either relatively peaceful protesters or local rebels supported by western military forces of NATO. Al-Qaeda was also not successful in the expulsion of all foreigners from Muslim countries. In fact, 9/11 resulted in an unprecedented (temporary) presence of foreign military, mainly from the US and its allies, in Muslim-majority countries like Iraq, Afghanistan, Libya and Mali. The organisation of the late Osama bin Laden did manage to do what its 1998 fatwa called for: 'to kill the Americans and their allies – civilians and military'. If we look at the casualty lists of 9/11 and that of the US troops and their allies who died in what the Americans called the 'Global War on Terror', the number adds up to over 10,000 fatalities.

In this figure lies the only 'success' of al-Qaeda in terms of stated goals. Obviously, the group has managed to drag the US and its allies into a very costly war in Afghanistan and Iraq and several military operations in other parts of the world. And the terrorist acts of al-Qaeda and its affiliates and sympathisers have managed to force many countries around the world into a difficult and lengthy struggle against terrorism. Despite all counterterrorism efforts, the organisation has survived, and more than that. It is still making headlines, even after many of its leaders and followers have been captured or killed – including Bin Laden himself. The same holds for Islamic State. It was temporarily successful in establishing a caliphate, but lost it at the cost of thousands of fighters and supporters killed in battle and CT operations, including its leadership. Nonetheless, Islamic State still exists and, despite its failures, some elements have continued the fight and the group also still has many supporters around the globe.

This validates the question raised earlier: whether or not one should measure the success of terrorist groups solely by looking at the extent to which they have reached their stated goals. What about the high levels of fear, the enormous investments in counterterrorism or the fact that the threat posed by terrorism is still high on political agendas? Should that not also be considered a sign of success? And if so, how successful has terrorism been in recent decades? If we look at the success of terrorism in terms of making headlines, it is clear that terrorists are good at that. Or perhaps this needs rephrasing: terrorists *and* the media are very good at that. After all, it is not the terrorists who write the headlines or decide what is breaking news, but journalists do so in order to serve an audience that expects them to do exactly that.

There are several studies that have looked into this topic, for instance by analysing the use of the word 'terrorism' in media reports. These studies show that terrorism has indeed been making headlines almost on a daily basis in many parts of the world, not just after 9/11, but for decades. A study by

Iyengar (1987, p. 27) shows that 'between 1981 and 1986, more news stories were broadcast [by the three major American TV networks, ABC, CBS, and NBC] on terrorism than on poverty, unemployment, racial inequality, and crime combined'. There are also many studies that have looked at the media coverage in the immediate aftermath of the attacks on the US in 2001. Not only was the attack on an unprecedented scale, the media attention in response to it was also unprecedented. The reporting of the attacks on 9/11 was breaking news everywhere around the globe and the reporting of its aftermath was the opening news story for many radio and TV bulletins for weeks, if not months.

The reporting of the attacks on 9/11 was no exception though. Other large terrorist attacks have attracted a lot of media attention around the world: think of the attacks in Bali in 2002, Paris in 2015 and Christchurch in 2019. Smaller-scale attacks, such as the 2013 Boston Marathon bombings, also received worldwide attention, even though it was a minor attack in terms of the number of fatalities. The attack caused five fatalities – three spectators, one police officer and one of the two perpetrators. But even on the other side of the globe in Fiji it made headlines. The *Fiji Times* produced a lengthy article with pictures that read as follows: 'Fijians living in Boston, United States, remained indoors as authorities began investigation into two bomb blasts targeting thousands of people participating in the Boston Marathon yesterday'. Apparently, even with relatively limited means terrorists can receive a lot of attention from the media, and therefore from the general public and politicians, and many terrorists have been successful at that.

When defining the success of terrorism in terms of spreading dread and fear, opinion polls offer a valuable source of data. The polls by Gallup, for example, include information on how worried respondents in the US are that they or a family member could become victims of a terrorist attack. About a quarter of the American respondents had this concern in April 2000, a decrease compared to the figure of 42 per cent in 1995, when the poll was taken just after the Oklahoma City bombing. Quite understandably, in the first few weeks after the attacks on 9/11, the number of people who were very or somewhat worried went up to highs of 58 per cent. In the following decade, the level varied between 28 and 48 per cent. In April 2013, just after the Boston Marathon bombings, this number was 40 per cent, which indicates that the numbers go up and down depending on whether or not there has been a recent major terrorist incident.

Fear of terrorism according to Eurobarometer

The standard Eurobarometer was established in 1973. Each survey consists of approximately 1,000 face-to-face interviews in EU member states and associated countries. One of the questions asked is the following: what do you think are the two most important issues facing the EU at the moment? In the first ten years after 9/11, countries in which relatively many people mentioned 'terrorism' included the United Kingdom, Spain and Turkey. EU member states and associated countries in which people did not think terrorism was a very important issue for them included Finland and the Baltic countries, and countries such as Slovenia and Luxembourg. Somewhere in between the most worried and the least worried about terrorism were Greece, the Netherlands, Denmark, France and Germany. This changed with the rise of IS and a number of major attacks in Europe, think of the ones in France, Belgium and Germany. In more recent years, the trend has shifted again, and terrorism is seen as a less important issue in most European countries. In 2022, only 6 per cent of interviewed citizens mentioned it as being among the two main issues for the EU.

BOX 4.11   FEAR OF TERRORISM ACCORDING TO EUROBAROMETER

The same holds true for Europe. Eurobarometer, a public opinion survey conducted regularly on behalf of the European Commission, shows that concern over terrorism has also had its ups and downs in recent decades (see box 4.11). Jeanine de Roy van Zuijdewijn and Jessica Sciarone studied how the salience of terrorism as an important issue developed after major jihadist attacks in Western Europe between 2014 and 2017. They observe that terrorism was seen as a more important issue in the years after 2014, when Europe was confronted with several attacks, such as in Paris (2015), Brussels (2016), Berlin (2016), London and Manchester (2017). Since 2017, however, numbers have gone down substantially. In 2021, only about 8 per cent of EU citizens considered it to be among the most important issues for the EU.

What about the rest of the world? What about worries in those countries that are most often hit by terrorism? It is sad to note that there are only a few public opinion polls outside the western world that specifically focus on terrorism, and that ask questions about terrorism on a regular basis. Thus, we have to base our answer to this aspect of the success of terrorism solely on western sources.

Conclusion

This brings us to the overall assessment of what to make of all these ideas and facts about the success of terrorism. It all depends on your definition

Assumptions about terrorism

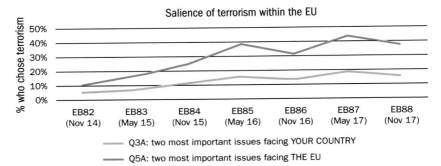

Figure 4.03   Salience of terrorism within the EU

of success. Very few terrorist organisations have managed to achieve their stated political goals ... and in some cases, one might wonder if they have managed to do so thanks to or in spite of the use of terrorist tactics. However, terrorists have been successful in getting attention from the media and thus have managed to spread fear and intimidate societies. However, the levels of fear do not last and fade out after a number of years. So, in the short run terrorists may get the attention they seek, but otherwise they are not very successful. Therefore, we should label this assumption as partly true.

Key points

- Terrorist organisations are not successful in terms of achieving their political goals.
- They do manage to receive a lot of attention.
- Their actions can lead to high levels of fear which, after a while, fade out.
- The assumption that terrorists are successful can be labelled as partly true.

Bibliography

Abrahms, M. (2006). Why Terrorism Does Not Work. *International Security*, 31(2), 42-78.

Australian Government Department of Foreign Affairs and Trade. (2004). *Transnational Terrorism: The Threat to Australia*.

Bakker, E. (2006). *Jihadi terrorists in Europe, their characteristics and the circumstances in which they joined the jihad: an exploratory study*. The Hague: The Netherlands Institute of International Relations Clingendael.

Bakker, E., & Boer, L. (2007). *The Evolution of Al-Qaedaism: Ideology, Terrorists, and Appeal*. The Hague: The Netherlands Institute of International Relations Clingendael.

Bakker, E., & Graaf, B. A. de. (2011). Preventing Lone Wolf Terrorism: Some CT Approaches Addressed. *Perspectives on Terrorism*, 5 (5-6), 43-50.

Bergen, P. L. (2006). *The Osama bin Laden I know. An oral history of Al Qaeda's leader*. New York: Free Press.

Bloom, M. M., & Horne, C. D. (2009). 'Is Terrorism the "Poor Man's Patent"?: Evaluating the Causal Connection between Education, Poverty, and Political Violence'. *Paper presented at the annual meeting of the ISA's 50th annual convention "Exploring the Past. Anticipating the Future"*, New York.

Burke, J. (2007). *Al-Qaeda: The True Story of Radical Islam* (Third edition). London: Penguin Books.

Bush, G. W. (2001). *Address to a joint session of Congress and the nation*. Address presented at the U.S. Congress, Washington D.C., United States.

Cheney, D. (2004). *Campaign Address*. Address presented at the 2004 Bush Campaign, Carroll, OH, United States.

Clancy, T. (1991). *Sum of all Fears*. New York: Putnam.

Crenshaw, M. (2000). The Psychology of Terrorism: An Agenda for the 21st Century. *Political Psychology*, 21(2), 405-420.

Cronin, A. K. (2009). *How Terrorism Ends: Understanding the Decline and Demise of Terrorist Campaigns*. Princeton: Princeton University Press.

Davis, A. (2013). *Americans Say Economy Is Top Worry for Nation's Future. Federal debt ranks as second-most common worry*. Gallup, http://www.gallup.com/poll/163298/americans-say-economy-top-worry-nation-future.aspx.

Ellis, C. et al. (2016). Lone-Actor Terrorism. Final Report. Countering Lone-Actor Terrorism Series No. 11. London: RUSI.

European Commission. (2001). *Eurobarometer 56*, Autumn 2001, https://europa.eu/eurobarometer/.

European Commission. (2004). *Standard Eurobarometer 62*, Autumn 2004.

European Commission. (2005). *Standard Eurobarometer 64*, Autumn 2005.

European Commission. (2013). *Standard Eurobarometer 80*, Autumn 2013.

European Commission. (2022). *Standard Eurobarometer 96*, Winter 2021-2022.

Fiji Times. (2013). *Boston bombs*. April 17, 2013.

Gill, P. et al. (2014). Bombing Alone: Tracing the Motivations and Antecedent Behaviors of Lone-Actor Terrorists. *Journal of Forensic Sciences*, 59(2), 425-435.

Gruenewald, J., Chermak, S., & Freilich, J. D. (2013). Distinguishing "Loner" Attacks from Other Domestic Extremist Violence. A Comparison of Far-Right Homicide Incident and Offender Characteristics. *Criminology & Public Policy*, 12(1), 65-91.

Hewitt, C. (2003). *Understanding Terrorism in America: From the Klan to Al Qaeda*. London: Routledge.

Hoffman, B. (2006). *Inside Terrorism (Revised and expanded edition)*. New York, Columbia University Press.

Horgan, J. (2005). *The Psychology of Terrorism*. London: Routledge.

Huntington, S. P. (2007). *The Clash of Civilizations and the Remaking of World Order.* New York: Simon and Schuster.

Iheonu, C. O., & Ichoku, H. E. (2021). Poverty and Terrorism in Africa: Understanding the Nexus Based on Existing Levels of Terrorism. *Poverty & Public Policy, 13*(3), 254-272.

Institute for Economics & Peace. (2021). *Global Terrorism Index 2020. Measuring the Impact of Terrorism.*

Iyengar, S. (1987). *Is Anyone Responsible? How Television Frames Political Issues.* Chicago: University of Chicago Press.

Jenkins, B. M. (1975). International terrorism: a balance sheet. *Survival: Global Politics and Strategy, 17*(4), 158-164.

Jenkins, B. M. (1975). *Will Terrorists Go Nuclear?* Santa Monica: RAND Corporation.

Jenkins, B. M. (2006). The New Age of Terrorism. In Kamien, D. G. (ed.), *The McGraw-Hill Homeland Security Handbook: The Definitive Guide for Law Enforcement, EMT, and all other Security Professionals* (117-130). New York: McGraw-Hill.

Johns Hopkins Medicine. (2022). *Mental Health Disorder Statistics*, https://www.hopkinsmedicine.org/health/wellness-and-prevention/mental-health-disorder-statistics.

Jones, S. G., & Libicki, M. C. (2008). *How Terrorist Groups End: Lessons for Countering al Qa'ida.* Santa Monica: RAND Corporation.

Kessler, R. C. et al. (2005). Lifetime Prevalence and Age-of-Onset Distributions of DSM-IV Disorders in the National Comorbidity Survey Replication. *Arch Gen Psychiatry, 62*(6), 593-602.

Krueger, A. B., & Maleckova, J. (2002). Education, Poverty and Terrorism: Is There a Causal Connnection? *The Journal of Economic Perspectives, 17*(4), 119-144.

LaFree, G. (2011). Using Open Source Data to Counter Common Myths about Terrorism. In Forst, B., Greene, J. R. & Lynch, J. P. (eds.), *Criminologists on Terrorism and Homeland Security* (411-442). Cambridge: Cambridge University Press.

Ministère de L'Europe et des Affaires Étrangères. (2022). *Terrorism: France's International Action,* https://www.diplomatie.gouv.fr/en/french-foreign-policy/security-disarmament-and-non-proliferation/terrorism-france-s-international-action/

Moskalenko, S., & McCauley, C. (2011). The Psychology of Lone-Wolf Terrorism. *Counseling Psychology Quarterly, 24*(2), 115–126.

National Consortium for the Study of Terrorism and Responses to Terrorism (START). (2022). *Global Terrorism Database,* https://www.start.umd.edu/gtd/.

Neumann, P. R. (2009). *Old & New Terrorism.* Cambridge: Polity Press.

Piazza, J. (2006). Rooted in Poverty?: Terrorism, Poor Economic Development, and Social Cleavages. *Terrorism and Political Violence, 18*(1), 159-177.

Piazza, J. (2009). Is Islamist Terrorism More Dangerous? An Empirical Study of Group Ideology, Organizations, and Goals Structure. *Terrorism and Political Violence, 21*(1), 62-88.

Post, J. M., Sprinzak, E., & Denny, L. (2003). The terrorists in their own words: Interviews with 35 incarcerated Middle Eastern terrorists. *Terrorism and Political Violence, 15*(1), 171-184.

Post, J. M. (2007). *The Mind of the Terrorist: The Psychology of Terrorism from the IRA to Al Qaeda.* New York: Palgrave Macmillan.

Richardson, L. (2006). *The Roots of Terrorism.* New York, Routledge.

Roy van Zuijdewijn, J. de, & Bakker, E. (2016). Analysing Personal Characteristics of Lone-Actor Terrorists: Research Findings and Recommendations. *Perspectives on Terrorism, 10*(2), 42-49.

Roy van Zuijdewijn, J. de, & Sciarone, J. (2021). Convergence of the Salience of Terrorism in the European Union Before and After Terrorist Attacks. *Terrorism and Political Violence, 33*(8), 1713-1732.

Saad, L. (2013). *Post-Boston, Half in U.S. Anticipate More Terrorism Soon: Confidence in U.S. Government to Protect Citizens from Terrorism is Down Slightly.* Gallup, http://www.gallup.com/poll/162074/post-boston-half-anticipate-terrorism-soon.aspx.

Spaaij, R. N. (2010). The Enigma of Lone Wolf Terrorism: An Assessment. *Studies in Conflict and Terrorism, 33*(9), 854-870.

Sprinzak, E. (2000). Rational Fanatics. *Foreign Policy, 120,* 66-73.

Stern, J. (2003). *Terror in the Name of God: Why Religious Militants Kill.* New York: HarperCollins.

Tutu, D. (2007). *Opening Address.* Address presented at The World Social Forum 2007, Nairobi, Kenya.

United States National Counter Terrorism Center. (2012). *Country Reports on Terrorism 2011.* U.S. Department of State.

Walker, A. (2012). *What is Boko Haram?* Washington D.C.: United States Institute of Peace.

Wilkinson, P. (2006). *Terrorism versus Democracy: The Liberal State Response.* London: Routledge.

World Islamic Front. (1998). Fatwa *'Jihad Against Jews and Crusaders'.*

143

5

Assumptions about counterterrorism

5.1 Introduction

In the previous chapter we analysed five assumptions about terrorism. In this chapter we will investigate five popular assumptions about counterterrorism we consider interesting either because they are challenged or because of the opposite: they are considered true and constitute the basis for policy-making. As witnessed in the previous chapters, terrorism is a dynamic phenomenon and subject to continuous change, which means that theories and hypotheses regarding this phenomenon and the policies for dealing with it need to be regularly evaluated and possibly revised. This also holds for the following assumptions about counterterrorism which we will investigate in this chapter:

1. Profiling works.
2. Deradicalisation of terrorists is possible.
3. Decapitation of terrorist organisations works.
4. Terrorism cannot be defeated.
5. Terrorism can best be dealt with by way of a holistic or wide approach.

But before we move on to these assumptions, we first have to define the term 'counterterrorism'. What exactly do we mean by this? Basically it refers to actions and policies to deal with the phenomenon of terrorism. That concept was discussed in detail in the first three chapters of this textbook. From that discussion we learned that there is no universally accepted definition of terrorism and that its meaning is to some extent a matter of personal opinion. Similarly, there are different opinions about counterterrorism. In this chapter we simply refer to 'counterterrorism' as a set of measures and activities that are designed to prevent terrorism or react to terrorism.

5.2 Assumption one: Profiling works

As discussed in chapter 3, one of the major difficulties when researching terrorism is its secretive nature. This is a challenge not only to academics, but also to policy-makers in the field of counterterrorism. Obviously, they would like to discover terrorists before they engage in terrorist activities. This is, of course, very difficult and the comparison with the proverbial finding of a needle in the haystack has often been made. Nonetheless, there have been several successful attempts to recognise a terrorist based on certain clues or signs – in most cases this related to 'suspicious' behaviour, which resulted in foiled terrorist plots (see box 5.01). There are also various examples of statements by authorities that show that they believe in the idea that profiling works. The Metropolitan Police, London's main police service, for instance asks citizens on its website to help it out. It writes, '[y]ou can help by knowing the signs and behaviours of terrorists and being vigilant about their activities, both online and in your community'.

Not only do authorities seem to believe in profiling. Terrorists themselves also think that profiling is possible. From the early days on, terrorists have tried their best not to look suspicious in order not to be noticed. Or they have changed their appearance and behaviour in order to avoid fitting any profile that others might have in mind. Some terrorist organisations also use (pregnant) women for certain roles as they are believed to look less suspicious.

Finally, there is a technological side to the idea that profiling works. With the increased possibilities of gathering, storing and analysing large numbers of data, there is a lot of optimism that that may help us to solve all kind of societal issues, including seeing patterns in terrorist behaviour and other possible common and particular characteristics of terrorists.

Detection of suspicious behaviour

Examples of 'suspicious' behaviour that have proved to be the starting point for further investigations into what later turned out to be preparations for terrorist attacks pertain to target probing and surveillance. There are several examples of such activities that have caught the attention of ordinary people, guards or law enforcement personnel. A report by Kevin Strom and others (2010) that examined successes and failures in detecting terrorist plots in the US gives several examples of trespassing in and photographing military barracks; breach or attempted intrusion; eliciting information; testing or probing of security, and observation or surveillance. The authors argue that '[m]ore than 80% of foiled terrorist plots were discovered via observations from law enforcement or the general public. Tips included reports of plots as well as reports of suspicious activity, such as pre-operational surveillance, para-military training, smuggling activities, and the discovery of suspicious documents'.

BOX 5.01   DETECTION OF SUSPICIOUS BEHAVIOUR

Despite a number of success stories it remains unclear if, how, or to what extent profiling works and if one can recognise a terrorist. Ideally it would be possible for counterterrorism agencies to make a distinction between the general population on the one hand and radicals and terrorists on the other, based on prior experiences of using certain characteristics. This would make it possible to focus counterterrorism efforts only on violent groups and individuals. Such characteristics could pertain to age, education, socio-psychological characteristics, ethnic or religious background, socio-economic status, relative deprivation, physical features, travelling patterns, behaviour on the internet, etc. The process of profiling aims at singling out people or groups as (potential) terrorists from a larger population based on known traits or behaviours. What does this mechanism encompass and how does it work – that is, if it works?

There are different types of profiling. A main distinction can be made between profiling based on personal characteristics and profiling based on behavioural patterns. The prevalent method of attempting to make a distinction between an offender, either a criminal or a terrorist, and a non-offender is a combination of these two approaches. Basically, it starts by collecting data on terrorists we already know and deriving from these cases a set of typical attributes that can tell us what yet unknown terrorists might look like. The set of characteristics or features could also provide an indication of certain behavioural or personality traits. Together these attributes make up a terrorist profile. Often, this exercise is followed by data mining or data searching, a process that extracts information from a dataset to discover certain statistical correlations between the different attributes. Ideally, these correlations can be transformed into an understandable structure or, even better, an indication or 'picture' of what, in general, 'the terrorist' might look like. The next step is to compare this picture with the traits or behaviour of people. For instance, in relation to international travels this may involve looking at flight patterns, behaviour at border controls, the age of travellers and their nationality, the way tickets were purchased, etc. Doing so might lead to cases in which specific travellers are asked additional questions at the border or confronted with additional checks of their luggage.

Why does it matter to know whether or not profiling works?

In an ideal world, data mining discovers these patterns of terrorism in terms of personal attributes which, in turn, allows us to craft profiles of these individuals. Whenever this profile is compared to a certain population – or run through a database – ideally it should result in a list of potential terrorists. If it really works, it might offer counterterrorism agencies the perfect tool for discovering terrorists without much prior information about this individual or group. Obviously, there is a great demand for such a tool, as it could make counterterrorism much more efficient. For instance, it could make security checks at airports easier and quicker. Even more important, it may help to reduce the number of terrorist attacks. At the same time, we have to answer the question, what if it does not work while we believe it does? In that case it could lead to false positives or false negatives. In the former case, people might be wrongly taken for terrorists. In the latter case, over-confidence in the profiling tool might lead to a situation in which a terrorist is not recognised as one and excluded from further investigation because he or she did not fit the profile. Both cases can be very detrimental to the effectiveness and reputation of counterterrorism policies. Even if it works, the questions remain: is it proportional and is it ethical? In recent years we have seen an increase in awareness of the negative implications of profiling. Think of the Black Lives Matter debate in the US and elsewhere. It is obvious that some groups in society have fallen victim to profiling, with serious repercussions for those involved, sometimes leading to the loss of life. It is important to learn from lessons in the field of policing when looking at the practice of profiling in counterterrorism.

Does profiling work?

The basic idea behind profiling is the perception among many that terrorists are different from the general population. In the previous chapter we already argued that there is no empirical evidence that suggests that terrorists are crazy, but they could, of course, have other personal or behavioural characteristics that set them apart from non-terrorists. Whether true or not, this idea constitutes the basis of the assumption that profiling works and that it might be possible to recognise a terrorist. This notion is not only held by certain practitioners in the field of counterterrorism, but is also common among terrorists. Apparently, they have some idea of what terrorists look like or what we think terrorists look like and how they behave, as many of them have tried not to look suspicious and draw the attention of the police and intelligence services to them. As most terrorists are male, using women to stage an attack has a number of advantages. They can slip under the radar of counterterrorism and law enforcement agencies which primarily look out for male terrorists. In this regard, Anne Speckhard and Khapta Akhmedova (2006, p. 73) found that 'Palestinians only started to use women as bombers when the checkpoints became increasingly difficult for men to cross, and women initially had more success in arousing less suspicion and undergoing less rigorous searches'. In her book, *Bombshell*, Mia Bloom highlighted a case in which a woman pretended to be pregnant in order to work round safety precautions (2011, pp. 68-70). In other words, as counterterrorism efforts were mainly focused on males, terrorists worked their way round such mechanisms by using individuals who would not fit the profile or stereotype picture of 'the terrorist'.

Profiling of terrorists (and other criminals) is not a new phenomenon. The idea was already developed in the late nineteenth century. In those days in London, law enforcement agencies were desperately looking for a person popularly known as Jack the Ripper. This man was wanted for a series of murders of women in London between 1888 and 1892. The authorities tried to discover the person behind these murders by developing a profile according to which the police had to look for a physically strong, daring but quiet and mentally unstable, sexually deviant middle-aged man, probably an eccentric loner without an occupation. This effort, however, did not result in the arrest of Jack the Ripper. Nonetheless, this case has been credited as the starting point in modern criminal profiling.

Another famous historical case in which profiling became a central component was the so-called 'Mad Bomber' case. On 16 November 1940, workers at the Consolidated Edison building in New York found a homemade pipe bomb carrying a note which read, 'Con Edison crooks, this is for you'. In the following one and a half decades, over 30 small bombs in and around New York City were detonated, targeting movie theatres, phone booths and other public areas. The Mad Bomber managed to dodge investigators for 16 years. Eventually, after the criminal psychiatrist sketched a profile of the suspect, the authorities were able to arrest George Metesky (see box 5.02).

George Metesky, the 'Mad Bomber'

After 16 years of unsuccessful investigation, the authorities turned to criminal psychiatrist James Brussel and asked him to sketch a profile of the Mad Bomber. While some elements of the profile were simply the result of common sense, others were built on more advanced psychological concepts. Based on the notion that paranoia tends to peak at around the age of 35, Brussel suggested that, 16 years after his first bombing, the suspect would be somewhere halfway through his 50s. Additionally, based on historical evidence, the bomber was most probably male and, given his rancor against Con Edison, most likely a disgruntled former employee. Brussel's most fascinating prediction was that the bomber would wear a buttoned double-breasted suit the moment he was caught. Brussel's profile proved dead on, as it led the authorities to George Metesky, a 54-year-old sacked employee. Most strikingly, when the police ordered Metesky to change clothes for his arrest, he came out wearing the predicted buttoned double-breasted suit.

Greenburg, M. (2011), *The Mad Bomber of New York. The Extraordinary True Story of the Manhunt that Paralyzed a City*. New York: Union Square Press.

BOX 5.02   GEORGE METESKY, THE 'MAD BOMBER'

Another historical example of profiling that has been regarded as a success by some was the efforts of the German Bundeskriminalamt (German Federal Criminal Police Office) to catch members of the Red Army Faction (Rote Armee Fraktion, RAF). According to Beatrice de Graaf (2009), in the late 1970s the president of the Office, Horst Herold, launched a hunt for members of this left-wing terrorist group using both profiles and data screening. Based on interviews with relatives and acquaintances of RAF members, they were able to develop a profile consisting of personality traits and other characteristics. Additionally, it was discovered that these terrorists rented apartments under false names and paid their electricity and gas bills in cash. With this knowledge, the authorities asked various energy companies for further information on clients who paid their bills in cash. This allowed the Bundeskriminalamt to narrow down their pool of suspects. Then they compared the set of people with the data of register offices and other agencies. Consequently, only people with false identities remained, whose apartments could then be checked using conventional means. The authorities managed to locate one RAF apartment. This quite huge and costly operation thus resulted in the arrest of *one* member of the RAF.

All three cases catch our imagination, but what can we actually learn from them? Was Brussel's profile nothing more than a fluke? Can we call the arrest of one single RAF member by the Bundeskriminalamt a success, given the enormous effort? And is it really possible to effectively single out people or groups as criminals or terrorists from a larger population based on certain attributes of people that are as yet unknown to the authorities?

The academic literature on this topic is not very positive about this possibility. In fact, it did not offer clear-cut examples of the successful profiling of terrorists. Moreover, virtually all important academic studies say profiling based on personal characteristics or attributes is impossible. This clear 'no' to the possibility of profiling on the part of academia is linked to the widespread assumption that there is no standard (type of) terrorist or terrorist personality. According to Crenshaw (1981, p. 390), the 'limited data we have on individual terrorists ... suggest that the outstanding common characteristic of terrorists is their normality'. Thus, terrorists are not only not crazy, they are also not very different from others in society, or at least not different enough. Given this 'normality', Geoff Dean (2007, p. 175) would go as far as to stress that identifying a terrorist in a mass of people would be a 'naïve and futile task'. Additionally, even if they were very different, in many countries – especially in the western world – the authorities would be confronted with the fact that (fortunately) there are too few terrorists to be able to gather enough data to construct profiles of possible terrorists that are distinct or precise enough to be used in profiling.

Perhaps attempts like that of the Bundeskriminalamt might lead to more results as it did not focus on personal attributes but on certain behaviour. This would also require a lot of data on known cases that can be used to discern suspicious behaviour or combinations and patterns of behaviour. In particular in recent years there has been a revived interest in this so-called behavioural profiling, which is partly explained by the increasing possibility of gathering, storing and comparing enormous numbers of data (or 'big data') thanks to information technology and the internet. Behaviour on the World Wide Web in particular leaves behind a trail of digital information of users that could tell us a lot about an individual. According to Quirine Eijkman and Daan Weggemans (2012), open source information derived from digital sources, such as web-based communities (social-networking sites, video-sharing sites, blogs, etc.), constitutes a vital component of the information gathered by certain intelligence agencies. But even with regard to this so-called behavioural profiling, most academics are highly sceptical as there are many practical and technological obstacles. Obviously, there are also many risks pertaining to ethics, privacy, human rights and the governance and control of such profiling efforts. Moreover, there are serious negative side effects in the legal domain. According to Newton Minow and Fred Cate (2006, p. 1082), data mining not only violates privacy rights, but it is also undermining national security by targeting innocent individuals, failing to identify real suspects or otherwise wasting scarce resources. They argue that it creates 'liability for businesses and others that provide, or fail to provide, the government with requested data, or otherwise fail to comply with often detailed and burdensome laws; and interfering with transnational data flows or subject U.S. companies to liability under foreign international laws'.

Despite the above-mentioned risks and negative side effects, also for the private sector, the security and aviation industries still show much interest in further exploring new ways to arrive at a truly effective and efficient tool for recognising terrorists before they manage to stage an attack. Theoretically, a profiling tool that really works and can help to recognise terrorists out of a larger population could have enormous benefits. However, while we have not seen concrete cases of success of profiling attempts by counterterrorism agencies, we did see cases in which the above-mentioned risks have materialised. In several cases, intelligence agencies and law enforcement agencies have made serious and deadly mistakes as a result of relying on profiles and data mining. Some of these mistakes are related to the possibility that incorrect information from profiling can lead to so-called false positives or false negatives; concepts that originate from the study of statistics. Both can have serious consequences (see box 5.03).

False positive: the case of Jean Charles de Menezes
Jean Charles da Silva de Menezes was a Brazilian, aged 27, who was shot dead by the London Metropolitan Police on the London Underground, a day after a failed suicide attack on the London Underground in 2005. Menezes was misidentified as one of the fugitives from the failed attack that the police were after. One police officer saw Menezes and thought he looked like one of the suspects, and a number of surveillance officers followed him when he caught a bus with the order that the suspect was to be prevented from entering the London Underground. Menezes, when arriving at the station, noticed that it was closed because of the previous day's attempted bombings. He made a phone call and took the bus to the next station. The surveillance officers believed that this behaviour suggested that he might have been one of the previous day's failed bomb suspects. Menezes left the bus, took the escalator and boarded a train, directly followed by three of the surveillance officers. When armed officers arrived on the platform, one of the surveillance officers shouted 'He's here!'. These officers boarded the train and it is not exactly clear what happened the minute after that. The fact is that Menezes was shot seven times in the head and once in the shoulder at close range. It was later revealed that police officers had been ordered to fire directly at the suspects' heads when confronted with suspected suicide bombers, the idea behind that being that shooting at the chest could conceivably detonate a concealed bomb.

BOX 5.03   FALSE POSITIVE: THE CASE OF JEAN CHARLES DE MENEZES

As mentioned earlier, in the case of a false negative the profile might provide information that leads investigators to rule out the actual perpetrators while focusing on a wrong individual or group of people. A false positive refers to a situation in which an innocent individual is identified as a suspect based on an incorrect profile. The consequence of such a false alarm could be that a person is investigated or, in the worst case scenario, arrested and convicted on terrorism charges. Obviously, arresting people on vague grounds not only violates fundamental rights, it is most likely counter-productive as it could lead to distrust in the authorities in general and counterterrorism agencies in particular. This is an especially serious risk when profiling is based on characteristics of a person that relate to religion and ethnicity. Profiling on such criteria could be discriminatory and a violation of the law. Although a common argument is that technology does not discriminate, the parameters of such systems are all human-made and could be based on stereotypes rather than carefully selected attributes of both personal characteristics and behavioural patterns which are known and tested to be relevant. Moreover, the fact that a system might not discriminate does not mean that it is not discriminatory by nature.

In the years after 9/11 several governments were criticised for adopting racial profiling mechanisms. Amnesty International (2004) reported that following the attacks on the US in 2001, racial profiling at public sites by US law enforcement agencies had increased significantly. Approximately 32 million Americans had been subjected to racial profiling. Of these 32 million people, individuals of Middle Eastern and Southern Asian descent were targeted most often, but it also affected Native, Hispanic and African-Americans. Racial profiling did not just result in false positives and false negatives. According to Amnesty International, it also had considerable ramifications for the individual liberties of the population being monitored, as it violated fundamental rights, such as the right to privacy, freedom of religion and the freedom of movement.

Efforts to profile terrorists in the West in recent years have often proved to be examples of racial profiling, mainly monitoring Muslims and immigrants. This is highly problematic for many reasons. It has not only resulted in false positives and false negatives, but it has also had considerable ramifications for the individual liberties of the population being monitored. It created and fostered stereotypes, the idea of a struggle between Islam and Christianity, and a loss of trust in the authorities among Muslim and immigrant communities. This tends to become even more problematic when authorities try to 'team up' with the wider population in their search for terrorists, For instance, the

British 'Prevent' programme, which is part of the national counterterrorism strategy, aimed to motivate citizens to report suspicious behaviour to the authorities. According to several studies, this has led to Muslim communities being seen as 'suspect communities' (see box 5.04).

Suspect students pushed to the edge

In 2003, the UK government established the Counterterrorism Strategy (CONTEST) to reduce the threat of terrorism in the UK. Its 'Prevent' programme aimed to reduce the threat of home-grown terrorism by calling upon individuals in public-facing roles to report anyone they suspected of being vulnerable to radicalisation and terrorism. In 2015 the programme was extended with a new law on higher education institutions to prevent individuals from being drawn into violent extremism and legally obliging them to report any individuals that they suspect of being vulnerable to radicalisation. This requirement was heavily ciritised by many. Tahir Abbas et al. (2021), in his study on the impact on British Muslim university students, observes that they are 'pushed to the edge'. It has led to self-censorship and self-silencing, has done damage to staff-student relations and to the mental health of individuals.

BOX 5.04   SUSPECT STUDENTS PUSHED TO THE EDGE

This might have even further alienated some people who were already on the brink of extremism or made them more receptive to us-them narratives. Thus, profiling based on parameters such as nationality, ethnicity, race, age or gender not only has a negative effect on the daily life of certain groups of minorities, it also affects relations between different countries and communities. It creates and fosters stereotypes and concrete grievances. Such grievances are grist to the mill of terrorist organisations as, according to Sageman (2004) and others, feelings of being discriminated against make youngsters more likely to engage in terrorism.

Conclusion

There is no doubt that there is a demand for a tool that can make an effective distinction between terrorists on the one hand and non-terrorists on the other. Although there is a long history of attempts to profile individual criminals and terrorists, there are, with few exceptions, no clear-cut success stories. This is related to the fact that terrorists are not very different from us in terms of personal characteristics or appearance, which makes it extremely difficult, if not impossible, to sketch a distinct profile of a terrorist. There are similar challenges pertaining to behavioural profiling. Current parameters are simply too broad and might create an overload of information, including inaccurate information or intelligence. Adding the examples of false positives and false negatives and looking at the debate on racial profiling, it seems that, today, profiling should be regarded as a technically and politically risky endeavour, and it is likely to remain so in light of the current research. According to scholars, it is futile or almost impossible to do personality profiling. Behavioural profiling might offer more opportunities on paper, but there are a lot of obstacles in practice. The enormous efforts have not led to clear-cut successes. Therefore we label the assumption that one could recognise a terrorist by means of profiling false. However, given the rapid progress in information technologies that can analyse 'big data' and with an eye on the many negative side effects of the current use of terrorist profiles, it is important to continue to conduct research into the field of behavioural profiling.

Key points

- Profiling refers to the process of singling out people or groups as (potential) terrorists from a larger population based on known traits or behaviours.
- There are no concrete cases of clear-cut successes.
- In theory, profiling allows security actors to reduce the pool of potential suspects, which makes it easier to find a suspect or unknown offender.
- There is no standard terrorist and therefore also no distinct profile, which makes profiling extremely difficult.
- Profiling could lead to discrimination and can cause false positives or false negatives.
- Given these difficulties we label the assumption that profiling works as false, though more research is needed.

5.3   Assumption two: Deradicalisation of terrorists is possible

The second assumption pertaining to counterterrorism is that terrorists can be deradicalised. In other words we will look into the possibility of individuals leaving terrorism behind and no longer engaging in violent activity, or even changing their attitudes and behaviour. Is that possible or just wishful thinking? While radicalisation and recruitment have received much attention from both scholars and experts in the field of counterterrorism, deradicalisation has for long remained under-researched. There is, however, a lot we can learn from the relatively few experts who have studied the topic and from those who have tried to deradicalise terrorists and extremists in practice. Before we address the body of literature on this topic, we first have to define the term. What is deradicalisation? And how does it relate to the notion of radicalisation?

The term 'deradicalisation' can mean different things and there is no consensus about its definition among academics or experts. The term can refer to an individual or group process or a (governmental) policy or programme. The rationale behind the deradicalisation of an individual as a process is that if an individual can radicalise and adopt a certain belief system that allows people to see terrorism as an acceptable means to achieve certain goals and to form or join a terrorist group, this process can also be undone. This is not to say that the process of deradicalisation is simply radicalisation in reverse. According to Angel Rabasa and colleagues (2010), deradicalisation has its own unique characteristics that can be rather different from the characteristics of the radicalisation process. The two processes are indeed very different. What they have in common is that they are very complex processes, and therefore difficult to define.

With regard to radicalisation, it is important to note that this process or phenomenon should not be immediately connected to the use of political violence, let alone terrorism. Although most terrorists are radicals, there are few terrorists among radicals, as most of them are not violent. We would go even further by saying that radicalisation as such could be a valuable process that has contributed to many positive changes in society. It has produced many non-violent and non-terrorist 'radicals' who have fought for the abolition of slavery, women's rights, the emancipation of discriminated against minorities, the democratisation of societies or have raised public and political awareness of child labour or the environment. Having said this, a critical distinction has to be made between non-violent and violent radicalisation. In this textbook we regard non-violent radicalisation as a social or psychological process that can be defined as an increase in extremism in sentiments, thinking and behaviour of an individual in relation to a political or politico-religious ideology. This process may not necessarily lead to violence – as is the case for most radicals – but is one of many factors that could lead to it. In other words, it could be a factor that leads to violent radicalisation and terrorism.

John Horgan (2009, p. 153) is arguably one of the main experts on radicalisation and deradicalisation, given his extensive research record in this field (see also box 5.05). He argues that deradicalisation is 'the social and psychological process whereby an individual's commitment to, and involvement in, violent radicalisation is reduced to the extent that they are no longer at risk of involvement and engagement in violent activity'. However, according to

Horgan, deradicalisation can also refer to a disengagement process 'whereby an individual experiences a change in role or function that is usually associated with a reduction of violent participation'. Such experiences could be getting a regular job or a new place to live, finding a new partner or starting a family. It is important to note that disengagement does not necessarily mean that people leave their radical ideas behind. Moreover, some disengaged terrorists might not even leave a movement or group. Sometimes people stay within these movements or scenes for a long time, even after they have become disillusioned about their leaders, the lack of success, the use of violence or the lack of concrete action. They may stay for many reasons, ranging from not wanting to be seen as a traitor, fear of repercussions or simply because they have nowhere else to go.

Walking Away From Terrorism

In *Walking Away From Terrorism: Accounts of Disengagement from Radical and Extremist Movements* (2009), Horgan investigates how and why individuals leave terrorist movements such as al-Qaeda or the IRA, and considers the lessons and implications that emerge from this process. He examines three major issues: 1) what we currently know about deradicalisation and disengagement, 2) how discussions with terrorists about their experiences of disengagement can show how exit routes come about, and how they then fare as 'ex-terrorists' away from the structures that protected them, and 3) what the implications of these findings are for law enforcement officers, policy-makers and civil society on a global scale. To this end, Horgan interviewed a number of people from 2006-2008 who had disengaged from terrorism. In fact, they had not entirely left terrorism behind, as none of them could be said to be 'deradicalised'. What they also had in common was their commitment to an underlying ideology and that their experience as terrorists could lead to disaffection and the desire to walk away from terrorism.

BOX 5.05   *WALKING AWAY FROM TERRORISM*

Before we start to explore the possibility of deradicalising a terrorist and promoting disengagement from terrorism, we have to make the distinction between deradicalisation and counterradicalisation. The latter term generally refers to a set of social, political, legal, educational and economic programmes that are designed to dissuade individuals from committing themselves to extremist ideologies, and in particular to prevent an increase in and reinforcement of extremism and becoming involved with a violent radical movement or terrorist group. Counterradicalisation programmes have a preventative character and tend to have a much wider target group – often labelled 'vulnerable groups' or 'groups at risk' – than deradicalisation programmes. The latter are mostly aimed at specific groups or even individual cases that have already been involved with violent radical movements or terrorist groups. In this section we regard as deradicalisation any process that leads to a situation in which someone's violent radicalisation is reduced to the extent that they are no longer at risk of involvement and engagement in violent activity. This could mean only disengagement, or a complete change of attitudes and behaviour.

Why does it matter to know whether or not deradicalisation is possible?

Many governments around the world spend a fair amount of their scarce resources on counterterrorism to prevent terrorist attacks from happening and to monitor and pursue (potential) terrorists. Such measures may help to prevent future terrorist attacks, but they are costly and do not contribute to long-term prevention of terrorism. Ideally it would be possible to deradicalise people who are involved in violent radicalisation and terrorism and to neutralise the potential threat they pose. Moreover, deradicalised terrorists – also called 'formers'— could be of help in preventing others from engaging in terrorism as they are probably the most credible people who can explain why one should not join a terrorist group and engage in violent activity. Hence, the benefits of deradicalisation of terrorists may be manifold. If it really works, governments should invest more in these types of programmes.

But what if it does not work, while we believe it does? We might not only misspend a lot of money on these kinds of programmes, but also run the risk that those whom we believe to be deradicalised secretly continue to be involved in terrorist activities. If the reward of participating in a deradicalisation programme for convicted terrorist is an early release from jail, governments run the risk of releasing from prison people who might one day surprise them by staging a terrorist attack. Think of the case of Usman Khan, who wounded several and stabbed two people to death on London Bridge in 2019. He and some of his victims were attending a conference on deradicalisation. Such tragic incidents put further pressure on the need to investigate this question.

Is deradicalisation of terrorists possible?

According to Angel Rabasa and others (2010), '[j]ust as there are processes through which an individual becomes an extremist, there are also processes through which an extremist comes to renounce violence, leaves a group or movement, or even rejects a radical worldview'. However, the last part is contested. Do people really give up their radical worldview and is it possible actively to deradicalise a person by way of deradicalisation programmes? And if so, how?

Evidence that it is possible to deradicalise a terrorist are those individuals who left terrorism behind, and who are now actively involved in counterradicalisation and deradicalisation projects. They turned from terrorists into experts on violent radicalisation who try to prevent people from joining terrorist groups. Well-known examples among terrorism experts of individuals who have deradicalised and successfully pursued professional careers in the field of counterterrorism include Daveed Gartenstein-Ross. As a youngster, he worked for the al-Haramain Islamic Foundation in Oregon, a Saudi-funded Wahhabi charity organisation that was eventually charged by the US government with financing al-Qaeda. Of American Jewish origin, Gartenstein-Ross gradually gained an interest in radical Islam while being enrolled in university. His entire journey can be read in his memoirs, *My Year Inside Radical Islam* (2007) (see box 5.06). Today, Gartenstein-Ross is regarded as an expert in the field of deradicalisation and counterterrorism, having published several books and countless other publications on (counter) terrorism and international security.

Daveed Gartenstein-Ross – *My Year Inside Radical Islam*
While attending college at Wake Forest University, Daveed Gartenstein-Ross became close to a charismatic fellow student, al-Husain Madhany, an Indian-American Muslim, who gradually introduced him to Islam. After converting to Islam, Gartenstein-Ross adopted elements of the Salafi variant of Islam during a summer job at al-Haramain, a foundation that supported Islamist movements throughout the world. When doubts about his faith started to arise, Gartenstein-Ross gradually disengaged from his Salafi beliefs and his former friends. Only after he had left al-Haramain did he discover the extremist nature of the organisation and its connection to terrorism. He decided to use this experience to start his own counterterrorism consulting business. In 2010 he became the director of the Center for the Study of Terrorist Radicalization at the Foundation for Defense of Democracies. He wrote the book *My Year Inside Radical Islam: A Memoir* (2007) to describe his experiences.
BOX 5.06   DAVEED GARTENSTEIN-ROSS - *MY YEAR INSIDE RADICAL ISLAM*

Another remarkable case of a former terrorist is Noman Benotman. After radicalising half-way into the 1980s, Benotman fought against the Soviet Union in Afghanistan in 1989. Once the Soviets were ousted, the former mujahidin was one of the founders of the Libyan Islamic Fighting Group (LIFG), the main goals of which included the establishment of an Islamic state and the removal from power of dictator Muammar Gaddafi. In the aftermath of 9/11, the LIFG was designated by the US Department of State as an al-Qaeda-affiliated organisation. Benotman became one of the leaders of the LIFG, but gradually moved away from that group's radical set of beliefs. He later became the president of the Quilliam Foundation, a London-based think tank on deradicalisation and Islamist extremism. In September 2010, he wrote an open letter to Osama Bin Laden, in which he appealed him to 'halt your violence and re-consider your aims and strategy'.

A third example of a terrorist who deradicalised and turned his back on terrorism is Henry Robinson. In the late 1970s, Robinson joined the Official IRA as a teenager and was sentenced to two years in prison after shooting two members of the Provisional IRA. However, after gradually leaving the ideas and methods of the Irish republicans behind, he eventually founded the organisation 'Families Against Intimidation and Terror' (FAIT). FAIT opposes the use of violence by paramilitary organisations, such as the Official IRA, and offers support to communities that have been directly affected by such organisations.

The above-mentioned people deradicalised largely on their own. There are, however, also several deradicalisation programmes and projects that help individuals to leave terrorism or violent extremism behind. In general, these programmes can be divided into two types: the first category focuses on individual ideological deradicalisation, using psychological and religious counselling to produce a change of mind. The second category aims for collective deradicalisation, using political negotiation to obtain a type of change of behaviour, such as ceasefires or the de-commissioning of arms.

There have been various deradicalisation programmes for individuals across Europe. Most of them are directed at right-wing extremists. Many of these programmes are in the Nordic countries – the 'Back on Track' programme in Denmark; 'EXIT' in Sweden, and 'Project Exit – Leaving Violent Groups' in Norway. The last programme was developed on the basis of research conducted by Tore Bjørgo. It focuses on the different factors that facilitate or obstruct an exit from right-wing groups and disengagement from violence (see box 5.07). This model was also used in Sweden where the programme consists of five phases: motivation, disengagement, settlement, reflection and stabilisation. In Germany, which has a relatively high number of right-wing extremists, there are several programmes that focus on these groups and individuals, including 'Exit-Germany' and the 'Violence Prevention Network'.

Tore Bjørgo's push and pull factors

Most of the designs of deradicalisation programmes, especially in the Nordic countries, are rooted in research by Tore Bjørgo (1997) on the radicalisation of youngsters in Scandinavia. He examined their motives for abandoning extreme right-wing groups. He identified three different types of factors that can facilitate or obstruct an exit: (1) 'push factors'; (2) 'pull factors'; and (3) 'factors inhibiting disengagement'. Push factors refer to the so-called negative social sanctions, such as social condemnation, physical insecurity and prosecution. Pull factors refer to positive social sanctions which makes it beneficial to leave a certain group. Some deradicalisation programmes actively facilitate such positive social benefits, for example by providing employment, housing or financial support. Furthermore, becoming 'too old' and losing status or motivation can also instigate a desire for a 'normal' life. Factors that inhibit disengagement include the valuable assets of the group such as friendship and material benefits, but also (fear of) potential retribution by fellow group members.

BOX 5.07   TORE BJØRGO'S PUSH AND PULL FACTORS

Similar programmes and projects aimed at deradicalising terrorists and violent extremists can be found in other parts of the world. In Indonesia, law enforcement authorities set up the 'Rehabilitation and Dialogue Process with Prisoners' project, which specifically aims to deradicalise jihadist prisoners. The results of this programme seem quite positive as the Indonesian police are now closely cooperating with former extremists. This programme offers not only psychological counselling and religious re-education, but also certain secondary benefits such as visiting arrangements with families and financial support in order to stimulate cooperation.

Some of the largest deradicalisation programmes in terms of budget and number of participants are to be found in Saudi Arabia. The 'Counselling Programme' intends to deradicalise extremist prisoners. This programme focuses mainly on the psychological aspects of deradicalisation through counselling and re-education. Although it has received extensive criticism, the Saudis point to the low (but widely disputed) recidivism rates of 10 to 20 per cent. Half of the 4,000 participants were released after Saudi law enforcement agencies believed that their deradicalisation had been successful. Nevertheless, despite the Saudi claim of success, a number of these people did return to violence and ended up in the ranks of various terrorist networks in the region.

While Saudi Arabia has developed the most well-structured official programmes, many other countries in the terrorism-troubled Islamic world have developed initiatives in deradicalising terrorists. Some countries, such as Egypt, Libya and Algeria, have gone through processes of collective disengagement from terrorism by entire groups, whereas others deal with individuals on a case by case basis. For an excellent analysis of the differences between the approaches of eight Muslim-majority states to countering and preventing jihadist radicalisation see the study by Hamed el Said for the International Centre for the Study of Radicalisation and Political Violence (ICSR) (see box 5.08).

Deradicalising Islamists: Programmes in Muslim Majority States
The study by El Said (2012) for ISCR lists five important factors that contribute to the effectiveness of programmes or initiatives aimed at deradicalising Islamists in Muslim-majority states:
National consensus – Lack of popular and political support has denied Jordanian deradicalisation efforts the social underpinning that contributes to their relative success in Saudi Arabia and Algeria.
Committed national leadership – Enthusiastic leadership by national governments can provide 'soft' counterterrorism policies with impetus, inject them with confidence, build trust in their purpose, and create and maintain the needed national consensus.
Civil society – The engagement of civil society can provide new ideas and reinforce the state's actions by empowering local communities and associations, especially those that are vulnerable and hard for the government to reach.
Non-religious programming – Religious dialogue alone will not eliminate violent extremism. Programmes must not ignore the social, economic and political factors that contribute to radicalisation and consider them in their mix of programming.
Cultural awareness – Deradicalisation programmes must be consistent with, and derive from, each country's mores, culture, rules and regulations, and take account of what is acceptable and not acceptable in their societies.
BOX 5.08   DERADICALISING ISLAMISTS: PROGRAMMES IN MUSLIM MAJORITY STATES

In Colombia, they tried to disengage not only prisoners, but also active members of the Revolutionary Armed Forces of Colombia (FARC), a (former) left-wing terrorist organisation. The Colombian judiciary tried to facilitate this by suspending trials in an attempt to encourage and sustain their demobilisation. In Colombia the keyword is demobilisation, and not deradicalisation. But the basic idea is to make sure that they leave terrorism behind, and perhaps also change their attitudes and behaviour. In Colombia they also 'deradicalised' the FARC as a whole. In 2017, the organisation decided to leave terrorism behind following years of negotiations with the government.

Many of the above-mentioned projects have been studied by scholars and have provided us with much more insight into deradicalisation processes and the challenges and possibilities regarding deradicalisation. These studies, however, also raised new questions. An important question is whether or not one can really speak of deradicalisation when a person leaves a terrorist group but not his or her radical ideas. The prevailing opinion is that leaving terrorism behind does not necessarily mean that that person is also deradicalised. Many so-called deradicalisation programmes are in fact primarily aimed at disengagement.

The distinction between deradicalisation and disengagement is an important one in relation to the question regarding the potential success of deradicalisation programmes. Disengagement refers to the situation in which a person leaves a terrorist organisation, but not necessarily his or her radical belief-system. While deradicalisation aims to accomplish a cognitive shift, disengagement generally only alters the attitude towards the use of violence. John Horgan and Mary Beth Altier (2012) emphasise that attitudes and behaviour towards the use of violence do not necessarily correlate. In their eyes, an individual might cut ties with his or her fellow terrorists, but does not abandon his radical beliefs or even reject the use of violence. This makes it difficult accurately to predict who are likely to relapse, as we do not know why certain individuals disengage. Without such knowledge of the motives of terrorists, it is impossible to assess the true effectiveness of deradicalisation programmes. Therefore, Horgan and Altier are sceptical about the success of programmes that aim for 'demobilisation', 'defection', 'de-escalation' and 'rehabilitation'. This, in their eyes, is not the same as deradicalisation. They would argue that many of the people who go through these programmes could still pose a risk in terms of involvement and engagement in violent activity in the future.

There are indeed quite a few examples of 'graduates' of these programmes who have returned to terrorism, especially in the case of Saudi Arabia. But it should be noted that the programmes in this particular country processed more than 4,000 detainees. Moreover, a survey of 13 deradicalisation programmes worldwide, conducted by the Institute for Strategic Dialogue (ISD) (2012), indicates that these programmes are useful in the struggle against terrorism. The study draws a number of important lessons from these cases. First of all, personal commitment of the individuals is vital as regards deradicalisation. Additionally, deradicalisation requires a certain level of mutual trust between the participant and the specific programme. Furthermore, 'formers' can play an important role in such programmes, as they tend to have a better understanding of the inner world of participants which makes it easier for them to earn their trust and respect.

Other studies also show that in a number of countries the overwhelming majority in deradicalisation programmes and terrorists released from prison do seem to leave terrorism behind. A recent study by Thomas Renard (2020) looked at terrorism recidivism rates and found that they are very low. He studied over 500 Belgians convicted of jihadist terrorism between 1990 and 2019 and found a recidivism and re-engagement rate of below 5 per cent.

Finally, it should be recalled that many people deradicalise totally on their own – because they have grown sick and tired of terrorism, or because of a new and better purpose in life, and for many other reasons. This means that some of those who participated in these programmes might also have been deradicalised without outside help.

Conclusion

There are various examples of terrorists who deradicalised, either on their own or through deradicalisation programmes. A number of these 'formers' have even actively contributed to preventing others from engaging in terrorism and to a better understanding of the process of deradicalisation. Thanks to their input and because of the increase in the number of deradicalisation programmes, today we know a lot more about the deradicalisation of terrorists than we did, for instance, five or ten years ago. We also know that some of these programmes have achieved more success than others and that it is important to make a distinction between programmes that aim at deradicalisation and those that aim only at disengagement. While the former attempt to generate a cognitive shift, the latter focus only on changing terrorist behaviour. Disengaged terrorists do not necessarily give up their radical beliefs. Although deradicalisation is obviously preferred, disengagement is often a more realistic target to achieve. Many of the so-called deradicalisation programmes are in fact primarily aimed at disengagement. There is something to say for that, as it is less intensive and therefore less costly. One could also argue that disengagement should be the first priority, and perhaps the only priority, as people have the right to have radical ideas. At the same time, there seems to be evidence that, as long as terrorists and violent extremists are only disengaged, the potential security risk to society remains. Nonetheless, many of those who went through the deradicalisation programmes or who disengaged from terrorism on their own did leave terrorism behind, and many of them for good. Therefore, the assumption that deradicalisation is possible can be labelled as true.

Key points

- Deradicalisation can refer to both a process and a programme.
- Deradicalisation aims to lead to a situation in which an individual abandons his or her set of radical beliefs and rejects the use of violence.
- Rather than deradicalisation, it might be more realistic to aim at disengagement, as disengagement does not necessarily change beliefs but aims to change behaviour.
- Deradicalisation cannot be enforced and requires the commitment of individuals.
- There are many examples of deradicalised terrorists; therefore, the assumption that deradicalisation is possible can be labelled as true.

5.4 Assumption three: Decapitation of terrorist organisations works

After the announcement by the Obama Administration that Osama bin Laden was killed in a raid on his compound in Abbottabad (see box 5.09), the American public spontaneously gathered in the streets throughout the US celebrating the death of America's most wanted. Some might have hoped that the death of the charismatic leader of al-Qaeda would mean the end of the War on Terror which started after 9/11, now that the man behind the organisation was no longer alive. Many took a more sceptical position, realising that the impact of the death of Bin Laden on al-Qaeda was probably very limited. Nonetheless, the 'National Strategy for Counterterrorism' of the White House (2011, p. 3) states that '[t]he death of [Osama] bin Laden marked the most important strategic milestone in our effort to defeat [al-Qaeda]'. It also reads, '[o]ur efforts in Afghanistan and Pakistan have destroyed much of [al-Qaeda]'s leadership and weakened the organization substantially'. At the same time, the strategy admits that in recent years the source of the threat to the US and its allies has shifted in part towards groups affiliated with al-Qaeda but separate from its core in Pakistan and Afghanistan. 'This also includes deliberate efforts by [al-Qaeda] to inspire individuals within the United States to conduct attacks on their own.' Today, al-Qaeda – its core, its affiliates and its supporters – is still very much alive and active in many parts of the world.

The same holds true for Islamic State. American forces also managed to decapitate the leadership of this terrorist organisation. In October 2019 its leader, Abu Baqr al-Baghdadi, blew himself up after he was surrounded by US forces in an isolated compound in northern Syria. Islamic State also lost several other high-ranking leaders, and the successor to al-Baghdadi, Abu

Ibrahim al-Hashemi al-Qurayshi, killed himself in February 2022 during a raid by US special forces. The capability of Islamic State to stage attacks has reduced in recent years. However, the organisation did survive and still has a presence in many countries around the world.

This raises the question: why is the White House still confident about the idea that the decapitation of al-Qaeda, Islamic State and other terrorist groups might work? And why do efforts in capturing and killing terrorist leaders feature prominently in the counterterrorism strategies of many other states, including Colombia, Israel, Yemen, Spain and Russia?

The killing of Osama bin Laden

The founder and leader of al-Qaeda, Osama bin Laden, US's most wanted man, had managed not to get caught or killed for almost ten years. However, in the early hours of 2 May 2011, US Navy SEALs entered the compound in which he had been hiding in the town of Abbottabad, Pakistan. The location had been identified as the house of Bin Laden, more than six months earlier, by following his courier. Using surveillance photos, intelligence reports and observations on the ground to determine the identities of the inhabitants of the compound, the Navy SEALs landed in and next to the compound using helicopters. There was some resistance that was quickly dealt with. They encountered Bin Laden himself on the third floor when he peered over at the Americans advancing up the stairs, who fired a shot at him. The SEALs found him lying on the floor with a head wound and fired more shots at him. Osama bin Laden was killed in the raid, as were three other men and a woman: his adult son, Khalid, bin Laden's courier and the latter's brother and sister-in-law. After the raid, his body was taken to Afghanistan to be further identified. After that it was taken to an aircraft carrier in the Persian Gulf where the body was buried at sea.

Owen, M. & Maurer, K. (2012), *No Easy Day: The autobiography of a Navy Seal*. Dutton Penguin.

Bergen, P. (2013). *Manhunt: The Ten Year Search for Bin Laden: from 9/11 to Abbottabad*. London: Vintage Books.

BOX 5.09 THE KILLING OF OSAMA BIN LADEN

Having given the example of the killing of Osama bin Laden and having mentioned targeted killings, it should be stressed that the decapitation of terrorist organisations includes more than the killing of terrorist leaders. Decapitation can also mean the arrest of such leaders and other key members of a terrorist organisation or network. What all these acts have in common is the taking out of the leadership with the aim or hope of weakening these organisations or even defeating them. In light of the fact that the US and other countries have put much effort into attempts to decapitate terrorist organisations, we will explore whether or not the White House strategy is right in assuming that decapitation of terrorist organisations works.

Why does it matter to know whether or not decapitation works?

The strategy and practice of decapitation of terrorist organisations in general and the killing of its leaders in particular have been heavily criticised for a number of reasons. Decapitation via targeted killings in particular has raised legal concerns. How does this relate to international humanitarian law, human rights law or domestic laws and regulations? Many human rights advocates and international lawyers challenge the legitimacy of the killing of terrorist leaders. They regard it as an illegitimate and inefficient means of state-imposed extra-judicial execution. Scholars and non-governmental organisations have also pointed to many different negative side effects of the decapitation of terrorist organisations in general and targeted killings by way of drones in particular. For instance, the International Human Rights and Conflict Resolution Clinic at Stanford Law School and the Global Justice Clinic at New York University School of Law (2012) have pointed to the 'collateral damage', resulting in death, injury and trauma, to civilians from US drone practices in Pakistan. Others have argued that the capturing and killing of the leadership of terrorist organisations may even lead to more violence, retaliating for the deaths of 'beloved leaders'. The leaders who are killed by the enemy may become martyrs and their deaths a boost to the recruitment of a new generation of terrorists. Add to all that the moral and ethical dimensions and it becomes very obvious that the practice of decapitating terrorist organisations is a highly sensitive issue.

If, on top of that, the practice or strategy does not work, the many critics are right in demanding an immediate halt to it. But what if it works? What if the capturing or killing of terrorist leaders may result in fewer terrorist attacks or even the end of terrorist groups? What would that mean for the acceptance of this tool? Would it motivate governments and societies to execute or demand an even more militaristic or repressive approach to terrorism?

Is decapitation of terrorist organisations successful?

As mentioned above, the capturing and killing of terrorist leaders is a widely practised counterterrorism measure that has been used around the globe. In fact, there have been many cases of decapitations of terrorist organisations from which we can learn (see boxes 5.09 and 5.10). Did these decapitations lead to a weaker terrorist organisation, fewer attacks or even the end of the terrorist group? Here are some examples from the past.

Perhaps one of the most notable successful cases has been the arrest of Abimael Guzmán, the commander of the Peruvian organisation, Shining Path (see also box 5.09). Starting its violent activities in 1980, this Maoist terrorist organisation wanted to overthrow the Peruvian government and install a regime more to its liking. In September 1992, the group was confronted with the arrest of its charismatic commander. In addition to the arrest of Guzmán, other high-ranked members of the Shining Path were captured. Although the organisation did not completely dissolve, active membership declined significantly in the months and years after the arrests. According to Sean Anderson and Stephen Sloan (2009, pp. 621-626), the number of active members went down from approximately 6,000 to 8,000 in 1990, to only 2,000 in 1995.

Captured terrorist leaders

Through military actions and the work of law enforcement officers, many terrorists have been arrested, including some important leaders or other key figures of terrorist organisations. The most well-known examples (in alphabetical order) include: Shoko Asahara (Aum Shinrikyo, Japan, arrested in 1995); Andreas Baader (RAF, Germany, arrested in 1968, 1970 and 1972); Abimael Guzmán (Shining Path, Peru, arrested in 1992); Sami Jasim al-Jaburi (Islamic State, arrested by Iraqi forces in 2021) Khalid Sheikh Mohammed (al-Qaeda, captured in Pakistan in 2003, held in Guantánamo Bay), Khair Mundos (Abu Sayyaf Group, Philippines, arrested in 2004 and 2014), Abdullah Öcalan (PKK, captured in Kenya in 1999, imprisoned in Turkey); Francisco Javier López Peña, a.k.a. 'Thierry' (ETA, arrested in France in 2008); Abu al-Hassan al-Hashimi al-Qurashi (IS, arrested in 2022); Mohammed Ahmed Sidibapa, a.k.a. Yasin Bhatkal (Indian Mujahideen, captured at the Nepal-Indian border in 2013) and Beate Zschäpe (NSU, Germany, arrested in 2011).

BOX 5.10   CAPTURED TERRORIST LEADERS

Another example that is often mentioned as a successful case of the decapitation of a terrorist organisation is the arrest of Abdullah Öcalan in 1999. After the leader of the Kurdistan Workers' Party (PKK) had tried to find asylum in a number of countries, he was arrested in Nairobi, Kenya, in February 1999 by Turkish special agents. Öcalan's arrest immediately resulted in a number of attacks on Turkish, Greek and Israeli diplomatic offices in many countries by followers of the PKK (Greece and Israel allegedly had been involved in the arrest). Although the leader of the Kurdish terrorist organisation was initially given the death penalty, this verdict was changed to life in prison, partly as a result of international pressure. Following Öcalan's arrest, the PKK withdrew from Turkey as part of a unilaterally declared ceasefire. According to the PKK itself, it switched to non-violent strategies and abandoned its terrorist methods. Despite the ceasefire, the PKK returned to violence in 2004 and launched a series of attacks on various targets. Since December 2012, the Turkish government has been in negotiation with PKK leader Öcalan, who remains in jail.

Unlike the Shining Path and the PKK, the Palestinian organisation Hamas has been less affected by decapitation by Israeli forces. Since its establishment in the late 1980s, Hamas has carried out a number of kidnappings and armed assaults, but it is perhaps most notorious for its suicide bombings, targeting Israeli military as well as civilians. After already being arrested in 1989, Sheikh Ahmed Yassin, founder and the spiritual leader of Hamas, was bombed by Israeli forces after his daily morning prayers in Gaza City (see box 5.11). Along with the senior Hamas leader, nine bystanders were killed in the attack. The assassination fuelled the rage among Palestinians against Israel and evoked international criticism. Not only Hamas, but also other terrorist organisations such as the al-Aqsa Martyrs Brigade, vowed retaliation. Nevertheless, Israeli government officials, such as Prime Minister Ariel Sharon and then Minister of Finance Benjamin Netanyahu, praised the attack and suggested that Yassin's death would paralyse Hamas. Yassin's successor, Abdel Aziz al-Rantissi, was also killed, only a month after the assassination of his predecessor. The recruitment of young Palestinian suicide bombers increased and Hamas remained capable of staging attacks against Israel. The Global Terrorism Database attributes well over 100 attacks to Hamas in the year after the assassinations, varying from armed assaults to suicide bombings and rocket strikes. Although the decapitation attempt on Hamas did not lead to paralysing the group, it did affect the organisation of its leadership. After the assassination of Yassin and his successor al-Rantissi, it did not publicly announce the name of its new leader.

The killing of Sheikh Ahmed Yassin

Sheikh Ahmed Yassin, co-founder of Hamas, was arrested by the Israelis in 1984 and 1989, but released some years later (in 1985 and in 1997) as part of a political deal – the second time in exchange for two Mossad – Israel's national intelligence agency – agents who had been arrested by Jordanian authorities. Following his release, Yassin resumed his leadership of Hamas and his calls for attacks on Israel. In September 2003, an Israeli fighter jet fired several missiles on a building in Gaza City in which the Israelis knew Yassin was present at the time. Yassin, who was tied to a wheelchair after a wrestling injury at the age of 12, was injured in the attack, but survived. In March 2004, while he was being wheeled out of an early morning prayer session, an Israeli helicopter fired missiles at him and his bodyguards. They were killed instantly and so were nine bystanders. Outside Israel, most reactions were highly critical. UN Secretary General Kofi Annan condemned the killing and so did the UN Commission on Human Rights which called it 'a tragic assassination'.

BOX 5.11   THE KILLING OF SHEIKH AHMED YASSIN

What do we make of these three cases? Can decapitation of terrorist organisations be considered a success in the cases of Peru, Turkey and Israel vis-à-vis Shining Path, the PKK and Hamas? And if so, what about other cases? If we look at the reactions of political leaders, such as Sharon and Netanyahu, there seems to be little doubt from their side. These two Israeli leaders are part of a large group of political leaders who have claimed success after an important leader of a terrorist organisation was captured or killed. Examples include the reaction by Spanish Prime Minister Zapatero (2008) after the arrest of the operational chief of ETA: '[w]ith this arrest, ETA has suffered a severe blow in its organization and capability. Today, ETA is weaker'. Another example is the remarks by Colombian President Juan Manuel Santos after the killing of FARC leader Alfonso Cano (2011): '[the killing of Cano is] the hardest blow to this organization in its entire history'. Rudy Giuliani (2011), former mayor of New York, explained how the death of Osama bin Laden would contribute to counterterrorism. He said, 'He was a symbol more than anything else right now but ... symbols are really important. ... In the long run this will be very helpful to us in defeating Islamic terrorism ... in the long run this is a much bigger step than people realize'. Why do these influential politicians think that decapitation works, even or especially in the long run?

Those who see it as an effective strategy assume that the success of a terrorist organisation depends greatly on effective leadership. Removing the leader will therefore weaken the organisation. This may be the case when a leadership struggle occurs that forces the organisation to devote all its time to choosing a new leader instead of carrying out attacks, or when a leader cannot easily be replaced because others do not have the right capabilities or experience. But it could also be related to ideas and theories about charismatic leadership. Some leaders, especially those of religiously-inspired groups, play a crucial role in explaining and safeguarding the group's ideology. Leaders like Osama bin Laden or Shoko Asahara, the leader of the Japanese Aum sect, have been regarded as highly charismatic. Many people therefore think that it is very effective to eliminate this particular type of leader because it will destabilise the entire group and weaken its appeal (see box 5.12). Furthermore, assassination is sometimes the only viable option as, for instance, capturing terrorist leaders in hostile terrorist- or rebel-held regions can be extremely difficult.

Murakami on Asahara and the Tokyo gas attack trials

In his book *Underground. The Tokyo gas attack and the Japanese psyche* (2000), Haruki Murakami describes the trials after the attack on the metro in Tokyo in 1995. 'I attended several of the trials of the defendants in the Tokyo gas attack. I wanted to see and hear these people with my own eyes and ears, in order to come to some understanding of who they were. I also wanted to know what they were thinking now. What I found there was a dismal, gloomy, hopeless scene, The court was like a room with no exit. There must have been a way out in the beginning, but now it had become a nightmarish chamber from which there was no escape. Most of the defendants have lost all faith in Shoko Asahara as their guru. The Leader they revered turned out to be nothing than a false prophet, and they understand now how they were manipulated by his insane desires. The fact that following his orders led to them committing terrible crimes against humanity has made them do some real soul-searching, and they deeply regret their actions. Most of them refer now to their former leader simply as Asahara, dropping any honorific title' (p. 359).

BOX 5.12   MURAKAMI ON ASAHARA AND THE TOKYO GAS ATTACK TRIALS

Available academic research on the effectiveness of decapitation is largely based on anecdotal rather than empirical evidence. Furthermore, these claims are often derived from single case studies, which makes it difficult to draw any valid, general conclusion. However, there are two important researchers who did incorporate statistical analysis – Jenna Jordan and Bryan Price. Interestingly enough, their studies claim different positions with regard to the effectiveness of decapitation tactics. For well-known examples of assassinated terrorist leaders see box 5.13.

Jordan (2009), in her article 'When Heads Roll: Assessing the Effectiveness of Leadership Decapitation', argues that decapitation is not only ineffective, but, under certain circumstances is also counter-productive. In her study she investigated over 300 cases of leadership decapitation between 1945 and 2004. She operationalised decapitation as 'successful' when the terrorist organisations remained inactive for two years following the moment of decapitation. Her assessment identified a number of important variables that determined the success of decapitation, such as the age of the group, its organisational size and its ideology. Generally, younger, smaller organisations were more often destabilised than older, larger terrorist organisations. Additionally, the data show that religious organisations seem to be more or less completely (96 per cent) resilient to decapitation. Separatist organisations remained active in 89 per cent of the decapitation cases. Ideological organisations were relatively more prone to organisational decline, as about one third of such groups were not able to overcome decapitation. All in all, decapitation proved to be effective in just 17 per cent of all cases.

Assassinated terrorist leaders

As a result of regular military operations, the use of special forces or targeted killings by drones, many terrorists have been killed in action or assassinated in the places they were hiding in or operating from. Among those killed or assassinated were important leaders of terrorist organisations. The most well-known examples (in alphabetical order) include: Abu Baqr al-Baghdadi (IS, killed in Syria in 2019); Alfonso Cano (FARC, killed in Colombia in 2011); Osama bin Laden (al-Qaeda, killed in Pakistan in 2011); Aslan Maschadov (Chechen rebel leader killed in Russia in 2005); Hakimullah Mehsud (Tehrik-i-Taliban Pakistan, killed in 2013); Thiruvenkadam Velupillai Prabhakaran (LTTE, killed in Sri Lanka in 2009); Abu Ibrahim al-Hashimi al-Qurashi (IS, killed in Syria in 2022); Indonesia's most wanted terrorist, Noordin Mohammad Top (Jemaah Islamiyah, killed in Indonesia in 2009); Sheikh Ahmed Yassin (Hamas, killed in Gaza City in 2004); and Abu Musab al-Zarqawi (al-Qaeda in Iraq, killed in Iraq in 2006) and his replacement, Abu Ayyub al-Masri (killed in Iraq in 2010).

BOX 5.13   ASSASSINATED TERRORIST LEADERS

Most notably, when Jordan compared these data with the data of terrorist organisations that had not experienced decapitation, she concluded that decapitated terrorist organisations do not have a particularly higher decline rate. This could imply that decapitation will not lead to faster dissolution, but that it may actually increase the lifespan of such organisations. Rather than 'killing' the terrorist organisation, it might result in the opposite: prolonging its life. Jordan attributes this consequence to certain side effects, such as the strengthening of the group's resolve. Following decapitation, these organisations grow stronger as a result of anger, as they vow to retaliate, supported by the general public. According to Jordan, decapitation is ill-advised, as the organisations that are targeted most regularly are generally unaffected by it, or possibly come out of it even stronger.

Unlike Jordan, Price (2012) in his article, 'Targeting Top Terrorists: How Leadership Decapitation Contributes to Counterterrorism', argues that decapitation can be effective. He criticises Jordan for focusing too much on the short-term effects, as she measures 'success' over the course of just two years. According to Price, such a timespan is too short to measure and appreciate the impact of decapitation. It is not necessarily a short-term instrument. He believes it can also have an impact on the organisation in the long run. Price also argues that decapitation of terrorist organisations could be successful, as these organisations differ greatly from other types of organisation, given their violent, clandestine and values-based nature. As a consequence of these characteristics, leaders of such organisations are more important than ordinary leaders of non-violent, profit-based organisations and businesses. He argues that succession is much more difficult, as their charisma and ability to pass over a certain ideological message are difficult to replace.

Subsequently, Price tested his anecdotal argument by assessing the effects of leadership decapitation on the mortality of terrorist organisations from the 1970s onwards. He concluded that decapitated terrorist organisations have a higher mortality rate than organisations that were not subjected to decapitation. Nevertheless, according to Price, organisational decline is not necessarily immediate, as only 30 per cent ended within Jordan's timeframe of two years after decapitation. Second, he acknowledges Jordan's claim that successful decapitation becomes more difficult when terrorist organisations grow older. Decapitation within the first year of the existence of a terrorist organisation is eight times more likely to result in organisational decline, and its effect tends to diminish sharply over time. Third, assassination as well as arrests that are followed by capital punishment increase the mortality rate of terrorist organisations. Fourth, apart from decapitation through assassination or arrest, other types of leadership turnover, such as natural death, banishment or voluntary resignation, also increase the mortality rate of terrorist organisations. Fifth, in contrast to Jordan's view, size does not necessarily affect the mortality rate of such organisations, as small groups are as equally affected by decapitation as larger groups. Sixth, and also contrary to Jordan's assumption, religious terrorist organisations were less resilient than nationalist ones. According to Price, religious terrorist organisations such as al-Qaeda, the Aum Shinrikyo movement, Hezbollah and the Taliban proved to be five times more likely to experience organisational decline resulting from decapitation than terrorist organisations in general.

Although Jordan and Price come to different conclusions, they both point out the importance of certain features of terrorist organisations. The character and composition of these organisations determine the probability of success of decapitation tactics. Success is highly dependent on the context. Decapitation may work in one case, while it could potentially backfire in another. The cases of the Shining Path, the PKK and Hamas, mentioned earlier in this section, show divergence in the effects of the arrest or killing of terrorist leaders.

Finally, the legal and ethical dimensions need to be addressed. Decapitation of terrorist organisations does not take place in a societal or political vacuum. Even if successful in terms of seriously weakening or even ending terrorist organisations, it may come at such a high price in other domains that the use of this tool may result in failure. Today, countries that employ leadership decapitation as part of their counterterrorism strategy, in particular the US, increasingly face criticism relating to the human rights dimension. This holds true in particular for the use of drones which has increased significantly under the Obama Administration.

Particularly relevant to the question whether decapitation of terrorist organisations works or not are indications, studies and reports that relate to negative side effects that seem to support Jordan's claim that in some cases the organisations that are targeted may possibly be strengthened. The earlier-mentioned report by the Stanford Law School and the New York University School of Law (2012) challenges the dominant notion in the US about the use of drones in Pakistan. According to this notion, the use of drones is a surgically precise and effective tool that makes the US safer by enabling the targeted killing of terrorists, with minimal downsides or collateral impacts. In contrast, the report shows how drone attacks in Pakistan are not only indiscriminate and unlawful, but also backfire, given their harmful impacts on Pakistani civilians and US interests (see box 5.14). A more recent report by Amnesty International, 'Deadly Assistance: The role of European states in US drone strikes' (2018), also looks at the case of Pakistan and even states that drone strikes in several cases could amount to war crimes or extrajudicial executions.

Conclusions Stanford/NYU Report on Drones

'Following nine months of intensive research—including two investigations in Pakistan, more than 130 interviews with victims, witnesses, and experts, and review of thousands of pages of documentation and media reporting—this report presents evidence of the damaging and counterproductive effects of current US drone strike policies. Based on extensive interviews with Pakistanis living in the regions directly affected, as well as humanitarian and medical workers, this report provides new and first-hand testimony about the negative impacts US policies are having on the civilians living under drones. Real threats to US security and to Pakistani civilians exist in the Pakistani border areas now targeted by Drones. It is crucial that the US be able to protect itself from terrorist threats, and that the great harm caused by terrorists to Pakistani civilians be addressed. However, in light of significant evidence of harmful impacts to Pakistani civilians and to US interests, current policies to address terrorism through targeted killings and drone strikes must be carefully re-evaluated.' The report (2012) also states that '[p]ublicly available evidence that the strikes have made the US safer overall is ambiguous at best'.

BOX 5.14   CONCLUSIONS STANFORD/NYU REPORT ON DRONES

By killing Osama bin Laden, the White House hoped it had achieved the most important strategic milestone in its effort to defeat al-Qaeda. It believed it had destroyed much of its leadership and weakened the organisation substantially. The same holds true for the decapitation of Islamic State. However, al-Qaeda and Islamic State did survive as organisations although their current strength is difficult to determine.

If measured by Jordan's standards, the killing of Bin Laden and al-Baghdadi cannot be labelled a success, as two years after the attacks both organisations still existed. Price, who uses a different criterion, has nonetheless argued that charismatic leaders like Bin Laden are not easily replaced and that, in the long run, the killing in Abbottabad could lead to a defeat of al-Qaeda. Jordan and Price agree that the impact of decapitation much depends on certain specific features of terrorist organisations and have stressed the need to look into differences in types of organisations that influence the success or failure of this measure. Whereas both scholars mainly focus on the question whether or not the terrorist organisation ceases to exist, the debate on success or failure should also include the legal and ethical dimensions and needs to look into efficiency, effectiveness and other possible (positive or negative) side effects. Targeted killings with the use of drones in particular are highly controversial, and it is essential that the public debate about the use of these instruments also takes the negative effects of current policies into account. Academics could contribute to this debate, for instance by looking into the effectiveness of decapitation as Jordan and Price did, but perhaps even more so into the negative side effects of the 'modus operandi' in decapitating the networks, whether it means arresting people or killing them in drone attacks. This may be helpful in determining whether or not short-term successes – as often claimed by politicians – can still be considered successes in the long term. Adding it all up, there are various ways to look at the success and effectiveness of the decapitation of terrorist organisations. Success depends on the size, the age and the type of group. There seem to be cases in which decapitation can work, but also cases in which it may backfire. Therefore, we label the assumption that decapitation of terrorist organisations works as partly true. But also for this assumption we have to add that more research is needed.

Key points

· Decapitation can refer to either the assassination or the arrest of a leader of a terrorist organisation.
· Critics doubt its effectiveness and argue that it can even be counter-productive as it fuels anger and tensions which may even strengthen terrorist organisations.
· Advocates of decapitation stress its effectiveness in the long term.
· Both using comparable statistical data, Jordan and Price arrive at different conclusions regarding the success or effectiveness of decapitation.
· In certain cases it may work; in others it may backfire.
· Therefore we label this assumption as partly true.

5.5   Assumption four: Terrorism cannot be defeated

The attacks on the US on 11 September 2001, led US President George W. Bush to declare a 'Global War on Terror' on 20 September. It set off a chain of events, including armed interventions in several countries, to begin with in Afghanistan. Its rulers, the Taliban, were considered to be one of al-Qaeda's primary allies. They refused to meet a set of US demands: the extradition of Bin Laden and the closure of terrorist training camps. In response, the US, in cooperation with its allies, launched Operation Enduring Freedom, which aimed at the ousting of the Taliban regime, the dismantling of al-Qaeda and the destruction of the training camps. Other interventions would follow that were directly or indirectly, rightly or wrongly connected to this war on terror.

As mentioned in chapter 3, the term 'Global War on Terror' was a misnomer as terrorism is not an enemy but a tool or instrument (see box 3.12). But the war was declared nonetheless, and now, more than two decades after 9/11, we would like to raise the question: who has won? We will focus not on this particular 'war', but on the fight or struggle against terrorism in general. On the basis of the observation that a war against terrorism does not make any sense as one cannot win a war against an instrument, we will investigate the assumption that terrorism cannot be defeated. It is related to the assumption that terrorism is successful, as discussed and analysed in the previous chapter. However, in this chapter we primarily look at the effectiveness of the whole range of counterterrorism measures – can they lead to the defeat of terrorism or not?

Interestingly, generals have been among the most pessimistic about the chances of a favourable outcome for their side. For instance, General Sir David Richards, Chief of the Defence Staff of the British Armed Forces (2010) put it this way when speaking about defeating al-Qaeda and Islamist militancy, '[f]irst of all you have to ask: "do we need to defeat it?" in the sense of a clear cut victory, and I would argue that it is unnecessary and would never be achieved'. Even more surprising is the answer provided by the man who officially 'declared' the War on Terror, former US President George W. Bush (2004). When he was asked whether we can win the War on Terror, the President answered, 'I don't think you can win it …, but I think you can create conditions so that those who use terror as a tool are less acceptable in parts of the world'. Even on a more fatalistic note, King Abdullah II of Jordan (2010) said, 'We're never going to be able to get rid of terrorism, because there is always going to be evil in the world'. After the fall of Kabul 20 years after 9/11 there were many experts and politicians who were very doubtful about the defeat of terrorism. Assaf Moghadam (2021), senior researcher at the International Institute for Counterterrorism in Israel, for instance, said, '[t]he objectives that it set for itself were unachievable. Terrorism cannot be defeated. The threat is constantly evolving'.

Getting rid of terrorism is, of course, not the same as defeating terrorism, which, in turn, is not the same as winning a war on terror. All these terms have different connotations and the notion of 'defeat' is difficult to define and to determine. Can we speak of a defeat when a terrorist organisation ceases to exist because of a lack of support from those it claims to represent? How can we know if certain policies led to the end of a group, and not, for instance, internal splits and quarrels? What are we talking about when we say terrorism cannot be defeated? Does that imply that it is impossible to bring terrorist groups to their knees, or that there will always be terrorist attacks? Or is General Sir David Richards right in saying that we do not need a clear-cut victory and can we agree with former US President George W. Bush that creating conditions that make terrorism less acceptable would already be a major achievement, perhaps even be considered a defeat for terrorists? Probably we have to make a distinction between individual terrorist organisations or networks and the phenomenon of terrorism as a whole. In this section we will read 'defeat' as 'cease to exist', and we will focus on both the possibility of defeating terrorists organisations and the phenomenon of terrorism as a whole.

Why does it matter to know whether or not terrorism can be defeated?

Obviously, it is important to assess the assumption that terrorism cannot be defeated. If that is widely believed – even among generals, kings and the president who launched the Global War on Terror – this could turn into a sense of 'defeatism' and strengthen the notion that we cannot manage the threat of terrorism. Given the enormous efforts in counterterrorism, the many who have died in the war on terror and the even larger number of people who have become victims of terrorism (or counterterrorism), the idea that terrorism cannot be defeated sounds dreadful, if not inexcusable. Were all these efforts and sacrifices in vain and will terrorists simply get away with it as they are undefeatable? These questions and feelings could not only scare a lot of people, they are also exactly what terrorists want. As explained and discussed in the first chapter, terrorists want to spread dread and fear, and the idea that they might be undefeatable can contribute to that. Thus, if terrorism indeed cannot be defeated governments may need to change their counterterrorism policies. It might imply that the primary focus should be not on fighting groups, but on trying to prevent terrorism from occurring in the first place, or investing in target hardening and research into the causes of terrorism.

And what if we find out that terrorism can be defeated? In that case we need to know what exactly leads to its defeat. There are many possible causes that can affect the three key actors in this game, or what Audrey Kurth Cronin (2009, pp. 7-8) calls the terrorist triad: the terrorist group the government and the audience. She argues that 'some pathways of decline are more likely to be under the control of the state, other mainly relate to a non-state group's activity and its tendency to implode, and still others reflect the influence and opinions of observers'. The only way to understand how terrorism ends is to analyse the dynamic relationship between all three actors. We primarily focus on the role of the state and its counterterrorism policies. If we know if and how these actors can contribute to defeating terrorism and under what circumstances, that offers opportunities to improve these policies or provide a clear warning not to make use of certain practices or strategies.

Can terrorism not be defeated?

The picture that has been painted by generals, politicians and heads of state regarding the chances of defeating terrorism has been rather bleak. Or perhaps we should call the remarks by General Sir David Richards, President George W. Bush and King Abdullah II realistic. Terrorism is not a war, as the general rightly points out. It is a phenomenon that perhaps cannot be defeated, but only contained. The terrorists may possibly defeat themselves. By attacking civilians, they may eventually discredit themselves, as Bush suggested. And King Abdullah II is probably right and realistic when he says that there is evil in the world and that it is here to stay. At the same time, he also suggests that a solution to the Israeli-Palestinian conflict would strongly contribute to stability within the region and reduce the threat of terrorism. So there are things governments and societies can do, even according to those who do not believe terrorism can be defeated.

A scholar with a different take on the defeat or end of types of terrorism and individual terrorist groups is the earlier-mentioned David Rapoport. He distinguished four waves of terrorism and concluded that those waves – after a few decades – gradually fade out. However, he also observed several examples of a defeated terrorist group and even of one particular type of terrorism. Rapoport (2004, p. 60) concluded that the new left wave of terrorism slowly started to peter out in the 1980s. He wrote, '[r]evolutionary terrorists were defeated in one country after another'. These terrorist organisations of the new left wave were cracked down on and dismantled by governments. The collapse of the Soviet Union and the end of the Cold War were arguably the final nail in the coffin, as leftist terrorist organisations lost a primary source of material support. Moreover, these groups lost their appeal as, in the eyes of many, communism had arguably failed.

Defeated 'new left wave' terrorist organisation

The Red Army Faction (RAF) can be divided into three separate 'generations'. The first was operative between 1970 and 1972, led by Baader and Ensslin. Their most well-known attacks include the bombing of the US military headquarters in Heidelberg in May 1972. After the arrest of the leaders of the first generation, RAF activities were carried on by several sub-factions. These people still acknowledged the authority of their predecessors and Baader and Ensslin were able to keep in touch with these new groups and coordinate some of the activities from jail. It is this so-called 'second generation' that was responsible for the most infamous RAF actions: the killings of German businessmen and a federal prosecutor. The suicide of the leaders of the first generation caused disillusion among many of the remaining members. A wave of arrests urged some of them to reconsider their future plans and start a new life abroad. The remaining members who were still active were labelled the 'third generation'. They were responsible for several killings and other violent acts. The last attack took place in 1993, and in 1998 the last members declared the RAF to be dissolved. The main factors that contributed to the decline of the RAF were a general fatigue and burnout that had struck the group that can be linked to the collapse of the communist regimes in 1989 and the subsequent end of the Cold War. Also the decline in support from the German public to almost zero resulted in a loss of motivation among the last remaining members for continuing their struggle.

BOX 5.15   DEFEATED 'NEW LEFT WAVE' TERRORIST ORGANISATION

To what extent can we, in the light of Rapoport's remarks, attribute the defeat of third-wave terrorism to counterterrorism efforts? Is there a way that allows us to measure the correlation between such measures and the gradual disappearance of leftist terrorism? Were these leftist terrorist organisations destined to perish as the third wave gradually petered out, or did these groups and networks cease to exist simply because of the fall of the Berlin Wall and the collapse of the Soviet Union? How can we know for sure that the end of the new left wave can be considered an example of defeat? (see also box 5.15).

One study that systematically analysed what causes terrorism to end is the report by Seth Jones and Martin Libicki of the RAND Corporation (2008), 'How Terrorist Groups End: Lessons for Countering al Qa'ida'. For this study which tried to answer the question at a more general level, they examined 648 terrorist groups that existed between 1968 and 2006 and determined if and how they had ceased to exist. In their report they distinguish four major reasons why terrorist groups ended:

1. because of the work of local police and intelligence services.
2. because of military force.
3. because they joined the political process.
4. because the terrorist groups were victorious – achieving their stated goals.

Jones and Libicki also mentioned a fifth – minor – reason: the splintering of groups. However, in that case the end of a group does not signal the end of terrorism. Additionally, its demise is the product of its own members, possibly with no connection with counterterrorism measures. Therefore it is excluded from our analysis on the issue whether or not terrorism can be defeated.

Let us have a closer look at the four major explanations. Do they provide reasons to challenge the idea that terrorism cannot be defeated? Have the groups investigated by Jones and Libicki ended because of successful counterterrorism policies?

The first major reason why terrorist groups end is, according to the RAND report, because of the work of local police and intelligence services. Counterterrorism measures include the collection of information on terrorist groups, penetrating cells, disruption and arresting key members. In this regard, Lindsay Clutterbuck mentions, for example, the efforts by US law enforcement officers who tracked down two members of Hezbollah who were raising money by smuggling tobacco (2004, p. 146). In addition to that, general police work can lead to the arrest of terrorists, as many terrorists are also involved in other criminal activities, as the example of the member of Hezbollah also indicates. Jones and Libicki argue that police and intelligence actors, unlike, for example, the military, are locally embedded and, therefore, have a better understanding of the environment. In other words, they see more and have better contacts with communities that constitute the additional eyes and ears on the ground. The cluster of law enforcement measures that have contributed to the end of terrorist organisations further includes developing anti-terrorism legislation and criminalising certain activities. The decapitation of terrorist organisations that we discussed in the previous section, in this case mainly the arrest of leaders, is also part of this category of reasons why terrorist groups ended. The short label for this category is policing, and according to Jones and Libicki the wide variety of measures under this label accounts for 40 per cent of the cases in which terrorist groups end (see also box 5.16).

Importance of policing in counterterrorism

In a volume on counterterrorism policing (2008), Sharon Pickering, Jude McCulloch and David Wright-Neville show the importance of the role of the police as well as its challenges and dilemmas when dealing with terrorism. According to the authors, 'Terrorist attacks on New York and Washington, European cities like London and Madrid, and the subsequent declaration of the "war on terror", are marks of a changed national and global environment in which the threat of terrorist attack and the need for effective counterterrorism policies have become issues of immediate political and social concern. Police organizations have a key role in the formation and implementation of government counterterrorism strategies. Accordingly, as part of national counterterrorism responses, police services are increasingly required to blend law enforcement with responsibilities for national defence. Incorporating law enforcement in national defence changes the nature of police work as traditionally conceptualised. The changed expectations in relation to law enforcement give rise to a number of opportunities and challenges particularly in relation to the community policing ideal that most police services adhere to and the sustainable and positive engagement with culturally diverse communities'. The book primarily looks at the Australian context, but also contains international comparisons with the US, UK, Canada and South Africa. It examines the nature and impact of counterterrorism on policing, diverse communities, legislation and policy and on the media.

BOX 5.16   IMPORTANCE OF POLICING IN COUNTERTERRORISM

The second strategy concerns the use of the military in dealing with terrorism. This particular counterterrorism measure or approach involves the use of military forces to capture or kill terrorist members or to fight against states that support terrorists. According to the RAND report, sometimes the threat of force or constant surveillance may be sufficient, pushing terrorist organisations to be always on the run. This age-old way of trying to defeat terrorist organisations is, however, not particularly successful. According to Jones and Libicki, only 7 per cent of terrorist groups that have ended since 1968 have ceased to exist because of military force. This relatively low number may come as a surprise, especially in light of the enormous efforts and sacrifices made in the Global War on Terror.

This limited success of the use of military force is related to the fact that most terrorist organisations are small and do not tend to employ conventional organised forces unless they are taking part in an insurgency against a government. In that particular case, military forces can be of more use, as they are generally larger and better equipped than police forces for going into battle. In the case of Islamic State, which managed to capture and occupy large parts of Syria and Iraq, it took several international coalitions with large military forces to deal with its thousands of jihadist fighters and successfully destroy the self-proclaimed caliphate. But this is an exception to the rule. In general, according to Timothy Hoyt (2004, pp. 172-173), 'traditional military methods are difficult to apply to terrorism', given the differences between conventional armies and terrorist organisations in terms of, among other things, size and tactical preferences. He argues that the military is poorly equipped to combat such a threat. Moreover, according to Hoyt, Jones and Libicki, the use of (massive) military power can alienate the local population and therefore be counter-productive.

Terrorist organisations joining a political process

Jones and Libicki show that terrorism can end after terrorist organisations join a political process. There are several well-known examples of this. In Europe, perhaps the ultimate example is the case of Northern Ireland. After much violence and a lengthy peace process, in 1998 most parties signed the so-called 'Good Friday Agreement'. This agreement regulated political, civil and cultural rights, justice and policing and the decommissioning of weapons. The last took time. In July 2005, after several rounds of negotiation, the IRA announced the formal end of its armed campaign against British rule in Northern Ireland. Other examples of terrorist groups joining the political process include the African National Congress (ANC) of Nelson Mandela in South Africa. In Nepal, the Communist Party of Nepal-Maoist, after a bloody struggle with the absolute monarchy, turned to politics in 2006. It even won the elections in 2008. In the Middle East, the Palestine Liberation Organisation (PLO) is probably the best example, and in Latin America since 2017 the FARC can be added to the list of terrorist organisations that disarmed themselves and joined a political process.

BOX 5.17   TERRORIST ORGANISATIONS JOINING A POLITICAL PROCESS

The third major reason why terrorism ends is that terrorist organisations join a political process. This possibility of entering politics depends on the terrorist organisation's goals. According to Jones and Libicki (2008, p. viii), 'The narrower the goals of a terrorist organization, the more likely it can achieve them without violent action—and the more likely the government and terrorist group may be able to reach a negotiated settlement'. In other words, the more societal and political changes a terrorist organisation tends to pursue, the more difficult it is for it to renounce violent tactics to achieve its goals and make the transition to conventional politics. The decision to join a political process is the outcome of a cost-benefit analysis and the conclusion that pursuing the goals through non-violent, political means will result in greater benefits and less cost than violent tactics. In other words, renouncing violence is simply a more cost-efficient way to achieve certain political goals (for examples of terrorist organisations that joined a political process see box 5.17).

The steps taken by terrorist organisations in joining a political process happen more often than many might assume. Of all the analysed endings of terrorist organisations, 43 per cent were caused by the fact that those organisations joined the political process. Does that mean that they are defeated? This is difficult to determine. Defeat implies that there is a winner and a loser. A move into politics as such cannot be called a defeat for a terrorist organisation. But it could be argued that it is a defeat for the use of violence because non-violent methods prove to be more promising and successful. Additionally, there are cases in which terrorist organisations were invited to join peace negotiations actually because of the use of violence. In these cases one could argue that the use of violence was rewarded and therefore successful. Hence, terrorist organisations joining a political process and thus abandoning terrorism provides only partial insight into the question whether or not terrorism can be defeated.

The fourth and last major reason for the ending of terrorist groups is that the terrorist groups were victorious. Ten per cent of the total number of groups that ceased to exist ended their terrorist activities because they accomplished their goals in some way or another. According to Jones and Libicki (2008, p. 33), '[w]hen they have achieved victory, it has usually been because they had narrow goals, such as policy or territorial change'. In fact, no terrorist group that sought empire or social revolution has achieved victory since 1968. It should be noted that Cronin (2009), in her book, *How Terrorism Ends: Understanding the Decline and Demise of Terrorist Campaigns,* re-examined the success rate of terrorist groups and found that less than 5 per cent of them prevailed over governments. Apparently, also in this case, there are different ways to look at the data, but the main conclusion remains the same. Very few terrorists achieve their stated goals, and among the 'successful' terrorist groups most had very limited or narrow goals (see box 5.18).

Victorious terrorist organisations

An important exception to the rule that terrorist cannot achieve wider social and political goals by using terrorism is the case of the African National Congress (ANC). This organisation carried out attacks from the 1960s until 1989 and managed to become a legal political actor in 1990, after which its leader, Nelson Mandela, became president of South Africa in 1994. What about other examples? Can you name other terrorist organisations that managed to achieve regime change or otherwise managed to achieve their political goals?

What about the IRA in Northern Ireland, what about the FARC in Colombia, and what about the Palestinian organisations in Israel/Palestine? Were they (partly) victorious? What about less well-known left-wing or right-wing groups and what about jihadist organisations? It seems that the list of victorious terrorist organisations is rather short.

BOX 5.18   VICTORIOUS TERRORIST ORGANISATIONS

What do we make of the outcome of the report by Jones and Libicki in relation to the assumption that terrorism cannot be defeated? Of the 648 groups that were examined, 244 were still active, 136 splintered (thereby ending the group but not ending the terrorism), leaving 268 that, according to Jones and Libicki, had completely ceased to exist. This represents more than 40 per cent of the total number of terrorist groups. Most of these 268 groups ended because they joined the political process (43 per cent of those that ceased to exist) and because of the work of local police and intelligence services (40 per cent). Of minor importance were victory (10 per cent) and military force (7 per cent).

These figures clearly support the argument that terrorism can indeed be defeated. The use of counterterrorism measures by the police, intelligence services and the military together explain almost half of the cases in which terrorist groups ended. We could question whether the most important reason for ending terrorist organisations, however, joining the political process, entails the notion that they were defeated. Defeat implies the presence of both a winner and a loser. In this regard, such a move into politics should not count as a defeat, as terrorists then decided their own fate. Nevertheless, although the terrorist organisation has not necessarily been defeated, the instrument of terrorism, as a phenomenon, has, since those who were previously engaged in it renounced terrorism and opted for non-violent means. In these cases, rather than an organisation, group or network, it is the tool of terrorism that has been defeated.

In order to make any valid claims with regard to the assumption that terrorism cannot be defeated, as stated by many politicians and even generals, it is important to define clearly what one means by 'terrorism'. When referring to terrorist organisations, empirical evidence suggests that terrorism can be defeated by counterterrorism measures. If we look at Jones and Libicki's findings, the assumption that terrorism cannot be defeated is clearly false and can even be called a myth.

However, when we refer to terrorism as a phenomenon we come to a different conclusion, as it seems unlikely that it can be defeated. Rapoport's four waves of modern terrorism show that, although waves generally tend to fade out, they will eventually be succeeded by new ones with their own unique characteristics. The anarchist wave has been succeeded by the anti-colonial wave which, in turn, was followed by the new left wave. Now, more than 30 years after the end of leftist terrorism, we mainly face religiously inspired terrorism, which could be followed by a new, as yet unknown wave of terrorism. Moreover, Rapoport has shown that even when waves fade out, some groups or movements that belonged to that wave may continue to exist for a long time.

Nonetheless, the study by Jones and Libicki proves that governments and societies should not remain passive, let alone be defeatist about the possibilities of dealing with terrorism and terrorist groups. This is important to note against a background of much pessimism regarding the possibility of forcing or convincing al-Qaeda, Islamic State and other large terrorist groups like the FARC in Colombia to end their terrorist activities. In this line of thought, partly depending on whether one puts the emphasis on individual groups

Assumptions about counterterrorism

or the phenomenon of terrorism as a whole, we can label the assumption that terrorism cannot be defeated either false or partly true. Yes, there will probably always be terrorism, but many terrorist organisations will end their terrorist activities as a result of the successful work of the police, intelligence services, military and other relevant actors. Hence, terrorists can be defeated.

Key points

· Leading experts and political leaders have expressed doubts about the possibility of defeating terrorism.
· Empirical evidence shows that terrorist organisations can cease to exist as a result of policing, the use of military force or because they join the political process.
· Nevertheless, Rapoport's theory regarding different waves of terrorism suggests that each wave will eventually be replaced by a new one. Hence, terrorism as a phenomenon cannot be defeated.
· Depending on the interpretation of the assumption, we can label the notion that terrorism cannot be defeated as either false or partly true.

5.6 Assumption five: Terrorism can best be dealt with by way of a holistic or wide approach

In the previous chapter we discussed and investigated five assumptions about terrorism. Some of these assumptions that are commonly believed to be true could not be labelled as such. Terrorism is not necessarily the consequence of poverty. Neither is it accurate to suggest that all terrorist are crazy and irrational actors. Furthermore, it sometimes proved difficult to state whether or not an assumption could be labelled false, a myth or partly true, as there are many ways to look at these notions and at terrorism in general. Its lethality and level of success, for instance, can be measured in different ways. Finally, also with regard to the assumptions about counterterrorism, there seem to be several possibilities for determining whether or not they are supported by empirical evidence and academic literature, leading to different outcomes. Decapitation might work in some cases, but not in others. Moreover the side effects could make it a practice that governments would do better to refrain from using, especially with regard to targeted killings using drones. In the previous section we learned that terrorism cannot be defeated, but that counterterrorism measures can defeat terrorist organisations.

Having discussed and analysed these assumptions about terrorism and counterterrorism, we see clearly that governments and societies are dealing with highly complex and ever changing phenomena. Given this complexity and the many different angles that can be and have been used to approach terrorism, what strategy or approach should be recommended when trying to counter terrorism? The final assumption will focus on this question. We will investigate the assumption that terrorism can best be dealt with by way of a so-called holistic, wide or comprehensive approach. To what extent is such an approach feasible or workable? What are the alternatives? And how can we assess the effectiveness of many different counterterrorism policies in order to see whether or not such a holistic or wide approach is indeed the best one? To answer these questions we will compare the assumption with empirical evidence and expert and scholarly literature on this subject.

It is first of all necessary to explain what is meant by a holistic approach in counterterrorism. It is also known as a comprehensive or wide approach or is sometimes referred to as a grand strategy. The last was defined by Martha Crenshaw (2004, p. 75) as 'a more inclusive conception that explains how a state's full range of resources can be adapted to achieve national security'. According to Crenshaw, such a strategy consists of three elements, as it identifies the interests of the state, the potential threats, and the tools available to deal with those threats. Moreover, a grand strategy or a holistic approach should allow for flexibility. The content of these three key elements must change when the shape, size and nature of terrorism changes. In general, descriptions of a holistic or wide approach to terrorism – or any other complex societal problem for that matter – often include the phrase 'involving a wide range of instruments' or 'involving a wide range of actors'. With regard to terrorism, they also often include the words 'preventive and repressive measures' or 'soft and hard measures'. According to Bruce Hoffman, a combination of both is required, given the complexity and multidimensional nature of terrorism (2001). In addition, the terms frequently refer to the need to deal with the complexity and multidimensional aspects of terrorism and counterterrorism, and most descriptions of the approach list a range of concrete policy areas – from the procurement of intelligence to the prosecution of the perpetrators of terrorist attacks. The question remains whether or not such a wide approach is the best one in dealing with terrorism.

Why does it matter to know whether or not terrorism can best be dealt with by way of a holistic or wide approach?

As we learned in the previous section, different policy instruments can have different outcomes. Jones and Libicki's research has shown that countering insurgencies generally requires military force. However, under other circumstances, military force is often not the best tool or instrument for dealing with terrorism. Therefore, relying just on a military approach does not seem to be the best approach. The same holds true for other approaches that focus on one or only a few instruments. Therefore, it seems obvious that a wide or holistic approach may be the best approach. But is it feasible and can we measure the effectiveness and efficiency of such an approach? There might be the risk that a holistic approach develops into a confetti approach consisting of many different micro-projects instead of dealing with the key and underlying issues. Additionally, there may be many other risks and challenges that could make this approach look good or logical, but impossible to implement. Hence, we need to know whether or not terrorism can best be dealt with by way of a wide or holistic approach and to compare it with empirical data and academic and expert literature on this topic.

Can terrorism best be dealt with by a holistic or wide approach?

A number of high-level politicians and well-known public figures have advocated a holistic approach to deal effectively with terrorism. One of them is the United Nations Secretary General, Ban Ki-moon (2013). In remarks delivered to the United Nations Security Council's open debate on combating terrorism in Africa in May 2013, he said that success in the fight against groups such as the Nigeria-based Boko Haram, al-Qaeda in the Islamic Maghreb, and the Somalia-based al-Shabaab would require greater and more holistic efforts. He said, '[m]ilitary advances, important as they are, will not by themselves bring an end to terrorism in Africa. This struggle must go forward on many fronts, including by addressing the conditions that are conducive to the spread of terrorism'. Ban Ki-moon added that the lack of development and the absence of the rule of law allow terrorist groups to recruit across communities and build their ranks. Furthermore, criminal activities, such as human trafficking and illegal arms and drugs trade, are an important source of income for such groups and networks. Ban Ki-moon argued that in order to crack down on terrorist activity in the region, it is important to improve the rule of law, spur economic development and induce political transformation. He finished by stating that a one-dimensional approach would relocate the threat instead of terminating it.

The urgency of a holistic approach is also felt in Pakistan. Early in 2013, Prime Minister Raja Pervez Ashraf stressed its importance with regard to the fight against terrorism during a ceremony at the National Police Academy in Islamabad. As Pakistan is one of the states most affected by terrorism, Ashraf advocated a wide approach for similar reasons to those put forward by Ban Ki-moon. Additionally, he stressed the essence of close ties between police forces and the community, as they would be able to deliver vital information about suspects and play an important role in the social condemnation of violent tactics. Such a relationship between (local) law enforcement agencies and civil society would be possible only if the former were to enjoy a certain level of credibility and respect. According to the Prime Minister, the culture of abuse among the police forces has severely damaged their reputation and limited their ability to combat terrorism effectively. What we can learn from these remarks is that a holistic approach is impossible if there is distrust between the different actors – the general public and the police being two very important ones.

The pleas of Ban Ki-moon and Raja Pervez Ashraf for a more comprehensive approach are very much in line with the counterterrorism approach of the United Nations (see box 5.19). In the autumn of 2006, the General Assembly unanimously adopted the 'United Nations Global Counterterrorism Strategy' (2006, pp. 3-23). This strategy was the first ever comprehensive, collective and internationally approved framework for tackling the problem of terrorism. It consists of four pillars: (1) measures to address the conditions conducive to the spread of terrorism; (2) measures to prevent and combat terrorism; (3) measures to build states' capacity to prevent and combat terrorism and to strengthen the role of the UN system in this regard; and (4) measures to ensure respect for human rights for all and the rule of law as the fundamental basis of the fight against terrorism.

The UN approach to counterterrorism

In its plan of action, the states members of the UN resolve to take urgent action to prevent and combat terrorism in all its forms and manifestations and recognise that international cooperation and any measures to prevent and combat terrorism must comply with obligations under international law. The measures are divided into four categories:

1) Measures to address the conditions conducive to the spread of terrorism: including prolonged unresolved conflicts, lack of rule of law and violations of human rights, ethnic, national and religious discrimination, political exclusion and socio-economic marginalisation.

2) Measures to prevent and combat terrorism: in particular by denying terrorists access to the means to carry out their attacks, to their targets and to the desired impact of their attacks.

3) Measures to build states' capacity to prevent and combat terrorism and to strengthen the role of the UN system in this regard: recognising that capacity-building in all states is a core element of the global counterterrorism effort, and enhancing coordination and coherence within the UN system in promoting international cooperation in countering terrorism.

4) Measures to ensure respect for human rights for all and the rule of law as the fundamental basis of the fight against terrorism: to reaffirm that the promotion and protection of human rights for all and the rule of law are essential to all components of the strategy, and recognising that effective counterterrorism measures and the protection of human rights are not conflicting goals, but complementary and mutually reinforcing.

United Nations General Assembly. (2006, September 20). GA resolution A/RES/60/288 on the United Nations Global Counterterrorism Strategy.

BOX 5.19   THE UN APPROACH TO COUNTERTERRORISM

The working titles of these four different dimensions indicate the breadth of their strategy, as it aims at various aspects of terrorism. These different pillars anchor the UN's counterterrorism activities into the broader agenda of this international organisation, which is active on many fronts and in many areas and countries. Furthermore, the UN encourages its member states to adopt similar holistic approaches when dealing with terrorism on the domestic level.

One country that has adopted a wide approach to terrorism is Indonesia. Its national counterterrorism strategy has been the subject of various studies by different scholars. According to one of them, Noorhaidi Hasan (2012), Indonesia has developed a balanced model for responding to Islamist radicalism and terrorism by carefully combining 'hard' and 'soft' measures (see also box 5.20). The main approach has shifted from one based on maintaining security – with a strong role for the military – to one based on law enforcement in which the police have become the lead agency. Nevertheless, the 'hard' approach is still important and not without controversy. In the aftermath of the 2002 Bali bombings which killed over 200 people, Indonesian law enforcement agencies were strengthened with a counterterrorism unit, 'Special Detachment 88', specialising in arresting terrorists and responding to terrorist attacks. This force in 2010 alone arrested approximately 100 and killed 16, the latter event resulting in questions being raised by human rights organisations at home and abroad. Notwithstanding these concerns, Indonesia today is less prone to major terrorist attacks than it was in the early 2000s, in part because of this 'hard' approach. However, the police also achieved a degree of success with soft measures such as their deradicalisation programme for detainees. This 'Rehabilitation and Dialogue Process with Prisoners' focuses on Islamic militants and offers counselling and guidance. It also pays additional attention to other aspects, such as education, employment and housing. According to the Institute for Strategic Dialogue (2012, pp. 17-18), the results have been rather positive, partly thanks to the offering of such benefits, which increased the willingness of the participants to cooperate and eventually to deradicalise.

Noorhaidi Hasan on Indonesia's balanced approach

In a report on counterterrorism strategies in Indonesia, Algeria and Saudi Arabia, Hasan (2012) evaluated the case of Indonesia. He shows how the country's approach to dealing with terrorism shifted from an 'enemy–centric' approach that was characterised by repression and gradually developed into a population–centric strategy that carefully combines 'hard' and 'soft' measures. Instead of the military, the police were designated as the leading agency in Indonesia's counterterrorism efforts, which were based on the notion of law enforcement. There is also a relatively important role for civil society in the campaign against radicalism and terrorism. Hasan argues that Indonesia has come a long way in the transition from a repressive approach to a balanced one, but still faces many challenges. Nonetheless, he believes the Indonesian experience in tackling the threats of Islamist radicalism and terrorism might be useful for other countries that are seeking inspiration for their own policies and programmes.

BOX 5.20   NOORHAIDI HASAN ON INDONESIA'S BALANCED APPROACH

191

The Indonesian approach and the United Nations Global Counterterrorism Strategy have been applauded by both politicians and scholars. But do they actually work? Or, in other words, how does one test the assumption that terrorism can best be dealt with by a holistic approach?

One scholar who has been very clear on this issue is Bruce Hoffman (2001), who is one of the leading scholars in the field of terrorism and counterterrorism studies. In his evidence before the 'Subcommittee on Terrorism and Homeland Security' of the US House of Representatives, which took place two weeks after 9/11, he stated that only a comprehensive or holistic approach would work. He said, '[t]he articulation and development of a "comprehensive, fully coordinated national strategy ... is not simply an intellectual exercise, but must be at the foundation of any effective counterterrorism policy'. Failure to do so historically has undermined the counterterrorism efforts of other democratic nations. Referring to the aftermath of the 9/11 attacks Hoffman stated, '[w]hat is now therefore clearly needed is a comprehensive effort that seeks to knit together more tightly, and provide greater organizational guidance and focus, to the formidable array of capabilities and instruments the U.S. can bring to bear in the struggle against terrorism'. The key words here are coordination and cooperation as well as focus.

One country that has invested a lot in improving the coordination between various relevant actors in the field of counterterrorism is The Netherlands. The authorities and many experts seem to agree on the need for a holistic or wide approach. The most noticeable product of this collective notion is 'National counterterrorism strategy 2011-2015' of the National Coordinator for Security and Counterterrorism and the subsequent 'National Counterterrorism Strategy 2016-2020' (see box 5.21). This document is clearly based on the assumption that terrorism can best be dealt with by a holistic approach. Its main point of departure is that an effective approach to terrorism can succeed only if not only the acts of violence themselves, but also the processes that preceded these acts are tackled. Different responses of a more repressive nature are required for those who have already taken the step towards being prepared to commit violence, or who are on the point of doing so. Thus, the strategy combines both preventive and repressive measures as part of the Dutch approach.

The Netherlands' counterterrorism strategy

As formulated in the Netherlands' 'National Counterterrorism Strategy 2011-2015', a cohesive and comprehensive approach is needed to deal with terrorism. Since 2005, changes in legislation have been implemented to increase the cohesion, coordination and effectiveness of Dutch counterterrorism policy. The most important achievement cannot, however, be expressed in terms of a law, rule or instrument. The fact that so many players are active in counterterrorism in such a wide range of networks requires cohesion, harmonisation and coordination. The cohesion between intelligence, policy and operation has grown in size and strength in recent years, thanks to a central coordination structure. A comprehensive and strategic vision of the future of counterterrorism is necessary in order to give direction to all parties involved in it and to maintain the strength of all the links in the security chain. The objective of the strategy is to reduce the risk of terrorist attacks and to limit any damage following a possible attack.

BOX 5.21   THE NETHERLANDS' COUNTERTERRORISM STRATEGY

A holistic approach seems compelling, if not necessary, in order to counter terrorism effectively. However, not all experts and scholars agree on the notion that a holistic approach is the best way to deal with the terrorist threat. They have pointed out a number of shortcomings.

The first problem of a comprehensive strategy is that it does not prioritise a finite amount of resources and attention. Governments do not have unlimited budgets and, in some periods, face the prospect of having to implement severe budget cuts, such as happened after the financial crisis in 2008 and the COVID-19 crisis. This makes it more difficult to fund a holistic approach that does not have a clear and demarcated focus but encompasses a wide variety of actors and measures across the public sector.

Second, the proponents of a comprehensive approach to counterterrorism tend to overlook the enormous pressure on governments and agencies to do something and to do it immediately. While a comprehensive approach may be vital to prevent terrorism in the long run, ad hoc security measures that detect, deter and disrupt terrorist operations still remain a preferred component in the fight against terrorism. Most of these preferred measures are hard measures and visible ones. Think of the arrest of alleged terrorists, hard security measures in front of embassies or increasing the number of patrols around airports.

Perhaps the most important criticism of a comprehensive approach relates to the chance to implement such a wide approach successfully. More often than not, comprehensive approaches leave unanswered important questions, such as who is responsible and who takes the lead, who has the financial and political means and how to make the various actors cooperate. In many countries, governments have established counterterrorism coordinators or so-called fusion centres designed to promote information-sharing at the national level between relevant agencies in the field of counterterrorism. But such agencies and coordinators can only do so much. The field of counterterrorism is, and has always been, a domain in which there are many challenges to cooperation. There is the obstacle of secrecy, there are legal barriers, and cooperation between certain actors does not come naturally. Think of cooperation between the public and the police in certain countries, as mentioned by Pakistan's former Prime Minister. Add to that the need for international cooperation to deal with this cross-border phenomenon and it becomes quite obvious that it is easier to draft a holistic approach than to implement one. In other words, it is easier said than done.

Finally, it is extremely difficult to measure its effectiveness. How does one do that, or how does one compare a wide approach with other, more one-dimensional approaches? These questions bring us to one of the most striking and serious flaws in both counterterrorism and the study of it: the lack of evaluation studies. In 2006, three authors, Cynthia Lum, Leslie Kennedy and Alison Sherley, published an often-quoted article in which they were looking for evaluation research. They discovered that there is an almost total absence of high quality, scientific evaluation evidence on counterterrorism strategies.

Academia has produced very little to evaluate strategies and measures. Even though this article was written in 2006, their main conclusion is still holds good today. This is also the case for governmental agencies. Despite the fact that governments have spent millions or billions on counterterrorism, only a very few of them – The Netherlands is a positive example – have looked into the effectiveness of their policies and approaches.

The independent evaluation of the first national counterterrorism strategy by Utrecht University (2016) observed that the comprehensive approach works when the threat is very visible, but that the plans unintentionally leave room for selective attention, leading to an emphasis on repressive and security-oriented measures. In the absence of a clear threat, partners also drift away from each other. The evaluation report also states that the effects of counterterrorism policies cannot be evaluated directly. The impact of measures is extremely difficult to determine because policy effects can also be attributed to other circumstances and because multiple instruments are applied simultaneously. This makes it difficult for an effect – such as a person deciding not to travel to fight with IS in Syria or Iraq – to be attributed to one specific measure, such as withdrawing a passport. The context of counterterrorism strategies is thus characterised by complexity: the developments are unpredictable, the number of actors involved is very large, and there are few scientifically supported standards which can be used to assess the quality or effectiveness of a strategy.

The extreme difficulty of measuring the effectiveness of counterterrorism policies and strategies is possibly one of the reasons that there are only a few scholars who have looked into this. In 2018, more than a decade after the study by Lum and others, Alex Schmid and James Forest still observed that there is a continuing dearth of evaluation studies of countering violent extremism programmes and counterterrorism policies in general. The authors also note that there are only a few evaluations of training manuals on counterterrorism: an evaluation of public- and private-sector products. There are a few exceptions, and in particular think tanks (RUSI in the UK, RAND in the US, and ICCT in The Netherlands) seem to have picked up on this (see boxes 5.22 and 7.07).

Handbook on monitoring and evaluation in CT

Laura Dawson, Charlie Edwards and Calum Jeffray (2014) observed that it is extremely difficult to demonstrate success in countering violent extremism (CVE). They noted that good monitoring and evaluation systems are crucial for effective implementation of policies and to ensure accountability. There are only a handful of examples in the public domain of CVE activities with monitoring and evaluation components. Therefore, they wrote a handbook designed as an introduction to this policy area. It examines the literature on useful practices in monitoring and evaluation, reflects current thinking in those governments conducting evaluation exercises, and provides a set of basic tools for policy-makers and practitioners working on CVE.

BOX 5.22   HANDBOOK ON MONITORING AND EVALUATION IN CT

It should be repeated that the complex nature of terrorism makes it very difficult to measure the effectiveness of counterterrorism measures, even when focusing on individual measures. The idea of assessing a country's holistic or comprehensive approach to terrorism should be considered extremely difficult. Peter Romaniuk and Naureen Chowdhury Fink (2012, p. 8) describe it well when they claim that the biggest challenge lies in the fact that evaluators are concerned with the measurement of a non-event (see also box 5.23). Without such a dependent variable, it is hard to assess which independent variables contributed and which did not. Furthermore, it is important to realise that solid evaluation mechanisms are not always in the best interests of policy-makers as evaluations could bring to light the fact that certain policies that are deemed politically desirable are actually not very effective. Or, worse, evaluations could serve as a political instrument to give legitimacy to politically desirable policies that do not work in practice or that have serious negative side effects.

'From Input to Impact: Evaluating Terrorism Prevention Programs'
In the years since 9/11, many countries have formulated policies or even a strategy to deal with terrorism. They have invested public money in a wide range of measures. Now, some years later it is time to look back and assess whether or not these measures were cost-effective and if they are also effective to counter the threats that states and societies face today. A report of the Center on Global Counterterrorism Cooperation (2012) 'From Input to Impact: Evaluating Terrorist Prevention Programs' focuses on these and other questions: how can the effectiveness of prevention policies be measured? What approaches have states advanced in evaluating the impact of terrorism prevention initiatives? In responding to this challenge, can lessons be gleaned from efforts to evaluate programmes in related policy domains? Their report provides an initial discussion of these questions. It draws on the discussions during an expert meeting on measuring effectiveness in counterterrorism programming, as well as discussions with experts and government officials and an initial literature review.

BOX 5.23   'FROM INPUT TO IMPACT: EVALUATING TERRORISM PREVENTION PROGRAMS'

Where do the above-mentioned observations lead us when trying to answer the initial question whether or not terrorism can best be deal with by way of a holistic, wide or comprehensive approach? As we have witnessed, there is relatively little empirical evidence that supports or challenges this assumption. Most among the relatively few evaluation studies focus on the impact and effectiveness of (sets of) individual instruments and not on strategies, let alone holistic approaches. However, most scholars seem to agree that terrorism does require such an approach or a grand strategy. The same holds for political leaders such as former UN Secretary General Ban Ki-moon and the UN itself. However, we have also observed that a wide approach has its shortcomings. The various strategies look good on paper, but sometimes fail to answer important questions, such as who takes the lead, how to coordinate the activities of all relevant actors and who carries the financial and political burden. Hence, we could argue that in theory a holistic approach might be the best approach, but that there are many obstacles when putting this into practice. Against this backdrop, we have to label the assumption that terrorism can best be dealt with by a holistic approach as partly true. We also should add that more evaluation studies are needed.

Key points

- Given the complexity of terrorism, it is important to deal with it in multiple ways, which is generally referred to as a holistic approach.
- Influential political leaders and important scholars have advocated a holistic approach.
- However, this approach also has it shortcomings, as it is costly, difficult to implement, and has not been properly evaluated.
- Based on these observations, we label the assumption that terrorism can best be dealt with by way of a holistic approach as partly true.

Bibliography

Abbas, T., Awan, I., & Marsden, J. (2021). Pushed to the edge: the consequences of the 'Prevent Duty' in de-radicalising pre-crime thought among British Muslim university students. *Race, Ethnicity and Education* [online first].

Al Jazeera. (2008). Eta 'military leader' arrested. *Al Jazeera*, 17 November 2008.

Amnesty International. (2004). *Threat and Humiliation: Racial profiling, Domestic Security, and Human Rights in the United States*. New York: Amnesty International.

Amnesty International. (2018). *Deadly Assistance: The role of European states in US drone strikes*. New York: Amnesty International.

Anderson, S. K., & Sloan, S. (2009). *Historical Dictionary of Terrorism* (third edition). Lanham: The Scarecrow Press.

Ashraf, R. P. (2013). *Opening Speech*. Address presented at Passing Out Parade of ASPs of 38th STP, Islamabad, Pakistan.

Ban Ki-moon. (2013). *Opening Debate Address to United National Security Council*. Address presented at the Security Council, New York, United States.

Benotman, N. (2010). Open Letter to Osama bin Laden. *Foreign Policy*, 10 September 2010.

Bergen, P. (2013). *Manhunt: The Ten Year Search for Bin Laden: from 9/11 to Abbottabad*. London: Vintage Books.

Bjørgo, T., & Horgan, J. (2008). *Leaving Terrorism Behind: Individual and Collective Disengagement*. New York: Routledge.

Bjørgo, T. (ed.). (1997). *Racist and right-wing violence in Scandinavia*. Oslo: Tano-Aschehoug.

Bloom, M. (2011). *Bombshell*. Philadelphia: University of Pennsylvania.

Bush, G. W. (2002). *State of the Union 2002*. Address presented at United States Congress, Washington D.C., United States.

Clutterbuck, L. (2004). Law Enforcement. In Cronin, A. K. & Ludes, J. M. (eds.). *Attacking Terrorism: Elements of a Grand Strategy* (140-161). Washington D.C.: Georgetown University Press.

CNN. (2010). Fareed Zakaria GPS: Interview with King Abdullah II of Jordan; Interview with John Yoo. *CNN*, 7 February 2010.

Crenshaw, M. (1981). The Causes of Terrorism. *Comparative Politics, 13*(4), 379-399.

Crenshaw, M. (2004). Terrorism, Strategies, and Grand Strategies. In Cronin, A. K. & Ludes, J. M. (eds.). *Attacking Terrorism: Elements of a Grand Strategy* (74-96). Washington D.C.: Georgetown University Press.

Cronin, A. K. (2009). *How Terrorism Ends: Understanding the Decline and Demise of Terrorist Campaigns*. Princeton: Princeton University Press.

Dawson, L., Edwards, C., Jeffray, C. (2014). *Learning and Adapting: The Use of Monitoring and Evaluation in Countering Violent Extremism: A Handbook for Practitioners*. London: RUSI.

Dean, G. (2007). Criminal Profiling in a Terrorism Context. In Kocsis, R. N. (ed.), *Criminal Profiling: International Theory, Research, and Practice* (169-188). Totowa: Humana Press.

Eijkman, Q. A. M., & Weggemans, D. (2012). Open Source Intelligence and Privacy Dilemmas: Is it Time to Reassess State Accountability? *Security and Human Rights, 23*(4), 285-297.

France 24. (2021). 'Total failure': The war on terror 20 years on. *France 24, 26* August 2021.

Gartenstein-Ross, D. (2007). *My Year Inside Radical Islam: A Memoir*. New York: Penguin Group.

Graaf, B. de. (2009). Counter-Narratives and the Unrehearsed Stories Counter-Terrorists Unwittingly Produce. *Perspectives on Terrorism*, *3*(2), 5-11.

Greenburg, M. (2011). *The Mad Bomber of New York. The Extraordinary True Story of the Manhunt that Paralyzed a City.* New York: Union Square Press.

Haaretz. (2011). Top Colombian Rebel Alfonso Cano Dies in Military Raid. *Haaretz*, 6 November 2011.

Haberman, M. (2011). Giuliani praises Obama's 'courage'. *Politico*, 5 February 2011.

Hasan, N. (2012). Towards a Population–Centric Strategy. In Meijer, R. (ed.). *Counter-Terrorism Strategies in Indonesia, Algeria and Saudi Arabia* (13-67). The Hague: Netherlands Institute of International Relations Clingendael.

Hoffman, B. (2001). *Testimony of Dr. Bruce Hoffman before the Subcommittee on Terrorism and Homeland Security, House Permanent Select Committee on Intelligence of the U.S. House of Representatives: Re-thinking Terrorism in Light of a War on Terrorism.* RAND Corporation: Santa Monica.

Hoffman, B. (2002). *Lessons of 9/11.* RAND Corporation: Santa Monica.

Horgan, J. (2008). From Profiles to Pathways and Roots to Routes: Perspectives from Psychology on Radicalization into Terrorism. *The ANNALS of the American Academy of Political and Social Science*, *618*(1), 80-94.

Horgan, J. (2009). *Walking Away From Terrorism: Accounts of Disengagement from Radical and Extremist Movements.* New York: Routledge.

Horgan, J., & Altier, M. B. (2012). The Future of Terrorist Deradicalization Programs. *Georgetown Journal of International Affairs*, *13*(2), 83-90.

Hoyt, T. D. (2004). Military Force. In Cronin, A. K., & Ludes, J. M. (eds.). *Attacking Terrorism: Elements of a Grand Strategy* (162-185). Washington D.C.: Georgetown University Press.

Human Rights Watch. (2010). *Letter to Prime Minister Julia Gillard: Australia: Press Indonesian Security Forces on Accountability.* 27 October 2010.

Institute for Strategic Dialogue. (2012). *Policy Briefing: Tackling Extremism: Deradicalization and Disengagement.* Copenhagen: Conference Report.

International Human Rights and Conflict Resolution Clinic (Stanford Law School) and Global Justice Clinic (NYU School Of Law). (2012). *Living Under Drones: Death, Injury, and Trauma to Civilians from US Drone Practices In Pakistan.*

Jones, S. G., & Libicki, M. C. (2008). *How Terrorist Groups End: Lessons for Countering al Qa'ida.* Santa Monica: RAND Corporation.

Jordan, J. (2009). When Heads Roll: Assessing the Effectiveness of Leadership Decapitation. *Security Studies*, *18*(4), 719-755.

Lum, C., Kennedy, L. W. & Sherley, A. J. (2006). The Effectiveness of Counter-Terrorism Strategies. *Campbell Systematic Reviews, 2*(1), 1-50.

Metropolitan Police. (2022). *Signs of possible terrorist activity*, https://www.met.police.uk/advice/advice-and-information/t/terrorism-in-the-uk/signs-of-possible-terrorist-activity/.

Minow, N. N., & Cate, F. H. (2006). Government Data Mining. In Kamien, D. G. (ed.). *The McGraw-Hill Homeland Security Handbook: The Definitive Guide for Law Enforcement, EMT, and all other Security Professionals* (1063-1088). New York: McGraw-Hill.

Murakami, H. (2000). *Underground. The Tokyo gas attack and the Japanese psyche.* New York: Vintage Books.

Nationaal Coördinator Terrorismebestrijding en Veiligheid. (2011). *National Counterterrorism strategy 2011-2015.* Den Haag: Ministerie van Veiligheid en Justitie.

Owen, M., & Maurer, K. (2012). *No Easy Day: The autobiography of a Navy Seal.* New York: Dutton Penguin.

Pickering, S., McCulloch J., & Wright-Neville D. (2008). *Counter-Terrorism Policing. Community, Cohesion and Security.* New York: Springer International.

Price, B. C. (2012). Targeting Top Terrorists: How Leadership Decapitation Contributes to Counterterrorism. *International Security, 36*(4), 9-46.

Rabasa, A. et al. (2010). *Deradicalizing Islamist Extremists.* Santa Monica: RAND Corporation.

Rapoport, D. C. (2004). Four Waves of Modern. In Cronin, A. K., & Ludes, J. M. (eds.). *Attacking Terrorism: Elements of a Grand Strategy* (46-73). Washington D.C.: Georgetown University Press.

Renard, T. (2020). Overblown: Exploring the Gap Between the Fear of Terrorist Recidivism and the Evidence. *CTC Sentinel, 13*(4), 1-11.

Romaniuk, P., & Fink, N. C. (2012). *From Input to Impact: Evaluating Terrorist Prevention Programs.* New York: Center on Global Counterterrorism Cooperation.

el Said, H. (2012). *Deradicalizing Islamists: Programs and their Impact in Muslim Majority States.* London: ICSR.

Sageman, M. (2004). *Understanding Terror Networks.* Philadelphia, University of Pennsylvania.

Schmid, A. P. (2013). Radicalisation, Deradicalisation, Counter-Radicalisation: A Conceptual Discussion and Literature Review. *ICCT Research Paper.* The Hague: ICCT.

Schmid, A. P., & Forest, J. J. (2018). Research desiderata: 150 un- and under-researched topics and themes in the field of (counter-)terrorism studies-a new list. *Perspectives on Terrorism, 12*(4), 68-76.

Strom, K., et al. (2010). *Building on Clues: Examining Successes and Failures in Detecting U.S. Terrorist Plots 1999-2009.* Institute for Homeland Security Solutions.

Speckhard, A., & Akhmedova, K. (2006). Black Widows: The Chechen Female Suicide Terrorists. In Schweitzer, Y. (ed.). *Female Suicide Terrorists* (63-80). Tel Aviv: Jaffe Center Publication.

The Telegraph. (2010). General Sir David Richards: Why we cannot defeat al-Qaeda. *The Telegraph*, 14 November 2010.

Today. (2004). *Bush: 'You Cannot Show Weakness in this World'. Today*, 30 August 2004.

Universiteit Utrecht. (2016). *Gericht, gedragen en geborgd interventievermogen? Evaluatie van de nationale contraterrorisme-strategie 2011-2015*. Utrecht: Universiteit Utrecht.

United Nations Commission on Human Rights. (2004). Commission holds special sitting on situation in occupied Palestinian territory following the killing of Sheikh Yassin. *UN Press Release, HR/CN/1057*.

United Nations General Assembly. (2006). *GA resolution A/RES/60/288 on the United Nations Global Counter-Terrorism Strategy*. New York: United Nations.

White House, The. (2011). *National Strategy for Counterterrorism*. Washington D.C.: White House.

6

Dealing with the impact of terrorism

6.1 Introduction

In the first chapter we discussed the definition and essence of terrorism. Although there is no universally accepted definition of the phenomenon, it is generally regarded as an instrument used by certain actors to achieve political goals by spreading fear and anxiety through violent acts. These acts are part of the practice and not a goal in themselves. We quoted Brian Jenkins, who said that terrorists like to see a lot of people watching, not a lot of people dead. This means that audiences are very important and that their reactions to a terrorism-related incident are what matters. Terrorism is about impact, about how you and I react to a bomb attack, hostage taking or a shooting spree. Of course it also depends on media coverage, statements by politicians, official responses and other factors. Spreading fear is a key aspect in this mechanism of how terrorism works.

6.2 Fear of terrorism

Fear features prominently in many definitions of terrorism. But what is fear and how does it 'work'? Scholars from many different disciplines have struggled to find answers to the fundamental questions. The difficulty lies, amongst other things, in the fact that fear pertains to a diffuse range of situations and behaviours. It ranges from an individual, psychological state of mind or a socio-cultural sentiment in society to political claims and rhetoric. In relation to the phenomenon of terrorism, Edwin Bakker and Beatrice de Graaf referred to fear as 'a sentiment of anxiety caused by the perception or presence of danger' (2014, p. 1). It should be stressed that fear in itself should not be considered merely as a negative reaction to threats and attacks. According to these authors, fear of danger is a very natural and useful emotion. It also functions as a survival mechanism that helps people to take the right measures and actions to protect themselves (p. 2). However, much depends on the level of or reasons for fear.

Fear is a complex and multidimensional phenomenon. One of the dimensions is time. To understand the complexity of fear of terrorism a distinction should be made between immediate fear responses to terrorism (fear after an attack) and enduring, sustainable fear of terrorism that is not ignited by a prevailing acute threat. On the one hand, fear of terrorism can be an affective state which is an immediate and automatic response to an acute terrorist threat. Under these conditions, fear is a natural and healthy response which allows people to make accurate and rapid decisions to save their lives. Functional fears like the fear of snakes or fires generally wear off when the immediate threat has disappeared. On the other hand, fear of terrorism can be imprinted as a persuasive state of mind which lingers on long after the actual threat has vanished. If unmonitored, perceived collective fear of terrorism can contribute to raising the real fear of terrorism, irrespective of whether or not the perception of shared fear is accurate. The feeling that others are afraid may be sufficient to intensify individual experiences of fear, which in turn may further strengthen the collective fear of terrorism.

Another dimension linked to fear is how relevant someone deems the threat to him- or herself to be. In other words, what do you think is the risk that you might become a victim of terrorism? Here, perceptions have arguably changed in recent decades. While terrorism is nothing new, as discussed in chapter 2, terrorism today takes different shapes and forms as compared to earlier. Terrorism is not a problem to just a handful of countries. It is a global phenomenon and there are very few countries that are not directly or indirectly confronted with it. Unlike in previous decades, terrorists often attack so-called 'soft targets': think of public transport, schools, places of worship, concert halls or the street. So the perception that terrorist attacks can target anyone anywhere has grown. Images are not only communicated by traditional media, but are instantly put out on social media. Some perpetrators try to make use of those communication tools: think of the attackers in Christchurch (2019) and Buffalo (2022) who tried to livestream their attacks. Furthermore, in various attacks, such as on the beaches of Sousse in Tunisia (2015) or the boulevard in Nice (2016) in the midst of the summer season, many tourists from various nationalities were among those targeted. In other words, we are increasingly confronted with images of attacks, even far away ones, that, due to the nationality of the victims, sometimes feel very close to home. Unfortunately, this has increased the fear and impact of terrorist attacks among the general public.

Fear of terrorism on the part of the authorities has led to drastic increases in investment in counterterrorism, particularly after the attacks on 9/11. Intelligence and law enforcement agencies were given additional means and sometimes additional powers and rights. The same holds true for many other governmental actors that play a role in dealing with violent radicalisation and terrorism. Also, new agencies were established. Most noticeable of these are the counterterrorism coordinators and fusion centres that were designed to promote information-sharing at the national or local level between relevant counterterrorism actors. Especially in the first five years after 9/11, these investments and measures, including immediate responses to concrete incidents, were very ad hoc. For good reasons, the emphasis was on preventing terrorist attacks, in particular a second attack of the magnitude of that on 9/11.

The possibility for terrorists to spread fear around the world, partly irrespective of the location of the attack, raises a fundamental question about the results of all these investments in counterterrorism and, more broadly, their effectiveness. Although difficult to prove, one might argue that the enormous investments seem to have resulted in the prevention of terrorist incidents, for instance if we look at the number of foiled plots or people convicted of (plotting) attacks. However, terrorist attacks and the number of victims are just one aspect of the phenomenon of terrorism, as we also discussed in the assumption of whether or not terrorism is successful. How successful has counterterrorism been if we are still confronted with relatively high levels of fear? If we look at fear and attention, the terrorists often get what they want. How do we limit this specific aspect of the impact of terrorism?

Negative consequences

Limiting the fear caused by terrorist attacks has, generally speaking, not been a key priority in counterterrorism. While billions of dollars have been spent on new counterterrorism programmes and actors, these mostly included more capabilities to stop and detect terrorists or to engage in costly military operations abroad. Countering the mechanism of terrorism, of which spreading fear is a key component, has long been overlooked. This is not without its consequences. If fear of terrorism is not proportional to the actual threat, it can have many unnecessary and unwanted consequences.

As Furedi and several other scholars observed, fear of terrorism can cause a shift towards dogmatic reasoning which is characterised by 'us versus them' thinking, stereotyping and discrimination. It can also lead to a lack of nuance, contributing to harsh, system-defending reactions that sometimes do more harm than good. In particular, fear related to terrorist attacks by groups and networks that claim to act in the name of Islam have provoked many of the above-mentioned reactions. Brigitte Nacos and Oscar Torres-Reyna demonstrated that the media's portrayal of Muslims and their religion grew more negative, unfair and stereotypical two years after the attacks on the US on 9/11. Thus, terrorist attacks not only contribute to fear in society at the time of the incident, but may also succeed in changing public attitudes for a longer period of time, as was already concluded in the 1980s. Amélie Godefroidt and Armin Langer (2020) showed how fear of future attacks, more than past terrorist attacks, can lead to a decrease in social trust between citizens.

A major negative consequence of fear of terrorism is that it can make societies more vulnerable to emotional, political and administrative overreactions. Fear may lead to a preference for action-oriented leaders with simple and sensational explanations for terrorism who call for immediate action. Encouraged by sensational media representation, the reaction of these leaders to terrorist incidents or acute threats is often one of strong focus on immediate security measures and repressive action towards perceived enemies. Immediately after attacks, the public is likely to support, or at least understand, drastic policy responses.

Though understandable, fear can lead to suboptimal policies and to overreactions in terms of states of emergency, false allegations, waves of arrests and specific legal or bureaucratic measures against members of suspected groups. Such reactions could lead to increased polarisation and even (violent) radicalisation; in other words a self-fulfilling prophecy adding to the damage done by the terrorist incidents themselves (see box 6.01). Donatella Della Porta (1995) and other terrorism scholars have argued that terrorists play to these vulnerabilities by way of (threatening) spectacular attacks.

A self-fulfilling prophecy

Joseba Zulaika in his highly critical book *Terrorism. The self-fulfilling prophecy* (2009) argues that counterterrorism has become self-fulfilling and is now pivotal in promoting terrorism. He stresses that the invastion of Iraq and the War on Terror have made the US far less secure than before. He focuses on what terrorism means symbolically and how it is used in political discourse. Primarily focusing on the US, Zulaika shows how terrorism has been used as a means of manufacturing consent for violent counterterrorism policies – the 'War on Terror'. That war became the sole mission of American politics after portraying terrorism as a constant risk that is omnipresent, a sort of chaotic principle always ready to strike, and that resulted in an unending struggle. In doing so, the US created a self-fulfilling prophecy in which those fighting the War on Terror were also those who were responsible for creating it in the first place.

BOX 6.01   A SELF-FULFILLING PROPHECY

Key points

- Fear is a key component in the mechanism of terrorism.
- Despite many counterterrorism measures, terrorists manage to create fear and attract attention.
- Fear can have a negative impact on counterterrorism policies, leading to repressive and ad hoc measures.
- Fear can also have a societal impact, leading to polarisation and, ultimately, even more radicalisation and terrorism.

6.3   A 'culture of fear' and resilience

Some authors would argue that, generally speaking, authorities have not only failed to devote much attention to limiting fear, they have what Furedi called become characterised by a 'culture of fear'. He analysed the effects of fear on western societies in the aftermath of 9/11 and explained how many of those societies, such as the UK and the US, have been caught in a so-called 'vulnerability paradigm'. In his book, *Invitation to Terror: The Expanding Empire of the Unknown* (2007), he investigated the reactions after 9/11 in the US and the UK. Furedi, Zulaika and others show how fatalistic attitudes, pessimism, vulnerability and fear of terrorism can lead to an invitation to terror. Describing terrorism as an almost apocalyptic threat that it is hardly possible to counter, as repeatedly stated by many politicians in the US and the UK in the wake of 9/11 and the 2005 London bombings, can produce a self-fulfilling prophecy. According to Furedi, slogans like the 'Global War on Terror' and talk about the 'Long War' show confusion about the threat and undermine our capacity to engage with it. It should be stressed that the culture of fear entails much more than just fear of terrorism. Many scholars have shown how (mainly) western societies have become what Beck (1999; 2002) coined 'risk societies', and how they have become more vulnerable to accidents, disasters, and violent incidents, including terrorism (see box 6.02).

Risk society

Two sociologists, Ulrich Beck and Anthony Giddens, developed the term 'risk society' in their writings in the 1980s and 1990s. They both referred to how modern societies deal with the notion of risk. Giddens argued that, due to technological developments, modern societies are increasingly preoccupied with the future and with safety, which generates the notion of risk. Thus, the notion of risk society was initially primarily used to refer not to security threats, but to changes in societies. They also referred to environmental risks. Beck published his famous book, *Risikogesellschaft,* in 1986, the year of the Disaster at Chernobyl, a nuclear power plant in the Soviet Union. In his article, 'The Terrorist Threat: World Risk Society Revisited', which was published after 9/11, Beck also referred to global financial crises and the threat of transnational terrorist networks. Today the term 'risk society' is frequently employed to examine the features of terrorism and how governments and societies deal with this risk.

BOX 6.02   RISK SOCIETY

By stressing vulnerability and showing how a 'culture of fear' could lead to an invitation to terror, Furedi was criticised for being a cultural pessimist. Nonetheless, his analysis of the consequences of the combination of fatalism and overreaction is relevant. In the years after 9/11, the Global War on Terror may indeed have obscured a proper analysis of the threat that countries faced by inflating the threat posed by terrorism. Political scientist John Mueller (2009) used the term 'overblown' to describe how he thought that politicians and what he called the terrorism industry inflated national security threats. Fatalism and overreactions make it hard to counter strong fears and extreme threat descriptions, or to raise questions about the necessity and proportionality of counterterrorism policies.

It should be stressed that after 2009 the concept of the Global War on Terror gave way to counterterrorism approaches that might do better in terms of not feeding fears in society. Today, most countries do not use the term 'war' or 'fight' against terrorism and often refer to prevention policies or use the more neutral term 'countering terrorism'. However, some of the responses after the rise of IS in 2014 and attacks in Europe seem to have indicated similar strong and often alarmist responses. The fear of returning foreign fighters perpetrating attacks might, arguably, also be called overblown or disproportional (see box 6.03).

The foreign fighter phenomenon and worries

The sudden influx of hundreds, later thousands, of foreign fighters into the conflict in Syria and later Iraq raised worries among many authorities across the world. Their main focus was not so much on the threat their citizens would pose on the battlefields in Syria and Iraq, but what would happen when they returned home. This was accompanied by very alarmist rhetoric. For instance, German Minister of the Interior, Hans-Peter Friedrich, called them 'ticking time bombs'. Former director of Europol, Rob Wainwright, spoke of hundreds of potential terrorists who were ready to strike upon return. While foreign fighters did indeed become involved in terrorist attacks, think of the attacks in Paris (2015) and Brussels (2016), these cases remained exceptional. Historical studies have also shown that foreign fighters only rarely execute terrorist attacks upon their return. Yet, if they manage to strike, the impact will be enormous. That is why Edwin Bakker and Jeanine de Roy van Zuijdewijn called this foreign fighter phenomenon a 'low-probability, high-impact threat' (2015).

BOX 6.03   THE FOREIGN FIGHTER PHENOMENON AND WORRIES

The fear of returning foreign fighters shows that countries remain vulnerable to overreactions to terrorism. Yet, the increasing awareness of this fact today has created the possibilities for policies and strategies that try to contribute to a mitigation of fear and anxiety, or that are even directed at increasing so-called 'resilience' in society.

Resilience

The concept of resilience has its roots in psychology, civil engineering and ecology, and conveys the capacity of a person, material or biotope to survive sudden shocks. Ecologist C.S. Holling was among the first the coin the term in relation to the capability of natural systems to deal with shocks. He explained that '[r]esilience determines the persistence of relationships within a system and is a measure of the ability of these systems to absorb changes of state variables, driving variables, and parameters, and still persist' (1973, p. 17). The term has been adopted in multiple disciplines. Norman Garmezy and Michael Rutter used the term 'psychological resilience' to describe children's successful psycho-social development in spite of multiple and seemingly overwhelming natural hazards. In general, the term 'resilience' thus indicates the capacity of people, materials or biotopes to deal with sudden changes or stress, as well as the capacity to recover and return to the previous situation. From the perspective of counterterrorism, resilience may be an important capacity for dealing with the negative impact of (the fear of) terrorism by individuals and societies as a whole.

According to Furedi, resilience could be regarded a counter trend to the dominant narrative of vulnerability in the face of terrorism. It could ensure that communities, corporations and countries have the capacity to withstand, respond, rapidly recover from and adapt to terrorism-related incidents, rather than being vulnerable targets. Edwin Bakker and Tinka Veldhuis (2012) stress that resilience to terrorism does not mean that individuals or societies are to be insensitive to the psychological impact of violent attacks: '[i]t means that societies have to develop the capacity to assess and attribute meaning to threats, as well as a set of coping strategies to recover from such traumatic events' (p. 5). According to Stephen Flynn and Sean Burke (2011), societies that manage to increase resilience to terrorism will make it much more difficult for terrorists to find a disruptive return on their effort.

Against this backdrop and given the earlier-described indirect and long-term costs of fear of terrorism, it seems high time to focus also on communication and resilience as integral parts of counterterrorism policies. We not only need to limit the chance that terrorists can attack us, we also need to make sure that when they do the impact of their violent acts will be limited. Or, as Jerrold Post in his article on the psychological dynamics of terrorism in 2006 puts it, 'if the goal of terrorism is to terrorize, terror is the property of the terrorized'. He also said, '[p]rograms that reduce vulnerability to terror and promote societal resilience represent a key component of antiterrorism'.

Fortunately, there has been an increase in research into this field. There is also a growing number of government reports that look into crisis communication after terrorism-related incidents as it can contribute to increased resilience to terrorism. This shows that, at least in some countries, the authorities are well aware of the need for an adequate reaction. Less fortunately, there are still too many cases of terrorist incidents where the authorities and other actors do not seem to pay much attention to fear management. In the next section we will discuss a number of concrete examples.

Key points
- Scholars have explained how a culture of fear can have negative consequences.
- Resilience, the ability to deal with the negative effects of an attack and retain a system's normal functions, is seen as a key antidote to this.
- In recent years, awareness has grown that this is an important dimension of counterterrorism in addition to preventing attacks.

Dealing with the impact of terrorism in theory

We have established that dealing with fear and other forms of impact is important, and discussed the role resilience could play in helping to reduce our vulnerability to terrorism. We will now explore a number of studies and concrete ideas that experts and scholars have come up with to improve the way authorities and the general public can deal with the impact of terrorism.

In recent years there has been an increase in research into the impact of terrorism and how to limit it. This is the work not just of scholars, but authorities have also realised that they should have clear ideas and strategies to respond to attacks. This response phase is considered to be a distinct element in various counterterrorism strategies. For instance, the Dutch 'Counterterrorism Strategy 2016 – 2020' lists 'being prepared for the consequences of terrorist violence' as one of the core goals.

The UK counterterrorism strategy also emphasises the importance of reacting appropriately. It says that 'terrorists attack us to create fear, to take revenge for real and perceived grievances, and to influence public opinion. We will respond proportionately and in a way that does not undermine our aim to enable people to live freely and with confidence'. In other words, they also warn of a culture of fear and an overreaction to attacks, because this might give terrorists exactly what they want, just as Furedi explained.

More studies

In 2014, Bakker and De Graaf noted that there was still a rather limited number of handbooks and strategies that deal specifically with the management of fear of terrorism. Studying these works, the authors hoped to derive a number of best practices that could help governments and other relevant actors to limit the impact of terrorism by reducing fear, anxiety and intimidation.

One of the studies they looked at was the British report by the 7th July Review Committee into the response to the London bombings in 2005. The report emphasised the importance of providing help to the survivors of the attacks. It showed that the majority of survivors were not known to the authorities or a support network of survivors and 'have been left to fend for themselves' (2006, p. 120). They also provided various recommendations related to efficient crisis communication. Other sources that Bakker and De Graaf studied were the Dutch 'National Counterterrorism Strategy 2011-2015', the 'US manual on Crisis and Emergency Risk Communication in 2012' and a report by COT-Leiden University from 2012 into limiting the impact of terrorism and extreme violence.

Fortunately, in recent years some more studies have emerged that provide insight into various elements of impact management. For instance, the 'US manual on Crisis and Emergency Risk Communication' was updated in 2018, looking into crisis responses after all types of emergencies, including terrorist attacks. It came up with six key principles of effective crisis and risk communication:

1. Be first: it is important to provide timely information.
2. Be right: make sure the information is accurate.
3. Be credible: honesty and truthfulness should not be compromised.
4. Express empathy: acknowledge the suffering.
5. Promote action: give people meaningful things to do.
6. Show respect: when people feel vulnerable, showing respect helps to promote cooperation.

Although the number of studies into impact management after terrorist attacks has increased in recent years, the topic can still be considered to be a relatively understudied one, as we will also discuss in the next chapter.

Noting the lack of research into impact management, De Roy van Zuijdewijn (2021) studied the aftermath of four jihadist terrorist attacks in Western Europe, focusing on the responses by both authorities and citizens. She used literature from adjacent disciplines to terrorism studies, such as crisis management, and zoomed in on the process of meaning- and sense-making. Crisis management scholars define meaning-making as a core task of crisis leaders: it refers to the process of attributing larger meaning to experiences, including terrorist attacks, for instance, stating that an attack is an attack on certain values, way of life, democracy or, alternatively, that it was just the action of a 'lunatic'. It differs from sense-making, which is simply getting the facts straight, for instance, how many people are injured, how many perpetrators are involved, was it an accident or done on purpose. She found that meaning-making is not always straightforward for authorities, as they need to balance juxtaposing goals: emphasising the abnormality of the event while also showing that the goal is to 'get back to business as soon as possible', in order not to give terrorists what they want. Interestingly, she found that citizens are often more capable of showing restraint in their responses than authorities.

Based on these and other studies, a number of best practices and lessons learned can be identified that can help governments and other relevant actors to limit the level of fear and the impact of terrorism. Before we present these, it should be noted that fear and impact management is extremely difficult. For example, Barbara Reynolds and Matthew Seeger in 'Psychological Responses to Terrorism' (2012) point out that the public will probably have a stronger reaction and a higher risk perception following terrorist incidents than after other types of crisis events. This is due to the intentionality and uncertainty that accompanies such events, the often intense media coverage of terrorist attacks (see box 6.04) and the frequent overreactions by governments and politicians mentioned earlier. De Roy van Zuijdewijn and Sciarone (2021) showed how the salience of terrorism increased in the EU in the years 2014-2017, when the region was confronted with various jihadist attacks.

Media, audiences and the spread of fear

As many scholars have made abundantly clear, the social impact of terrorism is not something that governments can fully engineer, let alone all by themselves. The impact of terrorist attacks in the 21st century is first and foremost influenced by the media, as people typically experience such terrorist incidents through news reports and the gripping images of dramatic terrorist attacks that the media disseminate. A study by Harley Williamson, Suzanna Fay and Toby Miles-Johnson (2019) shows that the public receives information about terrorism from multiple media sources and that this increases fear of terrorism. It also indicates that the types of media people consume and how they respond to media messages can heighten feelings of fear. Types of media that require active engagement – such as browsing websites or reading newspapers – may increase a person's fear of terrorism to the greatest extent. Moreover, deliberately seeking out information often serves to confirm what a person knows about a topic. The problem of confirmation bias suggests that someone who already fears terrorism is likely to seek out additional information that makes them fear it even more. These findings suggest that publishing accurate information is important in all journalism, but that it is particularly needed on platforms requiring active engagement. Audiences that search for information must be able to find sources that can productively shape and challenge their views, according to Williamson, Fay and Miles-Johnson.

BOX 6.04   MEDIA, AUDIENCES AND THE SPREAD OF FEAR

Moreover, there are several limitations to the idea of governmental management of fear that need mentioning. Bakker and De Graaf (2014, p. 6) present two of them: '[f]irst of all, coping mechanisms are individual mechanisms, mainly operating through personal psychological functions. ... Second, people may first seek support from family and friends rather than health professionals or other governmental employees' (see also box 6.05).

Notwithstanding this limited room for manoeuvre, Bakker and De Graaf (2014, pp. 7-8) argue that governments can affect the social impact of terrorist attacks all the same. 'Governments still have a monopoly on the use of violence and are the actor citizens turn to in times of national crises.' In short, strengthening resilience is difficult, but not impossible.

Defining fear management

In the *ICCT Research Paper*, 'Towards a Theory of Fear Management in the Counterterrorism Domain: A Stocktaking Approach', Bakker and De Graaf (2014) define the notion of fear management. The definition of management is 'the process of dealing with or controlling things or people'. In relation to business/staff management it can be understood as a manipulation of the human capital (or staff) of a business to contribute to the success of that business. This has a helpful application with regard to counterterrorism. Success in this domain could be divided into four distinct stages: successful preparation, prevention, response and recovery – pertaining to the physical (infrastructural, personal), social, economic and socio-psychological environment. 'Fear management' implies a form of manipulation of the human capital in society.

BOX 6.05   DEFINING FEAR MANAGEMENT

Recommendations for impact management

The first recommendation for impact management that many experts have shared is the importance of showing restraint in response to terrorist attacks. Positive examples of this include appeals for calm by politicians, religious leaders or community leaders. Of course, this is how it works in theory. In practice, some political leaders or citizens may have a different agenda and might benefit from increasing tensions, for instance. So while it is clear that from an impact management perspective an overreaction is to be avoided, we have to realise that from a political perspective this assessment may be different.

Second, appropriate crisis communication can help to limit the impact of terrorism. Given the indirect and long-term costs of fear of terrorism, it is important to focus on crisis communication as an integral component of counterterrorism policies. There are a number of important goals of crisis communication after terrorist attacks. The US manual on Crisis and

Emergency Risk Communication and other sources provided a number of key recommendations. Authorities should provide clear information in order to limit the spread of rumours. Furthermore, it is important to acknowledge and pay tribute to the victims and their relatives. Another goal or aspect is meaning-making: putting the incident in a wider perspective and explaining what it means to a society. It is also important to try to restore a sense of order. A phrase that is often quoted in this regard is 'back to business as usual as soon as possible'. Or, as the British would say, 'keep calm and carry on'. This slogan came from a poster produced by the British government in 1939, just before the Second World War, and intended to raise the morale of the public in the case of air attacks on major cities. Communication after an attack should also focus on portraying a feeling of solidarity and unity, to include various relevant communities in societies and to avoid stigmatising the community to which a perpetrator belongs. Crisis communication is important not only in the direct aftermath of an attack, or the 'golden hour' as some call it, but also in the following weeks and months.

Third, a number of studies have looked at ways to improve resilience, and these pertain to efforts prior to, during and after an attack, focusing on coping mechanisms. Coping mechanisms are strategies that people use to deal with stressful situations. A distinction can be made between negative coping mechanisms, such as anger, fear and distrust, and positive coping mechanisms, such as helping each other, showing solidarity and prayer. Positive coping mechanisms include ways of adapting behaviour and attitudes in order to minimise stress and negative emotions. They can foster positive emotions or increased feelings of strength or solidarity. The importance of gatherings, ceremonies and religious services is frequently mentioned. These can reaffirm a shared feeling of belief in certain values. Also important are sense- and meaning-making, the manner and extent to which government officials and politicians provide the public with a clear image of what is going on and give 'meaning' to it in a positive way. This increases the public's problem-solving capabilities and may reduce stress and feelings of trauma. The same holds true for visible acts of justice that function as a form of psychological education and sense-making. For example, a fair and public trial can play a significant role in helping people to cope with a terrible crime. At a later stage of the aftermath of an attack, providing attention and assistance to the victims and their relatives can satisfy the need for closure felt by individuals confronted with crises or traumas. Think of the commemorations that often take place directly after an attack or the annual commemorations.

There are also negative coping mechanisms. According to a COT-Leiden University report (2012) on limiting the impact of terrorism, counterterrorism efforts may unwittingly reinforce negative coping mechanisms by mobilising the public around images of fear, by rhetorically extending the spectre of terrorism to an enormous threat and projecting a warlike situation in society. These observations are very much in line with Furedi's findings mentioned earlier. Therefore this report and other experts and scholars advise authorities to refrain from or limit actions that might increase feelings of helplessness, fear and anger or fuel polarisation along ethnic, religious or cultural lines within society. Some positive examples to counter the negative coping mechanism of fear come from the general public, not from politicians or policy-makers. Think of the demonstrations after attacks in which people hold up signs reading 'we are not afraid', a slogan that was launched by citizens after a bombing in London in 2005.

A very important recommendation derived from studies and reports on crisis management in general and dealing with the impact of terrorism in particular is the need to facilitate self-efficacy. Self-efficacy, a term originally proposed in 1977 by the psychologist Albert Bandura, is the belief in one's capabilities of organising and executing the courses of action required to manage prospective situations. People do not want to be mere victims or bystanders, but generally express a desire to be able and willing to do something, or at least to do the right thing and not to play into the hands of the perpetrators.

Authorities can help to increase this belief in the ability to deal with such situations by asking the public not to remain idle but help the authorities and each other to make the best of the situation. Positive examples derived from responses to terrorist attacks in the past include calling upon citizens to upload videos, donate blood, provide shelter to people, and remain vigilant and report suspicious behaviour. There are quite a number of examples of people who felt capable and courageous enough to face the threat head on by stopping terrorists in time or apprehending terrorists immediately after the attack, risking their own lives (see box 6.06).

Apprehending terrorists

People rightly associate apprehending terrorists with special forces or specialised arrest teams. Think of the raid on Osama bin Laden's house by US Navy SEALs. Although this is often the case, quite a few terrorists are apprehended by ordinary police officers who happened to be in the right place at the right time. For instance, the perpetrator of the attack on the Berlin Christmas market was arrested by Italian police officers on a routine patrol who spotted a 'very suspicious' male walking through the city centre. In some cases ordinary citizens managed to apprehend terrorists. A famous case is that of Usman Khan who – wearing a fake suicide vest – threatened to blow up a building. He started stabbing people, killing two, but several citizens started fighting back. One of them grabbed a 1.5 metre-long narwhal tusk as a weapon and another a fire-extinguisher. Khan fled and began stabbing pedestrians outside on London Bridge. Several people were hurt, but in the end the attacker was driven back with the help of the tusk and the spray from a fire extinguisher.

BOX 6.06   APPREHENDING TERRORISTS

Key points

· Scholars and experts have provided suggestions for how to deal with the impact of terrorism in theory.
· Often-mentioned elements for authorities are the need to avoid overreaction, showing restraint, clear crisis communication, coping mechanisms and self-efficacy.

Conclusion

In this section we looked at studies and concrete ideas that experts and scholars have come up with to improve the way authorities and the general public can deal with the impact of terrorism, at least in theory. We discussed the importance of avoiding overreactions, showing restraint and crisis communication, coping mechanisms and self-efficacy. In the next section we will explore how relevant actors managed to put these recommendations into practice, focusing on five concrete cases from the US, France, the UK, New Zealand and Sri Lanka.

6.5   Dealing with the impact of terrorism in practice

We have discussed the concepts of fear and resilience and the negative consequences of a culture of fear. We also looked into reports and studies that contained advice on how to deal with the impact of terrorism. In this section we will discuss how this works in practice, based on five case studies: the Boston Marathon bombing in 2013, the November 2015 Paris attacks, the 2017 Manchester attack, the Christchurch mosque shootings in 2019 and the Sri Lanka Easter bombings in 2019. We will focus on the elements discussed in the previous section. How did relevant actors deal with the need to avoid overreaction and show restraint. What about crisis communication, coping mechanisms and the need for self-efficacy in these four cases?

Boston Marathon bombing

On 15 April 2013, the city of Boston was hosting its annual marathon. Over 23,000 runners were participating while hundreds of thousands spectators were present along the 42 km route. Four hours after the start, two brothers detonated two bombs near the finishing line. They killed three people and injured almost 300. A frantic search for the perpetrators ensued, which was helped by the footage of security cameras and a call upon citizens to share their pictures and videos of the event with the authorities. This provided citizens with the opportunity to show self-efficacy. In fact, this case showed many examples of the public being willing to do something to limit the impact of the attack. Many bystanders helped the victims, with various iconic pictures going viral or making the front pages of newspapers.

Not all attempts were equally helpful, however. *BBC News* later wrote an article entitled 'How internet detectives got it very wrong'. Large numbers of people were trying to help the authorities find the perpetrators. The popular social news website and forum 'Reddit' had a sub-thread entitled 'r/findbostonbombers' where citizens were posting footage of the alleged attackers, leading to the identification of various 'perpetrators' who later turned out to be innocent. Three days after the attack, the FBI had discovered the identity of the perpetrators and released pictures of two Chechen-American brothers. They later explained that they did so publicly in order to respond to all the rumours on Reddit as well as traditional media that had hinted at innocent bystanders being the perpetrators (see box 6.07).

Citizens and journalists gone wrong
While citizens, and journalists were trying hard to help the authorities identify the attackers, not all attempts were successful. Journalists later wrote about various cases where this had gone wrong. One example was a Saudi student who was wounded in the attack, but who was then wrongly accused of being the perpetrator. A talk show host linked him to the attack, called him a 'very bad, bad, bad man' and claimed that the FBI was covering up the case. Another example that led to a lot of turmoil was the front page of the *New York Post*. It had printed a photo entitled 'Bag Men' of two clearly recognisable men, who later also turned out to have no link whatsoever to the attack. Another person who was wrongfully accused, this time because of citizen detective work, was 22-year-old student, Sunil Tripathi, who had gone missing the month before and whose body was found a week after the Boston bombings (a case of suicide). On Reddit people noticed that he looked like photos released of one of the actual perpetrators. The social media pages

of his family members were immediately harassed by various people who assumed he was the bomber.

BOX 6.07   CITIZENS AND JOURNALISTS GONE WRONG

An almost unprecedented manhunt followed. One of the brothers was killed after a shootout with the police. The manhunt continued for the second brother, with thousands of law enforcement officers searching a 20-block area in Boston whose residents were asked to stay indoors, in which the transport system and most businesses and public places were closed. Soon, one of the residents discovered the brother hiding in a boat in his backyard, after which he was arrested.

As already mentioned, the manhunt and the subsequent lockdown were unprecedented and the economic costs to the community were quite high. In hindsight this seemed to be a case of overreaction. The same holds true for a number of headlines of media outlets that spoke of 'the biggest terrorist attack since 9/11'. The comparison of the attacks in which 3,000 people were killed with one in which three people died is not a sign of showing restraint. One could say that the media had a field day. The mayor of Boston, Thomas Menino, however, did not use big and alarmist words and spoke of 'a bad day for Boston'. President Barack Obama in a first reaction to the attack stated, '[t]he American people will say a prayer for Boston tonight. And Michelle and I send our deepest thoughts and prayers to the families of the victims in the wake of this senseless loss', which can be regarded as an example of a positive coping mechanism.

Yet, more positively, the aftermath of this attack was also characterised by solidarity and resilience. The slogan 'Boston Strong', based on a Twitter hashtag, came to dominate the popular idea of the response to the attacks. This catchphrase has been turned into a slogan on t-shirts and mugs, and various Boston sports teams use the words as well. While some criticised its commercialised use, it is still generally used to refer to the resilience of many of its victims and the inhabitants of the city in dealing with the attacks. Various books and movies have emerged that discuss the response to these attacks (see box 6.08).

'Boston Strong'

Various books and movies have been released about the aftermath of the attacks in Boston. An example is the book, *Boston Strong: A City's Triumph over Tragedy,* by Casey Sherman and Dave Wedge that focused in particular also on how the victims tried to recover from the attacks. In 2016, the movie *Patriots Day* directed by Peter Berg appeared on screen. The movie was based on the book by Sherman and Wedge and focuses on the attack and the manhunt. A very different perspective was offered in the movie *Stronger*, directed by David Gordon Green and released in 2017. It follows the story of Jeff Bauman, played by actor Jake Gyllenhaal, who lost both his lower legs in the attacks. The movie portrays his struggle to continue and shows how he, whether he liked it or not, became a hero and symbol of hope after the attacks.

BOX 6.08 'BOSTON STRONG'

Paris attacks

In November 2015, eight terrorists linked to Islamic State executed multiple attacks in Paris. A total of 129 people were killed, which made it the most deadly attack ever perpetrated in France. The day after the attacks, French President François Hollande stated that the country was at war with the terrorists of IS. He intensified strikes against IS targets in Syria and Iraq and declared a state of emergency. This state of emergency would be extended multiple times in the years that followed. Many of the additional capabilities that the authorities obtained by declaring such a special situation were made permanent in 2017, when the French government proposed various legal changes that would allow them to use such powers permanently. Over 500 academics expressed their worries that this would effectively entail a 'state of emergency light version' and called this a threat to the rule of law (*Libération*, 2017).

So, looking at this reaction in terms of avoiding overreaction and showing restraint, one can argue that it was perhaps the strongest reaction possible and the opposite of limiting the impact in this regard. The declaration of war against IS portrayed it as an enormous threat, and in a way gave legitimacy to its claim of being a real state. In hindsight there was a lot of criticism of the way the French President reacted to the attack. An investigation report on the aftermath of the attacks presented to the French National Assembly in 2016 was especially critical of the effectiveness of the state of emergency in reducing the threat.

When we look at the coping mechanisms in the aftermath of the attacks, some things stand out. For instance, many citizens used the hashtag #OpenDoors in the hours after the attacks to offer shelter to people that were stranded. This is an example of solidarity, but also of self-efficacy: the desire to do something concrete after the attack, in this case helping others. Citizens also came together to commemorate the attacks, not only in Paris but all over

France. But there were also examples of negative coping mechanisms, such as citizens and politicians projecting fear and anger on Muslim communities and also dozens of attacks on mosques in the days and weeks after the attacks.

On 22 May 2017 a man detonated a backpack filled with explosives in the foyer of the Manchester Arena. Many parents were waiting there to pick up their children who had just attended a concert by US popstar Ariana Grande. 22 people were killed and hundreds were injured. Among the fatalities were 10 people under the age of 20, the youngest being an eight-year-old girl. The fact that so many young children had been targeted led to worldwide shock and horror.

In the aftermath of the attack, to some extent as in the case of Boston, a lot of emphasis was put on the character of the city and its inhabitants. During one of the vigils held in the week after the attack a woman began to sing 'Don't Look Back in Anger': a well-known song of the famous rock band Oasis which was founded in Manchester. This song became the symbol of the spirit of the city of Manchester. Local poet Tony Walsh read out his poem, 'This is the Place', during the vigil with thousands of people watching. His poem contained various references to the city and its character (see box 6.09).

'This is the Place' by Tony Walsh

Tony Walsh was commissioned in 2012 by the charity Forever Manchester to write a poem about the city of Manchester, encapsulating its spirit. This poem became one of the symbols of the city in the aftermath of the May 2017 attack. Walsh made several references to the city's history. In the year 1996, Manchester had been targeted by a particularly devastating attack by the Irish Republican Army that destroyed the commercial city centre, although it fortunately did not lead to any casualties. The city had also been facing severe economic challenges, with the decline of the once famous textile industry. References to the inhabitants' experiences of being able to deal with such difficult times were plentiful in Walsh' poem. Read, for instance, the following verse:
'Because this is a place that has been through some hard times
Oppressions, recessions, depressions and dark times
But we keep fighting back with Greater Manchester spirit
Northern grit, northern wit in Greater Manchester's lyrics'.

BOX 6.09   'THIS IS THE PLACE' BY TONY WALSH

In terms of self-efficacy, a widely publicised example emerged in the weeks after the attack. Many people visited tattoo shops to have the worker bee tattooed on their bodies: a symbol of the hard-working spirit of this former industrial town that had known a lot of hardships in the past. The proceeds that the tattoo shops made were then donated to the victims. Music artists also tried to contribute in terms of helping the victims. On 4 June 2017, a few weeks after the attack, they organised the 'One Love Manchester' concert where, in additions to Grande, famous stars such as Justin Bieber, Coldplay, Take That and Robbie Williams performed. This concert helped to raise over seven million pounds, adding to the more than 20 million pounds raised by the We Love Manchester Emergency Fund. As such, the aftermath of the attack was characterised by many attempts to emphasise resilience and solidarity and to help the victims.

The authorities, for their part, showed restraint by not resorting to (long-term) repressive security measures. In the first days after the attack, additional military personnel were put to patrol the streets as part of 'Operation Temperer'. The Joint Terrorism Analysis Centre raised the threat level to the highest, 'critical', the day after the attack, fearing that more attacks were imminent. A few days later, it decided to lower the threat level again and soldiers soon withdrew from various key sites. Then the idea of 'back to business as soon as possible' clearly surfaced. For instance, the local authorities decided to go ahead with the Great Manchester Run which attracted tens of thousands of people to watch and participate. Mayor Andy Burnham joined the race himself. The election campaign on the national level that had been suspended out of respect for the victims was also quickly resumed with the widespread support of politicians from all parties, who emphasised the need to continue the normal democratic process.

Yet, also in this case, clearly not all responses to the attacks symbolised resilience, solidarity and unity. The mosque that the attacker and his family had attended, Didsbury Mosque, was the target of an arson attack in the night after the attack. Leader of the right-wing English Defence League, Tommy Robinson, later visited the city and recorded a video posted on YouTube in front of the mosque, pointing at random houses next to the mosques and saying that 'in these houses are enemy combatants who want to kill you, maim you and destroy you'. In the weeks after the attack a spike in hate crimes reported to the police was observed. A report by the Radicalisation Awareness Network (2017) indicated a rise of 505 per cent in hate crimes targeting Muslims.

Christchurch mosque shootings

The third case is that of the aftermath of the attack by a right-wing extremist in 2019. The attacker shot and killed 51 people in two mosques in Christchurch, New Zealand. The response by the political leader of New Zealand was very different from that in the two other cases. Jacinda Ardern, the Prime Minister, told Parliament a few days later that the attacker had 'sought many things from his act of terror, but one was notoriety – that is why you will never hear me mention his name' (see box 6.10). Rather than taking strong measures and using words that would enlarge the perception of a threat, she focused on restraint and solidarity and unity among different communities in New Zealand. She started her speech in Parliament with the words 'As-Salam Aleikum, may peace be upon you'.

No notoriety for terrorists

Jacinda Ardern's speech has been widely credited with providing a strong example of not giving any attention to the terrorist, or perhaps setting an international example. She was not the first to do so. For instance, Norwegian Prime Minister Jens Stoltenberg also tried to limit his use of the name Anders Breivik in referring to the perpetrator of the 2011 attacks in Norway. While he explained to the German newspaper *Der Spiegel* that it was not a general principle, he said that he tried to avoid using his name; 'I don't like that he's had so much attention. And that's because one of his motives was exactly that: to get attention. So, I focus on the victims, on all those who lost loved ones, on those who have survived and lived through horrible things'. During the commemoration of the first anniversary of the attack in Nice that took place on 14 July 2016, in which almost 80 people were killed, French President Emmanuel Macron used the following words: 'we have forgotten the name of this anonymous killer, but we have learned the names of the dead, our dead'.

BOX 6.10   NO NOTORIETY FOR TERRORISTS

Looking at the reactions of citizens, we see several positive coping mechanisms such as showing support and solidarity with the Muslim community. About 20,000 people joined the vigil two weeks after the attack, some non-Muslim women were wearing headscarves to show their support for Muslims in the country. Interreligious services were held by various communities. There were quite a few other examples that showed that New Zealanders would not let themselves be divided by such an attack and showed the terrorist that he would not get what he wanted.

Attempts to limit the impact of the attack were also visible in the actions of social media companies. The perpetrator aimed to reach a global audience by live streaming his attacks. allowing them to be swiftly replicated online. Wearing a camera attached to a helmet, he broadcast his shooting spree on Facebook; the company later removed the video and trained its artificial intelligence systems to detect and block any attempt to do that in the future. Other social media companies followed suit.

Sri Lanka Easter bombings

On 21 April 2019, Easter Sunday, terrorists linked to the jihadist National Twowheeth Jama'ath (NTJ) group carried out seven coordinated attacks across Sri Lanka. Three churches and three luxury hotels were among the targeted locations. A total of 269 people were killed in those attacks, making them among the most deadly the country had ever experienced. At the time of the attacks, worshippers present in the churches were attending Easter services, which led to the deaths of many Christians, who constitute a small minority in the country. The attacks came as a big surprise to the country, which had not witnessed major jihadist attacks before, although it had been frequently targeted by the separatist terrorist organisation, Tamil Tigers, until 2009.

On the day of the attack, the Sri Lankan government announced that it would temporarily shut down major social media platforms and messaging services such as Facebook, Instagram, YouTube and Whatsapp. The authorities were clearly worried about the spread of misinformation and conspiracy theories. With a long history of communal violence, the authorities were afraid that the attacks might spark new waves of violence. Temporarily disabling social media services was not a new move in the country: the government had done the same after anti-Muslim riots in 2018.

Disabling such services limited the spread of misinformation, but it also limited the spread of useful information. For instance, the Facebook Safety Check that many people use to inform their family members and friends that they are safe in the aftermath of an attack was no longer available. It also made it harder for people to coordinate help and see what they could best (not) do. Furthermore, several journalists and human rights activists criticised the move as it also led to less transparency regarding the actions taken by the state in response. The ban was lifted only after ten days. This move was a positive example neither of showing restraint, nor of clear crisis communication (see also box 6.11). However, it was portrayed as being informed by the need to limit rumours and disinformation, as the authorities were worried about those consequences.

The blocking of social media companies did not prevent anti-Muslim violence. The aftermath of the attack was not characterised by displays of solidarity among various communities. Amnesty International reported how Buddhist religious leaders and Sinhalese groups had called for a boycott of Muslim businesses after the attack. Even worse, a wave of anti-Muslim violence followed: hundreds of people stormed mosques and Muslim-owned shops across the country and a man was stabbed to death by a mob. In response, the authorities declared a curfew.

In the aftermath of the attack the authorities took various repressive security measures, for instance leading to the increased militarisation of the country. President Sirisena declared the situation to be an emergency which broadened the security forces' powers of arrest and detention and led to more military personnel at checkpoints. In that sense, this response thus showed similarities to the Paris attacks when a similar state of emergency was declared.

Still no clarity

The response by the authorities in Sri Lanka, particularly the long process of starting the trial of the suspects, has been widely criticised by the families of the victims and the Catholic Church. Archbishop of Colombo, Cardinal Malcolm Ranjith, said that 'it is clear from this procedure that after such a long time the government has no interest in finding out the truth about the attack and they are going to cover it up and wash their hands'. The Cardinal also referred to the attack as a 'grand political plot' and accused the government of having political reasons for not ensuring a speedy and thorough investigation process. Pope Francis met a delegation of the victims of the bombings over Easter 2022. He gave a speech in which he urged the Sri Lankan authorities to tell the truth. The Pope said, '[p]lease, out of love for justice, out of love for your people, let it be made clear once and for all who were responsible for these events . . . . This will bring peace to your conscience and to your country'. This example shows the importance of having transparent and timely investigation procedures after attacks. Not only is this of crucial importance to the relatives of the victims, who are dealing with a lot of uncertainty and unprocessed trauma, but also to the legitimacy of the government.

BOX 6.11   STILL NO CLARITY

Reflection on these cases

So, looking at these five examples, what can we say about dealing with the impact of terrorism in practice? Well, that on paper many people would agree that it is important, but that in practice it is not so easy always to respond in a way that makes the impact as small as possible. In other words, limiting the impact of terrorism is easier said than done.

We should not forget that there is a lot of political pressure on leaders also to show strength and determination in response to attacks. This could actually lead to actions that have the opposite effect of limiting the impact. You could ask the question to what extent President Hollande really had the option to show restraint after the deadliest terrorist attack in France just over six months after the Charlie Hebdo attacks had shocked the country. Or one can doubt the legitimacy of blocking social media websites in the aftermath of attacks, but we know that social media can stir up tensions between groups after attacks. So while impact management may be straightforward in theory, its application in practice also depends on many other things, including politics and earlier experiences with terrorism.

We must add here that the examples we gave came predominantly from attacks in western countries that received a lot of public and scholarly attention. In the third chapter we discussed the western bias in terrorism studies. So we are very much aware that these findings cannot be applied worldwide. Think of the many terrorist attacks in Iraq, or the various kidnappings perpetrated by Boko Haram in Nigeria. These are examples of attacks and situations with far more casualties than in Boston, Paris and Christchurch and of cases in which terrorists tried new or renewed modus operandi like the use of drones and going after children. How did the authorities and citizens in these countries that are confronted with terrorism almost daily deal with such horrible attacks? These are important questions for the future research agenda of terrorism studies.

Key points

- Dealing with the impact of terrorism may sound easy in theory, but it is hard in practice.
- Studying the aftermath of five different attacks shows that there are clear differences in terms of how the authorities and citizens managed to deal with the impact of terrorism.
- Studying such cases, as well as more non-western cases, can help us to respond better to terrorism.

6.6   Conclusion

In this chapter, we discussed the concepts of fear and resilience and the negative consequences of a culture of fear. We also looked into reports and studies that contained advice on how to deal with the impact of terrorism. Finally, we investigated how authorities and citizens responded to terrorist attacks in practice, based on the study of the aftermath of five major terrorist attacks. We focused on the way these actors dealt with the need to avoid overreaction and show restraint. Concrete examples of crisis communication, positive and negative coping mechanisms and self-efficacy in Boston, Paris, Manchester, Christchurch and Sri Lanka were discussed. From the literature and from these cases, we have learned that dealing with the impact of terrorism is easier said than done. Finally, we observed that the academic body of knowledge on impact management is primarily based on western cases, and that a lot could be learned from cases elsewhere.

Bibliography

Al Jazeera. (2022). Sri Lanka cardinal seeks UN Probe into 2019 Easter Bombings. *Al Jazeera*, 8 March 2022.

Altheide, D. (2009). *Terror Post 9/11 and the Media*. New York: Peter Lang Publishing.

Amarasingam, A. (2019). Terrorism on the Teardrop Island: Understanding the Easter 2019 Attacks in Sri Lanka. *CTC Sentinel, 12*(5), 1-10.

Amarasingam, A., & Rizwie, R. (2020). *Turning the Tap Off: The Impacts of Social Media Shutdown After Sri Lanka's Easter Attacks*. The Hague: ICCT.

Amnesty International. (2021). *From burning houses to burning bodies. Anti-Muslim violence, discrimination and harassment in Sri Lanka*. New York: Amnesty International.

Bakker, E., et al. (2012). *Onderzoek naar maatschappelijke effecten van bestuurlijk optreden bij terreurdreiging en extreem geweld: Bevindingen uit vier casusstudies*. The Hague: COT & Leiden University.

Bakker, E., & Veldhuis, T. (2012). *A Fear Management Approach To Counter-Terrorism*. The Hague: ICCT.

Bakker, E., & De Graaf, B. (2014). *Towards a Theory of Fear Management in the Counterterrorism Domain: A Stocktaking Approach*. The Hague: ICCT.

Bakker, E., & Roy van Zuijdewijn, J. de. (2015). *Jihadist Foreign Fighter Phenomenon in Western Europe: A Low-Probability, High-Impact Threat*. The Hague: ICCT.

Bandura, A. (1977). Self-efficacy: Toward a unifying theory of behavioral change. *Psychological Review, 84*(2), 191-215.

Barber, E. (2014). Marathon bombing: Saudi victim sues Glenn Beck for defamation. *The Christian Science Monitor*, 1 April 2014.

Beck, U. (1999). *World Risk Society*. Cambridge: Polity Press.

Beck, U. (2002). *The Terrorist Threat: World Risk Society Revisited. Theory, Culture & Society, 19*(4), 39-55.

Centers for Disease Control and Prevention. (2018). *Crisis + Emergency Risk Communication. Introduction*. Atlanta: Centers for Disease Control and Prevention.

Della Porta, D. (1995). *Social Movements, political violence and the state*. Cambridge: Cambridge University Press.

Der Spiegel. (2011). Norway's Prime Minister Discusses Utøya Massacre. *Spiegel International*, 10 October 2011.

Élysée. (2017). *Discours d'Emmanuel Macron lors de la cérémonie d'hommage aux victimes de l'attentat de Nice*. Paris: Élysée.

Flynn, S., & Burke, S. (2011). *Brittle Infrastructure, Community Resilience and National Security*. Washington D.C.: Transportation Research Board.

Furedi, F. (2007). *Invitation to Terror: The Expanding Empire of the Unknown*. London: Continuum Press.

Garmezy, N., & Rutter, M. (1983). *Stress, Coping and Development in Children*. New York: McGraw-Hill.

Giddens, A. (1999). Risk and Responsibility. *The Modern Law Review, 62*(1), 1-10.

Godefroidt, A., & Langer, A. (2020). How Fear Drives Us Apart: Explaining the Relationship between Terrorism and Social Trust. *Terrorism and Political Violence, 32*(7), 1482-1505.

Greater London Authority. (2006). *Report of the 7 July Review Committee*. London: Greater London Authority.

Holling, C. S. (1973). Resilience and Stability of Ecological Systems. *Annual Review of Ecology and Systematics, 4*, 1-23.

Lynch, C. (2013). Europe's New 'Time Bomb' is Ticking in Syria. *Foreign Policy*, 9 July 2013.

Mueller, J. (2009). *How Politicians and the Terrorism Industy Inflate National Security Threats and Why We Believe Them*. New York: Free Press.

Nacos, B., & Torres-Reyna, O. (2007). *Fuelling Our Fears: Stereotyping, Media Coverage, and Public Opinion of Muslim Americans*. Lanham: Rowman and Littlefield.

Nationaal Coördinator Terrorismebestrijding en Veiligheid. (2011). *National Counterterrorism strategy 2011-2015*. Den Haag: Ministerie van Veiligheid en Justitie.

Nationaal Coördinator Terrorismebestrijding en Veiligheid. (2016). *National Counterterrorism strategy 2016-2020*. Den Haag: Ministerie van Veiligheid en Justitie.

New Zealand Parliament. (2019). *Ministerial Statements – Mosque Terror Attacks – Christchurch*. Wellington: New Zealand Parliament.

Post, J. (2006). The Psychological dynamics of terrorism. In Richardson, L. (ed.). *The roots of terrorism* (17-28). Abingdon: Routledge.

Reynolds, N., & Seeger, M. (2012). *Crisis and Emergency Risk Communication – 2012 Edition*. Atlanta: Centers for Disease Control and Prevention.

Roy van Zuijdewijn, J. de. (2019). *Remembering Terrorism: The Case of Norway*. The Hague: ICCT.

Roy van Zuijdewijn, J.H. de. (2021). *The Aftermath:Meaning-making After Terrorist Attacks in Western Europe* (PhD thesis. Leiden University).

Roy van Zuijdewijn, J. de, & Sciarone, J. (2021). Convergence of the Salience of Terrorism in the European Union Before and After Terrorist Attacks. *Terrorism and Political Violence, 33*(8), 1713-1732.

Simpson, C. (2013). F.B.I. Released the Tsarnaevs' Photos Because of Reddit and the Post. *The Atlantic,* 21 April 2013.

Vatican News. (2022). Pope urges for truth behind Sri Lanka's Easter bombing. *Vatican News,* 25 April 2022.

Walt, V. (2016). Europe's Top Cop: It's 'Almost Certain' Terrorists Will Try to Strike Again. *TIME,* 16 May 2016.

Weimann, G. (1983). The Theatre of Terror: Effects of Press Coverage. *Journal of Communication, 1*(33), 38-45.

Williamson, H., Fay, S., & Miles-Johnson, T. (2019). Fear of terrorism: media exposure and subjective fear of attack. *Global Crime, 20*(1), 1-25.

Zulaika, J. (2009). *Terrorism. The self-fulfilling prophecy*. Chicago: The University of Chicago Press.

7

Trends and developments in (counter) terrorism and a future research agenda

7.1   Introduction

In the previous chapter we looked into the impact of terrorism and counterterrorism and how to limit that impact on societies and our daily lives. In this chapter we will reflect on what we know and what we do not yet know about terrorism and counterterrorism.

Let us first briefly go back to the previous parts of this book. In chapter 1 we explored the definition and essence of terrorism and looked into the question of why there is no generally accepted definition of the term and the consequences this might have. In chapter 2 we described and analysed the history of terrorism. This was followed by a chapter on the state of the art of terrorism studies in which we explained why it is so difficult to do research on terrorism and counterterrorism. In chapters 4 and 5 we explored and discussed assumptions on terrorism and counterterrorism. And, as mentioned above, in the previous chapter we looked into the impact of terrorism. In these different chapters we observed a need for further study on certain topics, a lack of consensus about certain assumptions and persisting challenges for policy-makers.

In this final chapter we stress the need for research into these domains. We look into un- and underresearched topics in terrorism studies and end with a suggestion for a future research agenda. First, however, we would like to emphasise that in order to be able to look ahead, it is important to grasp fully what is going on today and to try to see trends and developments. That is why we start this chapter by focusing on the importance of monitoring developments and analysing trends in an attempt to forecast what may be coming towards us.

7.2   Importance of monitoring trends and looking ahead

Why is it important to investigate developments and trends and to look ahead? In the first chapter of this book we mentioned that terrorism is a constantly changing phenomenon. One of the goals of studying terrorism and counterterrorism is to provide answers to the questions of policy-makers and politicians and those of the general public. They want to know what is happening today and what may happen tomorrow and in the years to come. With regard to counterterrorism, we also mentioned that prevention is one of the key elements of counterterrorism policies. Think of the measures for addressing the conditions conducive to the spread of terrorism mentioned in the UN Global Counterterrorism Strategy. In order to be able to do that, we need insight not only into current situations and developments but also into possible future ones.

Terrorism scholars and experts are fully aware of that need. There has been a large increase in attempts to come up with forecasts in the wake of the 9/11 terrorist attacks in the US in 2001. However, the track record of forecasting terrorism to prevent surprises or to develop proactive policies to mitigate future threats has not been particularly good. According to the intelligence and war studies expert Monica Czwarno (2006, p. 667), '[academia] failed to predict or warn government policymakers and the public of the possibility that events of 9/11 magnitude could take place on the United States homeland'.

Predictions and forecasts

Predictions and forecasts are not the same, although both aim to say something about the future. Predictions are mere statements about a possible outcome or future event. Forecasts are based on an analysis of data from past events and current developments and provide a calculated estimate to come up with a statement about the outcome of a future event. Forecasting is a process involving, among other things, analysts, statisticians and content experts. There are two general methods: quantitative and qualitative forecasting. Quantitative forecasting is a method of correlating variables using past records and trends to make forecasts using time series analysis, extrapolation of data or regression analysis. Qualitative forecasting relies on the judgement of content experts rather than numerical figures, using methods such as the Delphi method and surveys among experts. Forecasts often contain predictions as the final part of a methodological analysis. In the case of terrorism studies and the field of counterterrorism, we see quite a few predictions that are not supported by a forecasting methodology. Such predictions are risky and the actual future developments or possible future events may very much deviate from predictions made.

BOX 7.01   PREDICTIONS AND FORECASTS

This is not to say that scholars and experts have not tried to distinguish trends and forecast the future. They are often asked about their opinion regarding the future by politicians and in the public debate. Examples of the past include reports and articles with titles such as, 'Will terrorists go nuclear?' (Brian Jenkins, 1975), 'The future of terrorism' (Paul Wilkinson, 1988), *The Future of Terrorism: Violence in the New Millennium* (Harvey Kushner, 1998), 'Terrorism as a strategy of struggle: Past and future' (Ariel Merari, 1999), 'The new face of terrorism' (Walter Laqueur, 1998) and 'The Future of Terrorism' (Johnson, 2001).

Many of these studies are very interesting and valuable contributions to the debate about trends in terrorism, but they are not forecasts. They often raise assumptions or discuss scenarios. Most of them describe current affairs rather than systematically analysing factors and trends in order to forecast changes in terrorism. In general, the analyses of the future of terrorism before 9/11 showed an absence of methodologies and a lack of theoretical foundations.

As a result, scholars and experts were not very successful in forecasting terrorism, and this is particularly true for major changes in the modus operandi of terrorists. The attacks with aeroplanes on 9/11 is a case in point: according to Czwarno, methodological, and conceptual problems as well as a lack of a more systematic approach grounded in theory created a gap in the knowledge about Islamist terrorism and groups like al-Qaeda. In fact, the attacks on 9/11 and the operational capacity of al-Qaeda caught most members of the academic community by surprise.

Unfortunately, the same can also be said for the intelligence community. Although the '9/11 Commission Report' speaks of 'a shock, not a surprise', there were apparent analytical failures on the part of those who were supposed to keep the US safe from terrorism. The report of the Commission partly focused on operational failures: opportunities that were not or could not be exploited by the organisations and systems of that time. However, in the chapter entitled 'Foresight and Hindsight' the commission argues that the failure of imagination was the most important one: no-one seriously considered the possibility that terrorists would use planes not just as a tool to conduct hijackings – as they had done quite often in the 1970s – but also as weapons in a suicide attack (see box 7.02).

Failure of imagination
After the attacks on the US on 9/11 a National Commission was chartered to prepare a full and complete account of the circumstances surrounding the 11 September 2001 terrorist attacks. In its final report the '9/11 Commission' concluded that 'none of the measures adopted by the U.S. government from 1998 to 2001 disturbed or even delayed the progress of the al Qaeda plot, which had been in the making for several years. Across the government, there were failures of imagination, policy, capabilities, and management. The most important failure was one of imagination'. It also noted, '[a]s late as September 4, 2001, Richard Clarke, the White House staffer long responsible for counterterrorism policy coordination, asserted that the government had not yet made up its mind how to answer the question: "Is Al Qaida a big deal?" A week later came the answer'. A failure of imagination with terrible consequences.

BOX 7.02   FAILURE OF IMAGINATION

After 9/11 a number of excellent studies approached the possible future of terrorism in a more structured way. A good example of that is the study by Brynjar Lia (see box 7.03). However, in general, efforts after 9/11 to look ahead were not particularly fruitful either. In 2014, the quick rise of Islamic State and the proclamation of the caliphate came as a surprise to many (see box 7.04). The main conclusion in a study by Edwin Bakker (2012) of terrorism forecasts that were published between 2000 and 2012 was that there is no general consensus on the future of terrorism, and that there is a lot of room for improvement in the methodologies. Most forecasts seem to say more about the present state of terrorism and terrorism research than about the future. In most cases, current threats and latest incidents dominate terrorism foresights. This is not necessarily a bad thing as, in general, tomorrow looks very much like today and today is very similar to yesterday. But what about the day after tomorrow?

Systematic forecasting by Lia
In his book, *Globalisation and the future of terrorism. Patterns and predictions* (2005), Brynjar Lia shows how international terrorism is shaped, how it evolves and what we can expect in the future. Taking a theoretical approach and a

practical predictive perspective, he provides a valuable contribution to the field of forecasting terrorism. Drawing upon thorough research and scientific methods, he identifies long-term causes and driving forces in society. One of the basic assumptions in his study is that terrorists are usually integral players in local, national and global politics. Thus, terrorism changes when the local, regional and international contexts change, think of international relations, globalisation of the market economy, demographic factors, ideological shifts and technological changes.

BOX 7.03 SYSTEMATIC FORECASTING BY LIA

Unfortunately, from time to time terrorists manage to surprise us and strike us where we least expect it or in ways we could hardly imagine. Therefore, it does not suffice to expect future terrorism to be more or less the same as that of today. If we want to avoid unpleasant surprises, we cannot permit another 'failure of imagination'. We need to be able to look beyond today, or at least have some idea of what we can expect in the years to come. What type of terrorist group, type of attack, will we be confronted with in, let us say, five or ten years from now? Well, of course we do not have a crystal ball, and it is impossible to predict the future. But we can look at patterns, trends and developments that give us a little bit more insight into possible futures of terrorism.

This would require systematic monitoring and analysis of key aspects of terrorism that might shape the future. As argued by Joshua Sinai and others, to do so we need to utilise the latest and innovative conceptual methodologies and software-based systems that are based on social and behavioural sciences. Sinai (2004) argues that there is a lot to gain from theoretically grounded, conceptually precise, methodologically rigorous and analytically oriented research that can help us fully to understand the underlying conditions that give rise to terrorism.

This is, however, easier said than done. In the first chapter of this book we stressed the complexity of the phenomenon of terrorism. So what do we need to look at if we want to monitor and analyse trends and developments in terrorism rigorously and to understand patterns in how terrorism evolves?

Much depends on what we want to know. If we are interested in the fundamental or deeper dynamics of terrorism we need to focus on the structural or underlying aspects that shape it: think of geopolitical, sociological, demographic or technical aspects. By focusing on these aspects of the problem we can answer some of the more abstract questions about the terrorism of today and tomorrow, such as what type of circumstances might lead people to turn to this type of violence.

The fall of Mosul

In June 2014, an attacking force of about 1,500 men of the Islamic State organisation captured the city of Mosul from the Iraqi Army which officially had some 30,000 soldiers stationed there. Although Islamic State had gained momentum and notoriety in the months up to the attack, their victory in Mosul came as a major surprise. Enemies and supporters alike were flabbergasted, according to IS spokesman Abu Mohmmed al-Adnani. Apparently, the Iraqi authorities had not expected Islamic State to be willing and able to strike against Iraq's second biggest city. This unpleasant surprise cost the lives of thousands and resulted in no fewer than 500,000 civilians fleeing the city. Cockburn, P. (2015). *The rise of Islamic State: ISIS and the new Sunni revolution.* London: Verso Books.

BOX 7.04   THE FALL OF MOSUL

If we want to know more about concrete forms and manifestations of terrorism, perhaps we should start to look at more concrete aspects of the phenomenon, such as the characteristics of the perpetrators, their ideology and modus operandi, the impact of terrorism on societies and the facts and figures regarding terrorist attacks. And this is what we are going to do in the next section.

Key points

· It is important to forecast terrorism to avoid surprises and to mitigate future threats.
· The track record in forecasting terrorism has not been particularly good.
· Studies on the future of terrorism show an absence of methodologies and the lack of theoretical foundations.
· Most forecasts seem to say more about the present state of terrorism than about the future.
· A more systematic approach and new software systems might improve forecasts and responses to future threats.

In the previous section we explained the importance of monitoring developments and analysing trends in terrorism and counterterrorism. Here we will discuss how we can do this. We focus on key aspects of the ever-changing nature of terrorism that need to be monitored and analysed if we want to avoid unpleasant surprises and develop proactive policies to mitigate future threats. We will look at the following seven aspects:

1. Facts and figures of terrorism
2. Ideology
3. Perpetrators
4. Modus operandi
5. Impact of terrorism
6. Trends and developments in counterterrorism
7. Impact of counterterrorism

Facts and figures of terrorism

Of course it is important to monitor and analyse what is happening within countries and around the world and the facts and figures regarding terrorism. This enables scholars and practitioners to see developments and possibly discover trends in the growth of the phenomenon in terms of attacks and victims and the lethality of attacks. When mapping these attacks we can discover shifts in the geographical spread of terrorism and discover new hot spots of terrorism that we should pay more attention to.

When discussing the lethality of terrorism in chapter 4 on the basis of the data of the Global Terrorism Database, we already noted that there is no clear pattern regarding either the number of terrorist incidents or the number of people killed and wounded per attack. We observed that there are ups and downs regarding these figures, although more people are killed because of terrorism in the first two decades of this century than in the previous 100 years.

When discussing the map of terrorism in chapters 1 and 4 we noticed that the hot spots of terrorism in the past few decades were located in the Middle East and South Asia. In recent years we have seen an increase in terrorist attacks in Africa, which may be an important trend to monitor and analyse. Think of countries, such as Cameroon and Mozambique, that had not experienced much terrorism in the past, but which have in recent years been confronted with many attacks and casualties. Focusing on these and other countries

Terrorism and Counterterrorism Studies

Trends and developments in (counter)terrorism and a future research agenda

might provide us with insight into how terrorism spreads and why. Of course it is also relevant to focus on countries where terrorism is in decline and on the possible causes of such a positive development.

To be able to do so we need data and data series. As scholars, we need open-source databases that include information about attacks, casualties, perpetrators, modus operandi and locations. Besides the Global Terrorism Database there are other databases that can be of great help in monitoring and analysing facts and figures regarding terrorism or, for instance, in relation to certain types or aspects of terrorism and terrorist attacks.

A positive development is the fact that the number of terrorism databases has grown in recent years. In the journal *Perspectives on Terrorism*, Neil Bowie provided several inventories of such datasets. In a new inventory published in 2021, he observed growth in the subject coverage and the diversity in quantitative terrorism databases and datasets, including niches such as prisons and terrorism or lone-actor terrorism. He also noted that there are relatively few databases on state and domestic terrorism. Most of the 40 databases and datasets mentioned in the new inventory are academic, think tank and independent databases that are mostly open to the wider public. In addition, there are commercial and governmental databases that mostly require permission to access or that are not directly accessible to the general public or academic researchers.

Ideology

A second important aspect of the phenomenon of terrorism is the ideology of terrorist groups and individuals. Terrorism is aimed at achieving political goals that are derived from certain political ideas and world views.

Monitoring and analysing why and how these ideologies change over time could help us to understand what new groups or new factions within terrorist groups we need to worry about. The same holds true for possible changes in whom they see as the enemy and what type of actions and activities are linked to ideological changes within the group and its surroundings. It is especially important to monitor debates within ideological communities about the acceptance, usefulness or legitimacy of the use of violence. Think, for instance, of the hefty debate among Islamist and jihadist (religious) leaders on suicide terrorism. Some of them justified the attacks on 9/11 by al-Qaeda, the 'martyrdom operations' by Palestinian groups against Israel and the suicide attacks by IS, while others strongly condemned them on political, moral and religious grounds. Many scholars have, for instance, looked into these debate on suicide terrorism and the ideological discussions on the concept of violent jihad within and between Islamist and jihadist groups. Others have studied how debates within certain left-wing and separatist groups have resulted in them refraining from the use of violence.

Today, there are worries that ideological developments within certain right-wing groups increasingly foster the idea that terrorist attacks can provoke societal changes. Here we would like to stress that the use of violence, especially against ordinary citizens, is mostly not taken lightly and some groups, despite being very militant and condoning terrorism, attacked only buildings and tried to avoid casualties. In the Netherlands, for instance, members of the group called Rode Jeugd (Red Youth) visited terrorist training camps abroad and were behind several bomb attacks, but never attacked people, in contrast to their 'comrades' in Germany (Red Army Faction) or Italy (Red Brigades). Or think of animal rights activists who frequently carry out attacks on property and only rarely on people.

Perpetrators

What are developments with regard to the perpetrators of terrorist attacks? Are the personal characteristics of today's terrorists the same as in the past, and what can we expect in the future? Understanding possible changes in these characteristics is important if we want to know what people or what groups prevention policies should aim at and what individuals and groups in society should be closely monitored by intelligence and security organisations or other law enforcement agencies.

An important change in the last decade has been the rise of jihadist and right-wing lone-actor terrorists which took some authorities by surprise. Think of the attack on mosques in Christchurch, New Zealand, by a single terrorist. The same holds true for the high number of youngsters with an immigrant background or Muslim converts who travelled to Syria and Iraq to join the violent jihad. Many were also surprised to see so many young women among them.

Unfortunately, there are no clear patterns regarding changes in the background of perpetrators. The only constant element is that the majority of them are in their teens or early twenties when they join a terrorist group or link up to a terrorist movement. This means that monitoring general trends among youngsters and studying changes in attitudes and behaviours within this particular segment of society can help to forecast changes in the type of perpetrators of terrorist activities.

It is also good to look at more specific characteristics of these perpetrators and how they change over time. For instance, whether or not terrorists seem to suffer more often from mental health issues than they did in the past, as some argue with regard to lone-actor terrorism. Looking at such characteristics could help us to gain more insight into what groups or individuals might pose a serious risk and what to do about it in terms of monitoring or prevention policies.

Modus operandi

A very important aspect of terrorism to professionals who have to protect society from attacks is the modus operandi of terrorists: in other words their weapons, the ways in which they use violence and the targets they choose. Many scholars, think of David Rapoport, have looked into the question of how the modus operandi of terrorists have changed over time. He and others observed that terrorists use the newest technologies available. The so-called Islamic State is, unfortunately, a good example of a group that has managed to use the latest technological means, such as social media and drones for observation and to drop explosives upon their enemies.

Monitoring and analysing developments in the modus operandi of terrorists helps us either to take measures to make some of these means less easily available to terrorists or to prepare the right countermeasures. Think of the policies of social media companies to prevent or deny the use of their services to terrorist and extremist groups and technological tools to spot and jam drones (see box 7.05).

To be able to see changes in time we need data on modus operandi. The importance of that is reflected in the fact that many databases collect data on the targets of attacks and the weapons used by the perpetrators. A better understanding and forecasting of the target selection of terrorist groups will, for instance, help to determine what locations or individuals should receive additional protection and what possible measures are needed to protect them.

How terrorists innovate

In the book, *How Terror Evolves: The Emergence and Spread of Terrorist Techniques*, Yannick Veilleux-Lepage (2020) shows how innovations in terrorism occur as part of wider historical processes rather than in a vacuum. Drawing on evolutionary theory, he explains how terrorist groups innovate upon, transform and abandon techniques of political violence in order to advance their cause. He traces the processes through which the use of aircraft as weapons of destruction developed, from the first instances of aircraft hijacking in 1920s in Peru, through Palestinian terrorism in the 1970s and 1980s, to its adoption by al-Qaeda in the 1990s, culminating in the 9/11 attack in 2001. Veilleux-Lepage not only offers insight into the changing modus operandi of terrorist groups, but also shows the implications of counterterrorism on the evolution of terrorism.

BOX 7.05   HOW TERRORISTS INNOVATE

Impact of terrorism

A final key aspect of the phenomenon of terrorism that needs to be monitored and analysed is its impact on societies. That impact has differed in the course of time and between countries and target groups. Monitoring and understanding the development and differences in impact is important if we want to improve ways to limit that impact and mitigate its consequences. It may also give us insight into what changes in society make us stronger or weaker against terrorist attacks. Think of how many societies around the globe have become what Beck called 'risk societies' that seem to be more vulnerable to insecurity, including to the threat of terrorism. At the same time, there are countries or societies that have grown more resilient after many attacks and have found ways to more or less cope with their impact.

Helpful instruments for monitoring and analysing changes in the impact of terrorism are longitudinal studies of public opinion relating to things that worry people. Think of the Eurobarometer or the Gallup polls that have asked about these worries and terrorism for several decades. Understanding changes and possible patterns may help us to improve crisis communication in the aftermath of terrorist attacks or to increase societies' resilience to terrorism.

Trends and developments in counterterrorism

Developments and trends relating to terrorism will also influence the forms and manifestations of counterterrorism. They will, for instance, affect the actors who are involved in counterterrorism. If terrorist groups are increasingly participating in civil wars, such as in Syria and Iraq, military actors may become more important. Trends and developments in terrorism also have an impact on policy instruments. Some become more relevant, others obsolete. Think of the role of negotiators in hostage situations. There was a huge demand for these experts in the 1970s in the heyday of hostage taking and the hijacking of aeroplanes. Today, terrorists frequently intend to fight to the death and terrorists who manage to take over planes intend to crash them into buildings rather than to start negotiating with the authorities.

Changes in terrorism may also require new measures or new laws, for instance in relation to new technologies such as social media. We have already mentioned countermeasures by tech companies against the use of social media by terrorists, which is a good example of a new actor and new measures because of the adoption of new technologies by terrorist groups.

Changes not only in technology, but also in society have an impact on counterterrorism. Hardening of societies and overreactions of politicians after terrorist attacks might lead to changes in counterterrorism strategies, for instance a shift from a focus on prevention to one on repression. This could lead to an increased use of emergency laws and other extraordinary measures and less attention for social programmes to prevent radicalisation or long-term policies to gain the trust of certain communities. Monitoring these changes might help to mitigate or to stop trends that do not make societies safer or make them even more vulnerable to terrorism. This brings us to the impact of counterterrorism.

Impact of counterterrorism

Needless to say, changes in counterterrorism will also have an impact on societies and can have unintended side effects. Think of evoking emergency laws or lockdowns, or starting military interventions, as was the case after 9/11 under the title 'Global War on Terror'. Especially harsh and repressive counterterrorism policies could lead to more violence, more polarisation, more radicalisation and – in the end – more terrorism.

Monitoring and evaluation by think tanks

The International Centre for Counter-Terrorism (ICCT) is an independent think tank providing multidisciplinary policy advice and practical support for policies pertaining to the rule of law, prevention and threat assessment. One of the core areas of the ICCT is Monitoring and Evaluation – systematically assessing counterterrorism policies and strategies to provide feedback loops between policy and practice and to contribute to evidence-based planning and implementation. The ICCT observes that, given the political imperatives and speed with which counterterrorism policies and strategies are implemented, counterterrorism instruments are rarely evaluated and are often based on untested assumptions. To address the lack of systematic analyses of counterterrorism activities, the ICCT created a Monitoring, Evaluation & Learning programme to assess the effectiveness of various strategies, policies and individual counterterrorism measures. The programme is linked to the European Commission-funded project on Counterterrorism Monitoring, Reporting and Support Mechanism (CT MORSE), which is a project providing monitoring and support for activities in countering terrorism and violent extremism in countries outside the EU.

BOX 7.06   MONITORING AND EVALUATION BY THINK TANKS

Evaluation studies are important for gaining insight into how and to what extent counterterrorism policies contribute to less terrorism and the proportionality of these policies in terms of infringement of liberties and human rights. Increasingly, academia, think tanks and human rights organisations are interested in systematically monitoring and evaluating counterterrorism policies (see box 7.06). It is important to do so in a continuous and systematic way instead of only reacting to ad hoc and spectacular changes in counterterrorism policies, such as the effects of a declaration of a state of emergency after a major attack. We should continuously monitor and evaluate policies to see if there is perhaps a slippery slope, where these policies are gradually leading to a situation where we, while trying to protect our freedom and security, are actually selling out a lot of our freedom only to gain little additional security. Many human rights activists warn about such a trend. Similarly, it is important to see whether or not counterterrorism policies are moving in a direction where terrorism is wrongly seen as only a minor threat or something of the past. This can help to mitigate or reverse trends that do not make us safer. Think of budget cuts to counterterrorism actors in times of perceived quiet on the terrorism front, leading to a loss of expertise and capability to deal with terrorist groups that may have gone temporarily into hiding or are regrouping.

Key points

· When monitoring developments and analysing trends it is important to focus on a number of key aspects of terrorism.

· Key aspects of terrorism include facts and figures of terrorism, the ideology of perpetrators, their characteristics and their modus operandi.

· It is also important to look at the impact on societies to improve resilience to terrorism.

· It is important to monitor and analyse counterterrorism to be able to reflect critically on its effectiveness and possible negative side effects. Evaluation studies may help us to do this.

In the previous section we discussed important aspects of terrorism and counterterrorism that we should focus on when monitoring trends and developments in them. Although there has been much progress since 9/11 as we discussed in chapter 3, there are still quite a few topics that are under-explored. In this section we will look at what we do not know, or know too little about. In in other words, we will focus on un- and under-researched topics.

In chapter 3, we quoted Magnus Ranstorp, Andrew Silke and Alex Schmid, who have produced valuable publications on the state of the art of terrorism studies, including criticism of what has been produced since 9/11. Among the issues raised by these and other authors are a lack of primary data and comparative studies and a lack of theory testing. Also mentioned frequently is the event-driven nature of terrorism studies, which often leads to a focus on topical issues and niches. This prompted Schmid to establish the 'Terrorism Research Initiative' which aims to promote research into topics that are not so fashionable. He also came up with a list of 50 un- and under-researched topics in the field of terrorism studies in 2011. In 2018, the list had grown longer, as Schmid and Forest identified 150 un- and under-researched topics based on the input of some 20 leading academics.

They categorised the input they received into 14 main areas. Most of the topics fall into category 11 – 'counterterrorism by government and international organisations', as can be seen in the list below:

1. Terrorist organisations and terrorist group members (25 topics)
2. Radicalisation and de-radicalisation (7)
3. Causes of terrorism (10)
4. Religion and terrorism (10)
5. Internet/(social) media and terrorism (15)
6. Terrorism and the public/public opinion (6)
7. War and terrorism (6)
8. State and regime-linked terrorism (2)
9. Country and regional studies (6)
10. Prevention of, and countering (violent) extremism and terrorism – PVE/CVE (10)
11. Counterterrorism by government and international organisations (37)
12. Victim issues (7)
13. Conceptual issues (4)
14. The areas of terrorism and counterterrorism studies (5)

Regarding the 'terrorist organisations and group members' category, they noted that many scholars often study individual cases and groups. Schmid and Forest make a plea for more comparative studies or a broader focus in order to understand movements and campaigns of terrorist organisations. On the list we also see several topics in relation to the causes of terrorism. Another example of an un- and under-researched area is the relationship between the internet, media and terrorism. How do they affect each other? How do terrorists use new social media platforms and what role does the internet play in their recruitment efforts? Another topic on the list is victim issues. Think of research into how to improve coping and healing strategies for victims of terrorism. This is related to the category of terrorism and the public and public opinion. A research area that is linked to this is the domain of psychological and economic consequences of terrorism for various actors other than the direct victims. Or, more broadly, what is the impact of terrorism on various segments of the population? This is related to what we discussed in the previous chapter when we explored the concepts of resilience and impact management. Other topics on Schmid and Forest's list pertain to counterterrorism policies. For instance, what can we learn from counterterrorism in previous decades? Several authors mentioned a lack of evaluation studies and the problems with assessing the effectiveness of various measures.

Schmid, Forest and Lowe published another study in 2021 specifically focusing on the state of the art of counterterrorism studies. They asked current and former counterterrorism professionals various questions, for instance what they considered to be the greatest shortcomings and weaknesses in the field of counterterrorism. Some of the commonest issues related to research methodologies, a lack of comparative or interdisciplinary research, a lack of data or primary sources or a western-centric focus. Overall, the authors see much room for progress in counterterrorism studies.

Key points

- There are several issues in the field of terrorism and counterterrorism that need more attention and more research.
- Schmid and Forest produced a list of un- and under-researched topics in the field of terrorism studies and together with Lowe looked at shortcomings in counterterrorism studies.
- The list might inspire scholars when doing research on terrorism or when contributing to the debate on terrorism studies.

7.5   Future research agenda in terrorism studies

In this section we will discuss a few persisting challenges to research in terrorism studies and a number of remaining questions and suggestions for a future research agenda. We will focus on three challenges that need to be addressed to improve both research and policy-making:

1. The gap between academics and professionals in the field of counterterrorism
2. The western bias in terrorism studies
3. The state-focused nature of this academic field

Bridging the gap between academics and CT actors

Research into terrorism is conducted by a wide range of actors: academics, think tanks, NGOs, investigative journalists and, of course, various actors in the counterterrorism field itself, think of research by intelligence officers and police detectives. They are all experts in their particular field and they all have their own valuable insights into parts of the puzzle called terrorism. They can learn from each other, and putting the pieces of insights together might help all of us to understand terrorism and counterterrorism better. However, some actors do not come together easily, sometimes for good reasons – classified information, privacy laws, ethical concerns, amongst others. But often opportunities to share insights or test each other's views and assumptions are missed or not used to the fullest extent possible.

Academia and the policy and practice community

There is a long tradition of practice- and policy-oriented research in the field of terrorism studies. What do end-users think of this research? Are they satisfied with what academia offers them? The results of a survey by Bart Schuurman (2019) provide reason for some optimism. The policy and practice community holds the quality of research on terrorism in high regard and notes improvement in recent years. Nonetheless, the end-users criticise the relevance of these studies, seeing them as too theoretical and too removed from their daily reality to be of optimal practical value. Schuurman, however, warns that academic research is not there (just) to provide answers to practical problems and that – given the complexity of terrorism – the hope that any answers will be clear-cut should be tempered. The results of the survey also show that among the policy and practice community there is plenty of support for a constructive but critical engagement with the academic world.

BOX 7.07   ACADEMIA AND THE POLICY AND PRACTICE COMMUNITY

Unfortunately, there is still a gap, particularly between academics on the one hand and policy-makers and professionals on the other. To some extent they live in different worlds and they do not always trust or appreciate each other (see, for instance, box 7.07). The policy-makers and practitioners face direct pressure from parliament, the media and the public who want answers to pressing questions right now, especially after a terrorist incident. It is highly relevant for academics to understand the context of these counterterrorism actors and how dealing with terrorism works in practice: to understand the dilemmas and challenges of actually 'doing' counterterrorism.

And policy-makers and professionals could benefit from more rigorously testing assumptions and ideas that might form the basis for their work, as we also discussed in the chapters on assumptions on counterterrorism. They could make use of the input of academics to develop a more reflective and critical stand with regard to their daily work and the pressure they face. Therefore, we believe that bridging the gap between academics and counterterrorism actors is something to work on in order to improve both research and policy-making. For a concrete example of such an attempt see box 7.08.

EENeT

The European Expert Network on Terrorism Issues (EENeT) is an independent, non-partisan consortium of terrorism experts (see www. european-enet.org). EENeT is a purely informal network and has more than 150 experts from over 20 European countries. It came about as a result of the international symposium on 'Monitoring Terrorism/Extremism – Prospects for Phenomena Monitoring on European Level', initiated by the German Federal Criminal Police Office in 2007. At the end of the event, the majority of the participants recommended continuing to share experience and knowledge within the framework of an informal network. EENeT is dedicated to providing comprehensive insights into the complexity of the terrorist phenomenon which appears possible only on a multidisciplinary basis, in close cooperation with the specialist departments and experts from the law enforcement agencies, relevant authorities and the field of science.

BOX 7.08   EENeT

Western bias

This brings us to another broader issue in relation to terrorism studies that it is important to be aware of and that we should try to resolve. In the third chapter of this book we noted that the field of terrorism studies is dominated by western-based institutes and scholars and that this has resulted in a western-focused research agenda. The academic field mainly focuses on terrorism in the West or aimed against western interests. Hence, it misses important aspects of both terrorism and counterterrorism as they are mainly taking place elsewhere.

If terrorism studies as an academic discipline aims to understand terrorism and counterterrorism in all their contexts, facets, shapes and form, it is important that this situation changes. Academic institutes and those that fund academic research – mostly western state organisations – could also develop research projects that focus more on the situation in South Asia, Africa and other hot spots of terrorism beyond the West. Or they can support research institutes in those parts of the world. A good example of that is the Institute for Security Studies in Africa (see box 7.09).

ISS Africa

The Institute for Security Studies (ISS) is an African NGO with offices in Pretoria, South Africa; Nairobi, Kenya; Addis Ababa, Ethiopia; and Dakar, Senegal. ISS's goal is to enhance human security as a means to achieve sustainable peace and prosperity by way of research, practical training and technical assistance to governments and civil society (see issafrica.org). ISS covers, among others, transnational crimes, migration, peacebuilding, crime prevention and criminal justice, and the analysis of conflict and governance. Researchers of ISS have looked into how best to deal with jihadist groups in Sub-Saharan Africa. They show the importance of a broad strategy that addresses multiple reasons for joining jihadist groups – including social, security, economic and political factors – and that approaches to dealing with specific groups and individuals must be tailored. ISS also organises events for experts, for instance, on the role of NGOs, local communities and women in preventing extremism. The aim is to provide alternative pathways for dealing with violent extremist groups with international terrorism links.

BOX 7.09   ISS AFRICA

These projects should, of course, include scholars from these regions. Ideally such projects involve joint research teams in order to learn more about terrorism in other parts of the world, but also to learn from each other.

In addition, scholarships for students and academics from other parts of the world could help to bring their knowledge and experience to academic institutes in the West. In our digital age, there are also plenty of opportunities to share insights online and meet each other and exchange research findings, online through webinars and offline through workshops and conferences.

State-focused nature of terrorism studies

A flaw in the field of terrorism studies that is often mentioned by critical scholars is their state-focused nature. As we have seen in the list of un- and under-researched topics, only a few academic studies look at the negative side effects or unintended consequences of states' counterterrorism policies. In addition to that, the research agenda is to a large extent determined by policy-oriented questions. While this results in research that is very useful to policy-makers and practitioners in the counterterrorism domain, it also means that topics that are relevant to others receive less attention. Think of victims of terrorism or the consequences of counterterrorism measures for certain communities. There is also less attention – and funding – for critical terrorism studies or the development of rigorous methodologies and in-depth study into factors that are conducive to terrorism. Or think of the lack of attention for comparative or historical studies. An approach to dealing with this challenge is not only more (state!) funding for other topics and types of study, but also a more critical look at the research agendas of individual scholars – the authors of this book included. For an overview of topics that are funded by the EU see box 7.10.

EU funding of research

One of the most important funders of research on terrorism-related issues is the European Commission. In line with its 2020 'Counterterrorism Agenda for the EU', it funds research into factors causing radicalisation, extremist ideologies and recruitment mechanisms, with the aim of developing good practices and concrete guidance and tools for policy-makers and practitioners. Funding opportunities (EU grants and procurements) for research and projects on preventing radicalisation are regularly published by the Commission on its portal for funding and tender opportunities (see website ec.europa.eu/info/funding-tenders). The portal includes publication of calls as well as projects' results. Typing in 'terrorism', one can find (former) calls for research into, among others, 'technologies to enhance the fight against crime and terrorism', 'improved access to fighting crime and terrorism research data', and 'enhanced fight against the abuse of online gaming culture by extremists'.

BOX 7.10   EU FUNDING OF RESEARCH

Future research agenda

Having looked at the list of under-researched topics and given the state-focused nature of terrorism studies we think there are several topics that deserve more attention and should be on the future research agenda of

Trends and developments in (counter)terrorism and a future research agenda

terrorism and counterterrorism studies. So here are our personal suggestions for that agenda.

First, it is important not only to conduct ad hoc research into the latest developments in terrorism but also to pay more attention to long-term trends and developments in order to understand the underlying dynamics and factors that lead to terrorism or that help us to understand how terrorism ends. Historical studies could be part of that effort.

A second topic that we find very important is related to what we discussed in the previous chapter: the need to improve our understanding of how to deal with the impact of terrorism. We believe that more research on resilience, impact management and crisis communication could help to make sure that terrorists do not get what they want and, in the end, may help to make terrorism a less attractive strategy as we reduce its impact.

Third, as we also noted in the previous chapter, terrorism studies could benefit from more evaluation studies on the effectiveness and side effects of counterterrorism policies and strategies. We should critically explore the successes and possible negative consequences of counterterrorism efforts. We need to know what works in counterterrorism and what does not. How successful are these policies and are they proportional to the threat? And how can we limit possible negative side effects?

Key points
- Academics and counterterrorism professionals have a lot to offer each other and there are several opportunities to bridge the gap between them.
- If terrorism studies aims to understand terrorism and counterterrorism in all their contexts, facets, shapes and forms it has to deal with its western bias.
- The state-focused nature of this academic field overlooks the negative side effects or unintended consequences of counterterrorism policies.
- Topics for a future research agenda include long-term trends and developments, impact management and evaluation studies.

7.6   Concluding remarks

In this book we have provided you with a deeper understanding of some of the main topics and questions in the field of terrorism and counterterrorism. We have explored some of the main academic debates, theoretical ideas and assumptions and compared them with empirical evidence and practical experiences.

We hope that we have encouraged you to adopt a critical stance towards these topics and that you feel better equipped to analyse and understand terrorism-related issues and developments. After reading this book, we hope you are able to assess some of the dynamics behind these issues and developments and recognise and debunk myths about (counter)terrorism.

In this chapter we have demonstrated that there is still much to do when it comes to improving our understanding of terrorism and counterterrorism. Combining the forces of academics and practitioners is one way to achieve this. A critical attitude regarding what has been achieved so far is also needed. Much has already been said in chapter 3 when we discussed the current state of the art. Let us here recall the need for more empirical research and for conceptual and theoretical development. It is, however, also good to restate that today we do know much more about terrorism than we did before 9/11.

Let us conclude on this positive note and call upon academics, experts and practitioners to add to the body of knowledge and to continue to test and challenge existing assumptions regarding terrorism and counterterrorism. Thus, we might be able to make the world a safer place, perhaps one in which terrorism does not make headlines almost every day.

In the meantime, we hope this book has given the reader a concrete suggestion on how to respond to acts of terrorism: to show resilience and refuse to alter our lifestyles. Or, in other words, to simply say, 'we are not afraid and we will not give into the threats and violent acts by terrorists'. Unfortunately, in some places such as Syria and Iraq, this is easier said than done.

Bibliography

Bakker, E. (2012). Forecasting Terrorism: The Need for a More Systematic Approach. *Journal for Strategic Security, 5*(4), 69-87.

Bowie, N. G. (2021). 40 Terrorism Databases and Data Sets: A New Inventory. *Perspectives on Terrorism, 15*(2), 147-161.

Cockburn, P. (2015). *The rise of Islamic State: ISIS and the new Sunni revolution.* London: Verso Books.

Czwarno, M. (2006). Misjudging Islamic Terrorism: The Academic Community's Failure to Predict 9/11. *Studies in Conflict & Terrorism, 29*(7), 657-678.

European Commission. (2020). *Communication from the Commission: A Counter-Terrorism Agenda for the EU: Anticipate, Prevent, Protect, Respond.* Brussels: European Commission.

Jenkins, B. M. (1975). *Will Terrorists Go Nuclear?* Santa Monica: RAND Corporation.

Johnson, L. C. (2001). The future of Terrorism. *American Behavioral Scientist, 44*(6), 894-913.

Kushner, H. W. (1998). *The Future of Terrorism: Violence in the New Millennium.* London: Sage Publications.

Laqueur, W. (1998). The new face of terrorism. *Washington Quarterly, 21*(4), 167-178.

Lia, B. (2005). *Globalisation and the Future of Terrorism: Patterns and Predictions.* New York: Routledge.

Merari, A. (1999). Terrorism as a strategy of struggle: Past and future. *Terrorism and Political Violence, 11*(4), 52-65.

National Commission on Terrorist Attacks upon the United States. (2004). *The 9/11 Commission Report: Final Report of the National Commission on Terrorist Attacks upon the United States.* Washington DC.: National Commission on Terrorist Attacks upon the United States.

National Consortium for the Study of Terrorism and Responses to Terrorism (START). (2022). *Global Terrorism Database,* https://www.start.umd.edu/gtd/.

Schmid, A. P. (2011). 50 Un- and Under-researched Topics in the Field of (Counter-) Terrorism Studies. *Perspectives on Terrorism, 5*(1), 76-78.

Schmid, A. P., & Forest, J. J. (2018). Research desiderata: 150 un- and under-researched topics and themes in the field of (counter-)terrorism studies-a new list. *Perspectives on Terrorism, 12*(4), 68-76.

Schmid, A. P., Forest, J. J. F. & Lowe, T. (2021). Counter-Terrorism Studies: A Glimpse at the Current State of Research (2020/2021). *Perspectives on Terrorism, 15*(4), 155-183.

Schuurman, B. (2019). *Counterterrorism Professionals on Terrorism Research: An End-User Assessment.* The Hague: ICCT.

Sinai, J. (2004). *Utilizing the Social and Behavioral Sciences to Assess, Model, Forecast and Preemptively Respond to Terrorism.* Lecture Notes in Computer Science, 3073.

Veilleux-Lepage, Y. (2020). *How Terror Evolves. The Emergence and Spread of Terrorist Techniques.* London: Rowman & Littlefield.

Wilkinson, P. (1988). The future of terrorism. *Futures, 20*(5), 493-504.

Index

Printed in the United States
by Baker & Taylor Publisher Services